DESI QUEERS

Churnjeet Mahn,
Rohit K. Dasgupta
and DJ Ritu

DESI QUEERS

LGBTQ+ South Asians and Cultural Belonging in Britain

QUEER DIRECTIONS

First published by in the United Kingdom by C. Hurst & Co. (Publishers) Ltd in 2025

Published by Westland Books, a division of Nasadiya Technologies Private Limited, in 2025

No. 269/2B, First Floor, 'Irai Arul', Vimalraj Street, Nethaji Nagar, Alapakkam Main Road, Maduravoyal, Chennai 600095

Westland and the Westland logo are the trademarks of Nasadiya Technologies Private Limited, or its affiliates.

ISBN: 9789360452353

10 9 8 7 6 5 4 3 2 1

Typeset by Jojy Philip
Printed at Parksons Graphics Pvt. Ltd

CONTENTS

LIST OF ILLUSTRATIONS

A NOTE FROM THE SERIES EDITOR

Welcome to Queer Directions, a collaboration between Westland and the Godrej DEI Lab.

Under this label, we hope to offer a space for new kinds of books and writing that prioritises pride, progress, imagination and joy for queer people. Westland has supported queer writing under different formats for many years, and this imprint cements its commitment to breaking barriers through writing and publishing narratives that describe, as well as reshape, our present and future. The Godrej DEI Lab (including its previous avatar, the Godrej India Culture Lab) has worked to advance inclusion for LGBTQIA+ people and other historically excluded groups within and outside the workplace for more than a decade.

I serve as the hyphen between both these organisations—a Westland author who outlined and described the contours of a queer-inclusive India in my book *Queeristan*, and also as the head of the Godrej DEI Lab. Over many conversations with Karthika, Publisher at Westland, we decided to join forces to create this imprint in 2025 to serve as a meeting ground where contemporary and future queer writing could gather.

Queer Directions recognises and builds on decades of work by publishers, both independent and corporate, and will publish work by LGBTQIA+ writers from the Indian subcontinent and diaspora, as well as work about queer South Asia that matters to readers from these groups. We seek to be as plural as possible. We believe that the truly queer direction is forward, into the future.

Join us, collaborate with us and reach out to us, as writers, readers, allies. We're here to build a bridge, not a border—a bridge to a more beautiful, inclusive and queer-friendly world.

PARMESH SHAHANI

INTRODUCTION

On 2 May 1987 thousands of protesters gathered in London for 'Smash the Backlash', the first national black queer demonstration against racism and homophobia. Organised by Haringey Black Action, 'Smash the Backlash' called for a coalition of racialised gays and lesbians to unite against state-enabled right-wing attacks on progressive social and political movements, especially in London. One of the leaflets for the protest, entitled 'Black People Fight Bigotry', featured an image of the South Asian deity Kali and carried a call from the Black Panther Party to stand with all oppressed groups. Kali, derived from *kala* (black), was used as a figure evoking the revolutionary potential of destruction entwined with the creative potential of feminine energy. Behind her was a generation of queer South Asians in 1980s Britain, many of them migrants or the children of working-class first-generation migrants, facing down state-sponsored racism and homophobia. Their story is the beginning of the multi-generational account of desi queers in Britain this book sets out to capture.

From the early 1980s, the Labour-run Greater London Council (GLC) had pledged itself to distributing funding to minoritised groups in the city and setting up equality units as part of a co-ordinated approach to tackle key social inequalities. This would make the GLC a particular anathema to the Thatcher government, who made the council's closure a manifesto promise. The North London borough of Haringey had acquired a reputation for radical action. It had been the site of the Broadwater Farm Estate resistance in 1985 in response to endemic police violence towards Black and South Asian communities. London's first Lesbian and Gay Unit, focused on challenging structural heterosexism, was based in the borough, taking what we would now call an intersectional approach to incorporate the experiences of working-class, disabled, gendered, sexualised and racialised bodies in the heart of the unit's work.

It wasn't long, however, before the Haringey Lesbian and Gay Unit (HLGU) would find itself at the heart of a controversy that would change the shape of LGBTQ+ civil rights across the country. Many readers of this book will have lived through the consequences of what came next. The HLGU's policy to improve the positive representation of lesbians and gays included highlighting a book for primary school children that depicted a gay couple as parents. The media and political furore that followed depicted the initiative as a wholesale attack on the nuclear family. To use another word that has subsequently entered the cultural vocabulary of (anti-)equalities work, it was seen as woke gone mad. The local government leader of Haringey, Bernie Grant, was dubbed 'Barmy Bernie' for his own support of Haringey's equality work.

Haringey's small-scale initiative to provide positive images of queer life was successfully weaponised by right-wing political parties, media and organisations. The debates that started in parliament in response to this work would eventually result in an amendment to the Local Government Act of 1986 and would commonly be known as Section 28. Section 28 prohibited the promotion of homosexuality by local authorities. It would not be repealed until 2000 in Scotland, and 2003 in England and Wales. The defiant national protests in the lead-up to Section 28 have become part of a heroic narrative of queer resistance. If the Miners' Strike in 1984 has been imagined as the defining protest for working-class communities in the 1980s, the fightback against Section 28 was the definitive protest for queer life.

What's missing from this story is the fundamental contribution of Black queer and queer of colour resistance to Section 28. The resistance to Section 28 was not a single-issue protest. Haringey Black Action framed the lead-up to Section 28 as just one example in a series of assaults on minoritised life. The leaflets for 'Smash the Backlash' called for consciousness-raising across black and queer communities: 'State attacks on all working-class people—especially black people—are intensifying. Black resistance to these attacks will continue to increase. The resistance is not separate from fighting attacks on black sisters or on black lesbians and gays.'[1] The fightback against bigotry included pointing to evidence of queer sexualities across Asia, Africa and the Caribbean (challenging the notion that queer sexualities were a 'white disease'), thereby demonstrating that the real threat to black families were not queers, but white racists who had perpetuated genocide in 'Azania' (a term used for South Africa).[2]

A real threat, however, was the growing number of racialised minorities turning their back on progressive anti-racist activism: 'Some Asian and Afro-Caribbean organisations have aligned themselves with right-wing forces by attacking lesbians and gay men within their own communities.'[3] As we live through another moment with unlikely alliances between historically left-wing communities and right wing ideologies, past battles offer insights and resources for the ongoing work to create progressive coalitions. The 'Smash the Backlash' march has been largely forgotten in mainstream accounts of queer history in the UK and its omission from many accounts of the resistance to Section 28 is testament to the continual under-valuing of anti-racist contributions to delivering queer civil rights.

This book identifies the distinct contribution of South Asians to queer life in Britain, from activism to grassroots organising and culture. It's a move that critiques the heterowashing of migrant history and the whitewashing of queer history. We want to move away from deficit models of queer South Asian life that continually characterise us as isolated and at risk, to focus on what Anjali Arondekar has called in a different setting, the queer 'abundance' of South Asian life and sexualities.[4] We want to move from being framed as the passive beneficiaries of white-led projects for LGBTQ+ rights, to being recognised as part of the enabling infrastructure for larger projects of queer liberation. Queer South Asians helped to support key queer organisations and collectives in the UK. Gilli Salvat, who was born in British India and has Anglo-Indian heritage, worked to support the pioneering Young Lesbian Group in 1979, and would go on to be amongst the first workers in the Haringey Gay and Lesbian Unit in 1986. Savi Hensman, whose family arrived in Britain to escape violence in Sri Lanka, would become a long-standing worker at the Black Lesbian and Gay Centre as well as being involved in Haringey Black Action. Queer South Asians, whose routes to the UK were often determined by the legacy of Empire, were integral to shaping queer anti-racist movements, often drawn from working-class migrant communities, who had their own anti-imperial political inheritance.

Desi Queers offers a story of queer South Asian life in Britain from the 1980s to the present that draws on a wealth of archival, personal and creative material. Our work draws on three types of primary material. The first are archival collections that include the voices of, or are about, queer South Asians in Britain. When we initially started this project and approached various archives with enquiries, we were often met with non-replies or apologies. Part of what we address through this project is the obscurity of queer South Asian lives and community building in archives. However, thanks to the efforts of some archivists, LGBTQ+ collections, recent community-led archival projects (for example, Haringey Vanguard), and the informal archives held by individuals, we found far more than we could write about in this book. This has been part of the reason why London features so strongly throughout the book, as we had to find ways to narrow our focus. One of the finds that made this book possible was a collection of *Shakti Khabar*, the newsletter for Shakti, which is generally credited as the first queer South Asian organisation in Britain (and which acted as an incubator for leading charities such as the HIV/AIDS organisation the Naz Project, and Club Kali, a queer South Asian club night which has been running for thirty years). During the project, we came across several instances where material that researchers and archivists may define as 'of national significance' was being held on old floppy discs or in attics.

A few things were happening here. Material that had been 'useless' for so long was now finding itself to be useful for others. At a time when queer heritage projects have generated public interest, and interest from funders, these materials have potential value in parts of the heritage sector keen to do what the feminist writer and activist Sara Ahmed calls 'diversity work.'[5] When we were looking at material, we encountered the question of who the material might really belong to. The withdrawal of funding from key black-led and queer archives in the late 1980s and early 1990s left the material collections vulnerable. Some ended up in archives that moved to universities and museums, while others were broken up or lost. In some cases, records and archival material were informally passed along to queer friends in the community to safeguard. But what happens when these informal collections meet the copyright form of a depository? Who owns this work? We discuss some of the implications of institutional archives in Chapter 1.

The second type of material we draw on are interviews with queer South Asians who have or have had a substantial connection to Britain. With twenty-eight interviews spanning experiences from the 1970s to the present, we use these desi queer interlocutors throughout the book, commenting on the past, personalising some of the movements we describe, and acting as a point of connection for enduring conversations. We have been wary of using these voices as 'data' and we do not analyse them as such. Rather, we position our interlocutors in a networked inter-generational dialogue across types of sources that speak to queer South Asian life.

Finally, we draw on the art of queer South Asians in Britain whose experimental aesthetics produced a new style and vocabulary for watching, knowing, and feeling desi queer life in Britain. From iconic films such as *My Beautiful Laundrette* (1985), which explicitly dealt with the realities of homophobic and racist violence, to the queer subplots of *East is East* (1999), the near-queer misses of *Bend It Like Beckham* (2002), and the fairytales of *Nina's Heavenly Delights* (2006), mainstream British South Asian filmmaking has been peculiarly preoccupied with queer life. Some of Britain's foremost South Asian creatives have been part of queer communities. Sunil Gupta, Mumtaz Karimjee, Pratibha Parmar, Zahid Dar, Ian Iqbal Rashid, Parminder Sekhon, Poloumi Desai and Raman Mundair are just some of the artists whose work has straddled creative activism and the mainstream arts scene. Writers and artists such as Sharan Dhaliwal, Chitra Ramaswamy, Mohsin Zaidi, Raisa Kabir, Asifa Lahore and Mya Mehmi are just a few of the figures who demonstrate the breadth of queer South Asian representation today. We attempt to piece together a community story through the creativity and aesthetics that have engaged with the questions of nation, sexuality, and racialisation at the heart of being queer and South Asian in Britain.

Desiring histories

Queer coalitions and community spaces, particularly during the 1980s, have fuelled a nostalgia for the days of analogue activism. This looking back is often underpinned by the sneaking suspicion that things may have been better in the past through a romanticisation of earlier radical insurgencies. The availability of cheap or free accommodation for collectives, and the focus on voluntary efforts which often scavenged resources, can still be felt in countless carefully printed, assembled, and stapled queer and black feminist newsletters that survive from the period. The return to the activism of the past through reclaiming the urgency of earlier resistance can run the risk of smoothing over some of the real 'trouble and strife' of the time while excusing us from difficult conversations in the present.[6]

Films such as *Pride* (2014), which portrayed the work of Lesbians and Gays Support the Miners (LGSM) during the 1984 National Union of Mineworkers Strike, and series such as *It's a Sin* (2021), which focused on the experience of a London-based group of friends through the HIV/AIDS crisis of the 1980s, offer queer glimpses into communities that emerged at the intersection of desire, state violence and the machinery of neoliberalism. While present-day imperatives to diversify have influenced some of these contemporary projects in memory-work, the aesthetics of the queer '80s in Britain have portrayed some bodies as more desirable than others. As one of our interviewees put it, 'All the women had gone from both stories. And also the Asian women and the black women who actually were there.' The relative invisibilisation of women in high profile queer South Asian organising in Britain sits in contrast with the abundance of women's work, and their explorations of femininity as sites of resistance. Two examples of this in aesthetic practice can be seen in the work of Pratibha Parmar, who was a founding member of Shakti, and Mumtaz Karimjee, who as well as being known for her creative work, also documented queer activism in London. While Parmar and Karimjee were able to mobilise sophisticated narratives in artwork, text, and on film, we are also interested in everyday intimacies as sites of resistance, and forms of queer performance outside the conventional domains of art and culture.

Intimate diasporas

One of the interviews we conducted for this project was between Ritu and Ash (not his real name), a member of the London-based multi-generational South Asian drag house the Chutney Queens. It was a Friday night during one of the Covid lockdowns. Every other Friday night they had met as their alter-egos, Ritu as the DJ at Club Kali, and Ash as one of the Chutney Queen performers. Ritu had known Ash since the late 1990s when the Chutney Queens were at the height of their power, taking challenges from rival queer South Asian drag collectives on the stage, and often the floor, of Club Kali. As Ash put it, the 'drag wars' were 'Kinda like the Cold War. But very, very, hot.'

Talking about why dancing mattered to him, Ash turned his thoughts to his mother who had recently passed away:

> she was very, kind of, graceful and elegant with it as well, and there was a lot of power in that dancing [at community and family celebrations]. And I think maybe for her I think it was an outlet as well because, you know there was a lot of negative stuff going on at times, but I think that was her outlet. And I think it's something which yeah, it's sort of, it's an energy release and I find it very therapeutic.

Ash grew up in a working-class family in Southall, on the outskirts of London. Looking back at the adversity his mother had faced as a migrant woman, and the powerful release of that pain at family weddings and community functions, he saw a story that was partly his mother's, and partly his. Ritu picked Ash up on this later in the interview:

> But I think also, you used the word 'elegant' to describe your mum earlier, about the way that she used to dance. That there was the bold, and there was the energetic and the exhilarating aspect of what she was doing, but there was elegance. And that's always a word that I've used about you. I've never actually used it specifically about the way you dance, come to think of it, but I've always used it when I described you, because you do, you have, you've got her, your mum's elegance. There's a refinement.
>
> [...]
>
> Maybe I should have told you years ago. I don't know.

This book is filled with the stories we wish we had told, and we wish we had known. This encounter between Ritu and Ash captures the reasons we stayed with this book, and kept writing, despite the challenges in our own lives, and how daunting the task seemed. Partly it was to open a door between generations of queer South Asians in Britain to stage a vulnerability between the past and the present. But it was also informed by a desire to connect larger and longer histories of South Asian experience in Britain, to not see queer life in a silo, but to see it everywhere. The 'we' in this book is our collective authorial voice, but it is also a speculative reaching out to imagine the dimensions of queer South Asian life in Britain.

South Asian migration to Britain in the post-war/post-Partition period grew for several reasons, including calls for economic migrants and ongoing patterns of displacement (for example, the expulsion of South Asians from Uganda in

1972). Rising racial unrest in major cities, often involving far right organisations and unaffiliated individuals attacking or terrorising Black and South Asian communities, led to organised anti-racist resistance. Anandi Ramamurthy's work on Asian youth movements in the 1970s and 1980s[7] and Amrit Wilson's work on South Asian women's lives in the 1970s, particularly in the home and through unionised activism,[8] demonstrate the centrality of anti-racist and feminist consciousness-raising within predominantly working-class South Asian migrant communities. The wave of migrants arriving post-Partition to help bolster the British economy found themselves in diasporic communities that re-arranged geography in multiple ways. If Partition had segregated regional communities along religious lines, in the diaspora, the Muslim, Sikh, or Hindu neighbour you had lost might be your neighbour again. Working under the umbrella of 'political blackness,' South Asians challenged stereotypes of their status as the 'model minority,'[9] exemplified by the good, hard-working migrant who does not complain. The South Asian migrant generation of the 1970s and 1980s were within touching distance of Empire and the lasting effect of the 1947 Partition of India.[10]

Amrit Wilson's *Finding a Voice: Asian Women in Britain* (originally published in 1978, re-issued with new material in 2018) documents the struggles of working-class migrant women living in the climate of state-endorsed racism. Intended as a corrective to myths of 'silent and obedient' South Asian women, Wilson lays out everyday forms of care and resistance. By framing her work in the context of ongoing anti-colonial struggle in the late 1970s (namely in the north of Ireland) and legacies of racial capitalism (for example, processes of enclosure that turned land tenants in South Asia into small holders tied to land by debt), Wilson moves across the axes of power that locate working-class South Asian women within longer trajectories of colonial and post-colonial history. In her new introduction to the volume, Wilson posits *Finding a Voice* as a resistance to the systemic racism that undergirded the regulation of working-class South Asian family life:

> These probings [by social workers, health visitors and academics] led to the establishment of a host of 'experts' in the local authorities and at universities, who, by speaking to South Asian women, often via their husbands, found them to be 'passive,' to have inordinately low 'pain thresholds,' poor mothering skills and, of course, to be remarkably silent.[11]

The story of queer South Asians is a part of a longer history of gendered bodies who find themselves failing to properly reproduce good South Asian families (predicated on them staying quiet) that can be accommodated in the healthy imaginary of the nation (the slippage between the state's regulation of what a good mother is and the responsibilities of good citizens). The connections between the struggles of today's queers and yesterday's mothers are made by Camille Kumar, one of the contemporary respondents in the reprint of *Finding a Voice*. After reading the account of Manjula, a young woman who entered an inter-caste marriage against her parent's wishes, Kumar speculates on the parallels to her life:

> Where does a Fiji-Indian Australian lesbian living in England with her white British wife, engaged in feminist struggle and anti-violence work, fit into the hierarchy of *Khandan* [family/household] and *Izzat* [honour]? My triple crossing of the *kala pani* [literal: black water], the perceived double crossing of my family in being a lesbian has, to some extent, cut me adrift from all of it. When I read Manjula's story I am struck by the similarities of our experiences: The withdrawn affection, the closing of our worlds, the constriction of our beings, the atmosphere of guilt and disappointment. Yet I also feel far from her. I wonder what Manjula would think of my *Izzat* if she met me.[12]

If Kumar's triple crossing of the *kala pani*[13] (Fiji/Australia/Britain) represents a recursive move away from South Asia as the singular point of origin for identity, her queerness becomes another kind of figurative *kala pani*, a threshold that, once crossed, opens her body to be marked by a foreign social order. Kumar's reading of Manjula's words forty years later, her reach across varying scales of geographical, temporal and sexual difference, temporarily co-locates two very different accounts of exclusion grounded in the pain of family severance in the diaspora that renders two women unrecognisable, with their names unspeakable in their families. Crossing the *kala pani* becomes a more apt metaphor for desi queer life than 'coming out' of the closet. Instead of desi queer imaginaries and lives inhabiting the confines of the closet, the crossing of the *kala pani* sutures histories of migration, diaspora and social exile to the history of racialised and sexual difference. It is a threat, as much as a promise, of the rearrangement of social orders where old templates can be reworked and repurposed in the diaspora. Like Kumar, part of our work in this book is to think expansively about queer experience and to see connections between forms of marginalisation.

When we talked about the title of this book to other queer South Asians we were met by a mixture of intrigue, hesitation and a fair amount of correction. Our use of 'queer' was often mistaken for an identity category. At times, this was considered to be offensive, a deliberate erasure of more familiar terms like gay and lesbian. At other times, some worried about the risks involved in using the wrong word even though they did not have a supply of better ones. We use 'queer' in its most expansive sense to capture the real and imaginary experiences and formations of non-heteronormative life. 'Desi', which derives from the word *desh* (land), is a word loosely used to describe people with South Asian heritage who live in the diaspora. It holds the idea of a homeland alongside new terrains for home-making in the diaspora. In the British context, to some extent, it stood as the counterpart of *vilayat* (foreign), the word commonly used by first-generation migrants to describe Britain in the twentieth century.[14] For some South Asians we spoke to, desi was too exclusive, referring mainly to North Indian culture.[15] For others, the classed connotations were too uncomfortable (calling someone a 'desi' can describe lacking sophistication; this draws on 'local' being one of the connotations of desi).

The plasticity of 'desi', however, is part of its appeal. In 'Queer Desi Formations,' Gayatri Reddy riffs off a term which 'is used as a coded and affect-laden term of reference—self and other—for people from South Asia, including Pakistan. In that sense, the term accommodates the more capacious understanding of nation/place.'[16] The capaciousness of the concept, its non-allegiance to specific political histories, renders its edges malleable to coalition and solidarity, a version of 'desi' that Maya Bhardwaj uses in work on anti-racist solidarity and care amongst racialised minorities during Covid-19.[17] Naveen Minai takes the capaciousness of 'desi' and turns it into a promiscuous concept that can use the bifurcation of home/away held within 'desi' to reveal the normative work of discipline and surveillance across real and embodied borders of identity.[18] Kareem Khubchandani deploys 'desi' as a protean embodied cultural heritage ready to be reworked into a variety of diasporic forms, including the desi drag queen.[19] We use 'desi' in its most capacious sense as a designation which inscribes a shared terrain of a 'homeland' furnished by recognisable touchpoints.

What connects us as authors is Club Kali. For Ritu it is her club; for Churnjeet it was the first queer South Asian space she entered as a young woman in the late 1990s; and for Rohit it was one of the first queer clubs he went to when he arrived as a student in London from Kolkata. Rohit and Churnjeet had met in 2018 but started working together in 2019 on a project called

'Cross Border Queers' which was a precursor to this book. It was originally designed to give a comparative account of queer cultural production and community-making across the UK and India but had to fundamentally change in the face of lockdown. We return to this unfinished queer project in the Conclusion.

Churnjeet and Ritu met during the first lockdown when they joined the same online South Asian lesbian group, only to find themselves taken out of the group chat after the perennial question of 'can white allies and partners join?' fractured the group (thanks to a fellow exile, they formed another meet-up that still runs at the time of writing). Desire, trouble and strife are commonplaces in the social movements we describe from the past, and within the queer communities we live in now. This was felt, and was most apparent, in the interviews we conducted for the project. The majority of interviews were conducted by Ritu, whose professional life has included community research and radio interviews on the BBC, as well as other outlets. With a strong focus on individual storytelling, the semi-structured approach allowed us all to avoid arriving with a script geared towards queer revelation. Indeed, the explicitly queer content of each interview varies.

We interviewed twenty-eight people across during a two-year period running from 2020 to 2022. These included interviews conducted by Pawan Dhall in Kolkata with queer South Asians who had lived in Britain but had returned to South Asia. Asking people to share stories with us involved a looking back that was taking place during a time when 'real life' was on pause, a promise of something we would return to if we followed government guidance and used our own resilience to make it through. But as we saw, especially in the UK and other countries with stark socio-economic differences which affected racialised communities the hardest, the promise that we were all 'in it together' was hollowed out by statistics and stories showing the disproportionate suffering of Black and Asian heritage communities. Combined with the impact of Black Lives Matter on public debates around institutional and societal racism, and the growing visibility of an organised transphobia emboldened by unlikely alliances between sections of the gay and lesbian community and right-wing populists, our interviews took place in the context of a heightened sensitivity to the experience of discrimination and violence towards queer racialised communities. While many of the participants were multi-lingual, the interviews were conducted in English, which had its own drawbacks but which also represented the reality of spoken 'mother' tongues in the diaspora.

Speaking in English about being South Asian led to various kinds of looking back which often raised the issue of exactly where in South Asia their families were—to use a loaded word—'from'. These reflections followed, unsurprisingly, the historical routes of colonisation and empire. The Caribbean (Trinidad and Guyana), North America (Canada), the African continent (Uganda, Kenya, Nigeria, Somalia and Tanzania), Middle East (Kuwait and the United Arab Emirates), and East and Southeast Asia (Hong Kong and Indonesia) featured as prominently as Pakistan (Sindh and Punjab) and India (Punjab, Gujarat, Kerala, the North East and West Bengal). Nepal, Sri Lanka and Bangladesh were mentioned, but only by single interviewees. The majority of our interviewees were not born in South Asia, and for many, that was not the experience of their parents either. But despite national, religious, linguistic, ethnic, classed and caste differences, they recognised themselves in the term of 'South Asian' which has become an affiliation of convenience despite the term's tendency in Britain to over-emphasise the experience of economic migrants from North India, Pakistan and Bangladesh during the 1960s.

This was something the queer South Asian organisation Shakti addressed through calls for a more expansive imagining of South Asia that included people from Sri Lanka, Nepal and Bangladesh, amongst others. In their groundbreaking report on queer South Asian life in the UK published in 1991 as *Khush* (which we discuss in Chapter 3), they directly addressed the limitations of the word 'Asian' in the British context, but also highlighted the opportunity words like 'Asian' introduced to identify connections and solidarities across Asian culture.[20] A more recent example of the impetus to imagine counter-geographies of sexuality can be seen in the work of Queer Asia, a series of conferences festivals and a publication which have sought to parse what 'Queer Asia' means for activists and scholars, particularly in the UK.[21]

While 'British Asian' or 'South Asian' are useful ways of imagining communities, shifting emphases in regional or religious identities, often triggered by politics, have had a profound impact on the community networks people seek. Contemporary examples of this include the Farmers' Protests, where queer diasporic Punjabi Sikhs were part of a global fightback against the cycles of economically enforced industrialisation and debt that has shaped the Punjabi landscape in India.[22] Queer Muslims in Britain have been at the forefront of organising demonstrations to support the Palestinian cause, including partnering with Lesbian and Gays Support the Migrants, and Queers for Palestine in their call to opt out of London Pride 2024 to protest against the event sponsors who had direct links to Israel.[23] These responses expose some of the cracks within broader imaginings of the South Asian community in Britain. How far, for example, have Hindu and Sikh communities mobilised to collectively challenge Islamophobia in the UK? How possible is this when a transnational Hindutva (Hindu nationalist) movement has extensive social media penetration and fundraising from within

South Asian Hindu communities in the UK? In *Desi Queers* we look to the progressive queer coalitions that have used the South Asian diaspora as a platform from which to remake the possibilities of queer of colour life.

Black queer approaches

We locate our work in traditions that have responded to the specificities and immediacies of real and discursive violence in the UK. Our critical companions are drawn from researcher-activists such as Pratibha Parmar, Parminder Sekhon and Poulomi Desai, whose work we draw on conceptually, but whose lives are intimately entwined with some of the worlds we describe. Their own connections to the key figures in British cultural studies, including Stuart Hall and Paul Gilroy, alongside transnational networks of Black feminists including Audre Lorde, produce a critical genealogy for our work in the 1980s that took an active interest in cultivating common ground to challenge systems of oppression. An example of this can be seen in one of the seminal texts of the black women's movement in 1980s Britain, 'Many Voices, One Chant: Black Feminist Perspectives.'[24]

The production of this 1984 journal edition had, itself, been a notable process and event that recognised the role of white women in gatekeeping key forums of intellectual and cultural credibility in British feminism. The editorial was unambiguous in its refusal of cynical exercises in diversity that were happy to admit black women as case studies of women's lives without revealing how the lens of whiteness continually erased the specificities of racialised experience: 'We hope that in the future *Feminist Review* will include writings by and for Black women, so that this issue does not remain a token exercise. There is also an ongoing need for white women to take note of and act upon Black feminist critiques.'[25] The black feminist takeover of *Feminist Review* politically threaded Black and South Asian women together in a gendered resistance to imperialism and patriarchy that was articulated through the critical and creative work of black women which documented key achievements in activism led by, and for, black and South Asian women (examples of which included the Organisation of Women of African and Asian Descent, Awaz, the Brixton Black Women's Group and Brent Asian Women's Refuge and Resource Centre). The journal issue reflected on its own role in documenting a history and what it might mean to acknowledge the labour involved in building the affective communities of the future. The following footnote appeared at the end of an article:

> As an Asian lesbian I have been extremely privileged in participating in the production of this crucial work. I have learnt so much and gained so much strength from reading all the articles I typed. I have two requests: one, that my name be mentioned humbly in connection with this work and with these, my Black sisters, whom I respect greatly and two, that I have a copy of *Feminist Review* sent to me so that I can refer to these articles in my old age! Thank You, In Black Sisterhood, Ravinder Sethi.[26]

As we typed out this quote forty years later, we reflected on how much it continued to resonate. The request to be acknowledged, the hope for a future furnished with the words of our community. The work to acknowledge the contributions of South Asians to queer and feminist cultural politics continues. The article Sethi transcribed as 'Becoming Visible: Black Lesbian Discussion' was based on eight hours of audio recordings that documented an analysis of activism enabled by friendships and reflections shared over food. The article was built on the everyday praxis of community. The opening of the women's discussion brings together the potential of building solidarities through time spent together that sows strength in a vulnerability (which two of the discussants attribute to helping them make the decision to use their real names) that acts as an antidote to the fear and anxiety of how their words will be met in the world. Their words are prescient. Carmen parsed the risk of coming out on the page as becoming visible to the state and a hostile media:

> the drastic way things are going in this country, names in print are prime targets because of the threat our words make. It would also affect our freedom of travel into different countries. On the other hand, there's the way that names in print get taken up by the media, they like to pin mass movements onto a few individual 'heroes' or leaders.[27]

Pratibha [Parmar] similarly reflected on the consequences of entering a public discourse where the solid shape of words on the page could be used to fix, locate and target the women in the volume: 'I still don't feel sure about using my name... On the one hand I really want to use it and be who I am and be identified. My greatest fear is total rejection from my family.'[28] 'Coming out' as aspiration and requirement for a healthy queer visibility was its own target for critique by Pratibha: 'One is made to feel guilty if you don't come out. At one time in the gay movement there was this pressure that "You've not really come out till you've come out to your family" and I find that really oppressive.'[29] For Shaila, the role of the family in offering the simplest and most intimate insulation from the realities of everyday racism made the choice between 'coming out' and family impossible:

> The myth that Black families or people are more homophobic than whites should really be demolished, because really what is obvious is that the security links we need with our families/communities are stronger. But about using our names... I think it is important, it makes us accessible, which is very difficult and personal, but it would be nice for other sisters to be able to recognise us.[30]

Faced with the triple jeopardy of racism, misogyny and homophobia, the choice to 'come out' into a white-centric community, and male-dominated mainstream LGBTQ+ spaces, was to render yourself vulnerable to forces of a racism veiled by the language of gay and lesbian liberation.[31] In the forty years since its original publication, many of the debates in the volume are familiar.[32] The continual characterisation of Black and South Asian communities as 'problematic' has found a new expression in state-sponsored Islamophobia that lends weight to nativist ideologies that cast migrant communities and racialised minorities as the dangerous other of human rights-focused liberal Western democracies, a move which Jasbir Puar expanded upon in her 2007 argument on homonationalism.[33]

The (re)turn to identifying the significance of anti-racist activism and consciousness-raising to the project of making queer lives liveable involves a citational practice that names, and credits, the distinct contributions that have shaped the worlds we inhabit. As Sara Ahmed argues, 'Citation is how we acknowledge our debt to those who came before; those who helped us find our way when the way was obscured because we deviated from the paths we were told to follow.'[34] Naming becomes an act of recognition, a recognition of work done and a recognition of work yet to be done by us. The work done includes the labour which strikes minor notes in the present, but which forms everyday practices of resistance. Ravinder Sethi's footnote is just one example of this. Reading the words of fellow black women, taking the time to meticulously type them out, to rehearse the meaning of the words through touching every letter and space, became a material act of community building and consciousness-raising that relied on thinking with fellow black feminists in Britain. The request for the contribution to be acknowledged, and for a copy of the journal, act as their own tacit reminders of what kind of labour gets credit in knowledge economies (the authorial hand rather than the hands that carry the work) alongside the barrier to accessing academic publications which are behind paywalls or are prohibitively priced. One cannot help but wonder: forty years later, how does Sethi look back on this journal? What do we see when we look to the past encumbered with the weight of our expectations about what, or who, we want to find?

Many of the projects we describe in the first half of the book are influenced by political blackness. We do not use this term heroically, nor are we advocating for one its (many) returns. Rather, we view it as part of the complex ecosystem of racial politics and culture in Britain that holds the tension between the possibility of racial solidarity against the reality of anti-blackness, especially within South Asian communities. Stuart Hall's 'New Ethnicities' described a shift in racial cultural politics in Britain that moved from '*access* to the rights of representation'[35] to the politics of representation. This produced a turn towards proliferating aesthetic and cultural experiments and expressions which 'inevitably entails a weakening or fading of the notion that "race" or some composition notion of race around the term "black" will either guarantee the effectivity of any cultural practice or determine in any final sense its aesthetic value.'[36]

Unpicking the value in an essentialised black subject prone to romanticisation as always 'good' or the corrective to whiteness, Hall identified films like *My Beautiful Launderette* (1985) as part of a shift in focus to articulations of classed, gendered, sexual and ethnic difference that were producing forms of critique unbounded from a binary politics of race, but able to create new forms of belonging and longing in desiring and diverse trajectories of experience that could also, in concert, reveal some of the invisible operations of whiteness, and in the visibility, render them available for reckoning.

The political use of 'black' keeps making its own comebacks in British culture and politics and brings with it some familiar spectres. The scholar Tariq Modood attacked the concept in 1994 as, '"black" serves to obscure Asian identities and smother the basis of ethnic pride.'[37] The cultural turn produced new forms of emphasis for the study of Black and South Asian lives that inevitably focused on points of particularity that became incommensurable differences (for example, religious and cultural practices around marriage, tribal-caste affiliation, or language).[38] Claire Alexander's own reflection on her more recent encounters with the political use of 'black' during the formation of a Black Female Professors network in Britain highlighted the stark absence of racially minoritised women in universities, but also raised a discomfort around who gets to be called black, especially when the number of women professors from African and Afro-Caribbean backgrounds is comparatively lower than Indian heritage professors. However, Alexander points out that much of the discomfort came from South Asian women who worried about the risk of appropriation, a tacit act of solidarity through a recognition of the uneven forces of discrimination.[39]

The repeated return to political blackness in British political and cultural discourses is always a return to the site of a problem with a kernel of hope. Alexander underestimates the value of black feminism in exploring the affordances of blackness as a site of renewing and nurturing critique. In a discussion between Heidi Mirza and Yasmin Gunaratnam in 2014, Mirza pointed to attacks on black feminism as being 'anachronistic'[40] in the wake of neoliberal equality regimes where political demands for representation and the potential of what Hall called diversity can be churned into equality, diversity and inclusion policies that re-entrench the well-worn paths of structural discrimination.[41] But Mirza ends with a promising note, 'For me Black feminism is a stalwart tree with rich, deep roots, lovingly nurtured by a community of careful, critical gardeners. The wise embrace of its strong branches reaches out across time and space to shelter a multitude of voices.'[42] In this book we use black in its uncapitalised form to refer to specific political movements or configurations for racialised subjects.

For queer South Asians coming out in Britain in the late 1970s and early 1980s, political blackness and black feminism were more than coordinates for organising; they offered a critical vocabulary to begin naming the possibilities of solidarity as a way to survive in a society and media saturated in racist and heterosexist prejudice. Solidarity is an important strategy in this book, and we describe it in two different senses. In the first, we think of black feminist philosophy and action as what Sara Ahmed has described as a 'life-line' for various formations of queer feminist and anti-racist aesthetics.[43] Rather than seeing queer South Asian life as marginalised, we use the margin as a site of resistance and community. To imagine this, we draw on bell hooks's work on the margin as a space for improvised alternative cultural and aesthetic practice: 'For me this space of racial openness is a margin—a profound edge. Locating oneself there is difficult yet necessary. It is not a "safe" place. One is always at risk. One needs a community of resistance.'[44] Solidarities can take queer forms when they propose an aesthetic, critique or orientation that belongs to the 'profound edge', or periphery, that rests against, and resists, state-inscribed normative structures. The margins are where creative experiments in becoming and belonging celebrate the ex-centric relations between communities separated by distance but connected by their peripheral relationship to the healthy body of the state. To read the potential of the margin as a site of counter-hegemonic critique is to exceed the expectations of being heard, or included, by cultural and political elites. Asking for recognition from regimes of power bent on eviscerating bodies falling short of normative orders requires a visibility and legibility on someone else's terms. In her oft-cited work on borderlands, Gloria Anzaldúa uses the U.S.-Mexican border as the site of a 'border culture' where the, '*Los atravesados* live [...]: the squint-eyed, the perverse, the queer, the troublesome, the mongrel, the mulato, the half-breed, the half dead; in short, those who cross over, pass over, or go through the confines of the "normal."'[45] Solidarity in borderlands is an affective reach across differentiated positions that have the potential to realise community through proximal relations to one another that are not dependent on being routed through the powerlines of oppression. These turns to community outside the immediacy of ethnic, classed or place-based affiliation are impelled by a shared perspective from the periphery. A perspective that no longer finds a safe harbour in compliance.

While *Desi Queers* is orientated towards horizons of hope built on anti-oppressive coalitions, we remain vigilant for how and why identity politics becomes unmoored from the projects that precede them (is forgetting a necessary erasure?). The longer view of queer South Asian life in Britain is sparsely cited, if at all, in the grand histories of 'British Asians' or LGBTQ+ communities the UK.[46] When we began to consider the reasons for this, two quotes from recent books captured some of our thinking. The first documented an encounter between the queer geographer Amin Ghaziani and Ryan Lanji at Hungama, a queer South Asian club night that ran in London from 2018 to 2023:

> The South Asian experience is like 'mercury,' he [Ryan] reflected. 'We're shape shifters, and so at moments we become quite Black-orientated, or we can become quite queer, or we can become quite straight, or we can become quite White.' When my eyes returned, Ryan told me that at Hungama, people could 'embrace their chameleon.' The audience is like a 'color wheel,' he noted. Ryan was right—and there we were, spinning together.[47]

Lanji is part of an increasingly mobile community of queer creatives of South Asian heritage whose sampling of desi life is an aesthetic with the potential to erase the specificity of racialisation and obscure its conditions. We read these words against another recent evocation of 'mercurial' in relation to race and sexuality from Sita Balani:

> Cedric Robinson observes, 'race is mercurial—deadly and slick.' That race is deadly is easy to see—we see it in the deaths of migrants trying to cross the Mediterranean; we see it in the ongoing health disparities and mortality rates; we see it in the overrepresentation of racialised people in the criminal justice system.[48]

For South Asians able to mobilise different kinds of privilege within the diaspora (caste; skin colour; economic), the question becomes: What is mercurial? The ability of some South Asian communities to gravitate towards forms of economic and cultural capital, to shift and orientate towards varying power lines in diasporas? Or is racialisation mercurial in its ability to deploy ever-adapting tactics to ensure the brown body is marked? While we acknowledge the rich and productive work that has emerged to expand queer approaches to South Asia, *Desi Queers* is grounded in the specificities of local movements and issues. From the bombs planted in London by a Neo-Nazi in 1999 to target queer, South Asian and black communities, to the devastating impact of 9/11 and 7/7, which magnified existing tensions within British South Asian communities, evoking South Asian lives and communities in Britain is always and already political.

Routes through the book

Chapter 1 visits the queer and feminist black collectives and politics which acted as incubators for queer South Asian cultural politics, including Haringey Black Action and Southall Black Sisters. The spectre of the harsh reality of working-class life in the 1970s and 1980s, especially for people of colour, looms large in archival accounts where basic access to safety (from racism), housing and economic independence are recurring themes. Especially in the material from the 1980s and 1990s, we found class rather than caste to be the key element of structural oppression for South Asian communities, with gender and religion being the defining markers of difference (and discrimination) within communities. Class and caste are not synonyms in the British context, but they are structures of economic and cultural differentiation which can carve up and limit access to worlds and their resources. Where we do read an important similarity is in the way identities related to class and caste have become unmoored from their original meanings and contexts. Identifying as working class is no longer neatly tied to economics. And while the battle against caste-based oppression may have been subsumed by some of the anti-racist work of the 1970s to 1990s, a new generation of activists and artists are exploring queer approaches to caste-based life.[49]

Chapter 2 draws on our interviews, archive material on Shakti, and the work of DJ Ritu to describe the different political and cultural influences which facilitated the emergence of queer South Asian nightlife. This was more than a South Asian riff on existing queer nightlife; it was a distinct form that drew on counter-cultural music scenes developed by South Asian youth movements influenced by the full range of urban diasporic sounds, from the Caribbean to the Middle East. Chapter 2 also analyses the controversy around drag performances at Shakti Disco in the early 1990s. While early queer South Asian collectives turned to ancient India for coordinates to queer life in the Global South, we were surprised not to see more interest in gender non-confirming identities, communities and histories. Especially in the 1980s and 1990s, following the orthodoxy of mainstream LGB charities in the UK, the focus was very much on gays and lesbians. Scholars such as Sandeep Bakshi have been integral to exploring the opportunities in comparing different typologies of non-normative gender performance in community settings. As he pointed out in 2004, 'Drag queens, like Hijra performances, often make us think about the various ways in which gender is played out and "naturalised" in society.'[50]

It is only in the second half of the book that we focus on trans* life and expression more substantially, reflecting the minoritisation of trans* folk within queer communities. The relatively recent visible cultural, political and creative exploration of trans* South Asian lives and identities in the diaspora can be seen in the work of pioneers such as Sabah Choudrey who co-founded Trans Pride Brighton in 2013. Trans* scholarship and activism have become one of the most productive and creative intersections between the long lineages of gender non-conforming lives, histories and politics in South Asia, and its diasporas, despite, as Nat Raha and others point out, the precarity hard-wired into the labour of realising those lives.[51]

Chapters 3, 4 and 5 chart a lineage of desi queer community print (newsletters) and art in Britain that critiques oppression within the South Asian diaspora, and at the same time, places it in longer histories and legacies of imperialism. These chapters highlight the significance of transnational activism and cultural production. Through these platforms, new community spaces emerged for dialogue and cultural expression. South Asian queer organising and cultural creation are occurring across the global diasporas, a direct result of colonial exploitation. This creative resistance illustrates how South Asian queers documented their experiences, navigating racism and homophobia, and using their voices to challenge prevailing power structures. This effort was not just about increasing visibility for the community; it was also about asserting identity and resisting oppression. Researching queer South Asian diasporic life involves reading intimacy, culture and politics as part of the personal and public infrastructure that are the pre-conditions of queer racialised liveability. The Postscript is for researchers and students; it further explains and develops the critical and methodological frameworks we introduce in the book to explore these themes.

As we end this introduction, we want to reflect a little on friendship and what role it plays in research and especially doing 'queer research.' We are aware of the privilege involved in who gets to write and tell stories. As Matt Brim has demonstrated especially in relation to queer studies, the practices of radical hope and thinking otherwise at the heart of queer culture can be in opposition to the highly stratified and prestige-driven environments of academic systems.[52] However, as we see throughout the book, the relationship between education, culture, community activism, local authority policies and politics can be porous. We are interested in how forms of 'queer sharing'[53] can harness different kinds of institutional, cultural and individual labour to give imagined communities the stories, knowledge and resources to critique the worlds we live in, and imagine better ones.

This book is, in many ways, the outcome of a lifelong transformational project of working at the interstices of academia, social justice movements and cultural work. We carry the responsibility here of queer kin and allies who have entrusted us with their stories—memories, dreams and regrets. As Niharika Banerjea et al in their book *Friendship as Social Justice Activism* note, 'Friendship is integral to vitality. Friendship stokes imagination. Friendship fires rebellions. Friendship provides testimony.'[54] The stories we tell here are a testimony of the revolutionary work of queer friendship across generations.

1

BLACK, SOUTH ASIAN AND QUEER IN 1980s BRITAIN

In the years before the queer South Asian group Shakti formed in 1988, conferences such as the Organisation of Women of African and Asian Descent (a black feminist conference), Zami (for politically black lesbians),[1] and grassroots collectives such as the Black Lesbian and Gay Centre provided forums for queer South Asians invested in racial solidarity to meet, build community and organise. These were always politically charged spaces, where black, gay and lesbian and feminist struggles led to heated debate. But debates, political fractures, manifestos and everything that comes with activism were also the mechanism through which people worked the competing terrains of identity politics into solidarity-driven anti-oppression coalitions. These coalitions brought together learning from Greenham Common and the Race Riots of the 1980s alongside a quotidian exercise in care emerging from working-class, anti-racist and feminist life. These were also globally-minded coalitions. A united Ireland, Palestine, and Anti-Apartheid protest were just a few of the issues which formed an extended idea about the vectors and work of oppression. To put it another way, these were internationally-minded mutual aid-oriented projects bent on the equitable distribution of social and economic resources.

One of the important backdrops to this chapter is the work of the Labour-run Greater London Council (GLC), which from the early 1980s until its abolition in 1986 committed unprecedented funding to minoritised groups in London. If the 1980s marked the ascent of Thatcherite neoliberalism, it also marked a newly resourced group of minoritised groups with plans for change supported by prominent campaigns. For example, 1984 was the GLC's Anti-Racist Year and in 1987 Black History Month would emerge from anti-racist local authority work. While internal wrangling within the Labour party sought more socially moderate, and what they assumed were electable, positions, a much broader range of Left socialist politics was playing out in local branches and local authorities, especially in London.[2]

This chapter tells the story of how and why these scenes were so integral for what we call first-generation desi queers. We use this term to describe the formation of a generation whose belonging across migrant and queer communities produced distinct forms of social organising that have come to define the queer South Asian scene in Britain. South Asian queer activism in the late 1970s and early 1980s emerged in the context of rife anti-black and anti-South Asian racism that sought to categorise mostly working-class migrants and racially minoritised communities as a danger to Britain's public health, moral integrity and cultural coherency. It also emerged at a pivotal moment in British queer and feminist history. Hard-won basic civil rights had been established in British legislation through the Race Relations Act (1965), the Sexual Offenses Act (1967) and the Equal Pay Act (1970). This legislation found a balance between open state-endorsement of racism, homophobia and sexism and a significant body of public and political opinion about the need for appropriate limits to protect the already enshrined status of white heteronormative power. South Asian queer lives in Britain became visible through a range of anti-racist, feminist and queer praxis that sought solidarities between groups which had been historically oppressed and pathologised by the British state.

Successive waves of migrants had arrived in Britain in the aftermath of decolonisation and calls from Britain to the Commonwealth for workers to fuel economic growth. From the Caribbean Windrush generation of the 1940s to 1970s to South Asians arriving from Kenya (1968) and Uganda (1972), many of the people Britain 'welcomed' were, or were the descendants of, indentured labourers, refugees, 'double' migrants and displaced communities. Many of the Bangladeshi and Punjabi migrants arriving in Britain in larger numbers from the 1950s had witnessed or been impacted by the 1947 Partition of India. Through the 1980s, South Asians were protecting themselves from violence on the streets of Britain while seeing the consequences of faith and caste-based violence playing out in South Asia for their families and friends. 'Home', wherever it was, was not a guarantee of safety.

While the Race Relations Act 1976 made it unlawful to discriminate against individuals on the basis of race and ethnicity, it had a limited impact on communities who were facing state-sanctioned violence and intimidation through over-policing and racial profiling. Ruth Wilson Gilmore's definition of racism is particularly pertinent here: 'Racism, specifically, is the state-sanctioned or extralegal production and exploitation of group-differentiated vulnerability to premature death.'[3] The murder of Gurdip Singh Chaggar by white youths in Southall in 1976 led to the formation of the Southall Youth Movement and a growing action-based anti-racist consciousness within areas of significant South Asian settlement.[4] From the enforced bussing of Black and South Asian children, sending them to schools in different neighbourhoods, to increasing controls on immigration, and open discrimination in employment and housing, there was no aspect of life that remained untouched by racism.[5]

These were more than events or incidents. They were expressions of state-sanctioned disdain and violence towards Black and Asian communities that have left an indelible mark on the generations who lived through the fear of everyday violence. From the Brixton Riots (1981) to the protest in support of the Bradford 12 (1981), a generation of queer South Asians found their orientation through a language of anti-oppression and solidarity platforms.[6] As Savi Hensman pointed out to us, 'Perhaps we were something of an exception—yet queer South Asians coming out to ourselves and maybe others in the late '70s or '80s often interacted with older people in communities of colour who were themselves rebelling against patriarchal norms.' Despite the media interest in characterising South Asian communities as insular and conservative, the South Asian anti-imperial activism that developed in Britain from the late nineteenth century did not disappear after Partition. Instead, it took aim at the shifting strategies of cultural imperialism and state-sponsored racism that co-located with other movements, including the women's movement and the broader umbrella of political blackness.

The use of political blackness in the queer scene was strongly based in class politics, which South Asians used to complicate how affiliations across, and within, communities worked in practice. Via email correspondence, Savi explained this complexity through the following scenario:

> For instance a young Indian man from a prosperous Gujarati household, growing up in Wembley, whose parents were imbued with class and caste snobbery as well as an unconscious embrace of what might be described as Victorian values on top of other prejudices in a quest for

> respectability, might have faced a very different set of pressures from a young Bangladeshi woman on a council estate in Tower Hamlets whose parents were factory workers and trade unionists, with one or two African friends who went to the same mosque or whose children were at the same school. Affectional connections based on intimate relationships, along with what might be described as broader queer/black 'siblinghood', further complicate questions of personal identity and its shifts.

Savi's use of 'affectional connections' describes what Paul Gilroy termed conviviality: 'the processes of cohabitation and intersection that have made multiculture an ordinary feature of social life.'[7] Conviviality is not the celebratory side of multiculturalism. Rather, it describes the reality of people and communities who do not have obvious affinities, finding points of connection through sharing the same neighbourhood, or going to the same shops. Savi describes the emancipatory potential of these kinds of connections, forms of kinship that take on a more powerful relevance than more obvious ethnic or religious affiliations. This was a view shared amongst many of our interviewees. One described his time growing up in a London council estate in the 1970s that was home to several racist gangs, but never personally having any trouble from them, because they recognised him as part of a collective landscape structured by difference, but not always predictably defined by it.

In the quote above, Savi traces the complex interplay of faith, geography, caste and class as fluid categories that shift their emphasis in response to specific contexts. For example, while caste and class have very different operations and histories, their collusion in reproducing snobbery in Savi's quote temporarily locates them on the same terrain. The countermove to this is the space for solidarity or recognition amongst caste- and class-oppressed people who continue to be stigmatised in different ways, but often with the same consequences. Viewing longer histories of queer South Asian working-class history in the UK extends the work of scholars such as Yvette Taylor, who have shown the ways in which queer racialised subjects have continued to feel outside of the heroic narratives of working-class history (often viewed as part of a white working-class struggle) despite sharing, and recognising, politics conditioned by material precarity and working-class solidarity, for example through trade union movements.[8]

The realities of gendered and racialised economic precarity extended to sexuality for politically black-identifying queer groups in the 1980s. An example of this can be seen in the foundation of the Gay Black Group (originally called the Gay Asian Group for a few weeks) in 1981 as one of the first dedicated queer groups for racialised minorities in Britain.[9] With regular meetings at Gay's the Word bookshop in Bloomsbury, their collective slowly grew.[10] Their definition of black was: 'if you are of Asian or African descent; SE Asian, Chinese or Caribbean, if you have been culturally and economically colonised.'[11] An information leaflet for the organisation clearly framed sexual and racial minoritisation as an issue of class:

> Alongside the institutional racism we experience, there is the less overt racism that we encounter in the gay community. The priority placed on 'coming out' in the politics of sexual liberation, with its emphasis on rejecting the nuclear family, ignores the specific importance the extended family has for us. That is, we are urged to discard the solidarity and economic/emotional support which our families give us against a racist society.[12]

The list of support organisations at the back of the leaflet pointed to the Black Lesbian Group, Brixton Black Women's Group, Southall Black Sisters, and AWAZ (Asian Women's Movement) rather than white-led lesbian and gay organisations.

Their awareness of being a new queer formation was highlighted in their language, as more than once members of the Black Gay Group described themselves as 'first generation black gays',[13] an inventive riff that entwined experiences of migrant non-belonging with queer non-belonging.

A short documentary about the Gay Black Group, produced in 1983, interviewed several of its members, some of whom would go on to have prominent careers in art and/or activism, including Isaac Julien, Femi Otitoju, and Zahid Dar. The importance of the group was articulated by Femi Otitoju as a response to the lack of 'gay black empathy' in white-led queer spaces.[14] The South Asian men in the group framed the need for 'gay black empathy' through the impossible choice of family and community responsibilities which meant that being 'out' on the scene also meant being 'out' of the familial and community networks that had made you.

One of the South Asian men interviewed in the documentary spoke about the 'spark' of recognition in coming out in a (white) queer group, but that 'pushing the ideas of gay liberation' had been personally disastrous for him, as he came out to his family and subsequently became homeless. The self-fulfilling prophecy of homophobic South Asian communities displaced the reasons why the ties of family were so integral to social and economic resilience in hostile environments. He quietly stated his resentment of the 'white middle-class' terms of coming out, which he said he was slowly re-inscribing through his attempts to explain his sexuality to his family 'in Asian terms,' in order to find a way to return to them without giving up on his sexual identity. Filmed in Gay's the Word in Soho, in settings along the South Bank of the River Thames, and in the homes of the interviewees, the documentary sequences the queer scene/metropole/home as a triptych hinged on painful exclusions.

The absence of any queer South Asian women in the documentary was testament to an enduring issue in queer organising across the South Asian diaspora: the role and visibility of women. The documentary on the Gay Black Group is part of an important archive of black queer organising in UK. However, it also demonstrates the ease with which South Asian women can be removed from the frame of queer experience. This chapter responds to this invisibility by focusing on the black lesbian feminist organising and practice that would intellectually and materially support the development of long-standing queer South Asian networks and organisations from the late 1980s. The chapter begins by considering how we can surface and write these alternative queer histories, before moving through a series of case studies that demonstrate the ways in which black queer and feminist solidarities produced the political sensibility and cultural aesthetics that would be foundational for queer South Asian community organising.

Scavenging for queer South Asian activism

No matter how well catalogued or organised an archive is, you can't get away from the fact that you will need to patiently trawl through material to find what you're looking for. More often than not, material you weren't necessarily looking for will come and find you. Looking for lives deemed invisible in conventional archives and research always involves exercises in scavenging: scavenging for anecdotes, scavenging for evidence, scavenging because the value of this cultural history has not yet been felt. Here's one example: On 18 June 1987, Museum and Library Staff in Haringey Council were invited to a workshop on lesbian and gay inclusion. The training session was structured around practical scenarios including the following:

> Having seen an exhibition and book display, a member of the public comments, 'The council's only bothered about these lesbians and gays… and blacks… we're sick of having all this homosexuality shoved down our throats… why doesn't the council spend its money on ordinary decent people?' How do you reply?[15]

The session was an outcome of the coordinated work of the Haringey Lesbian and Gay Unit to challenge heterosexism in council services. Almost forty years later, this scenario remains strikingly relevant in the face of the right-wing backlash to prominent campaigns and movements, including Rhodes Must Fall and Black Lives Matter, that have used museums and monuments as examples of how the state values symbols and legacies of racism. More importantly, this example shows the real problem in approaching minoritised histories. The problem is not that minoritised communities and cultures have nothing of cultural value but rather that institutions do not have the expertise, infrastructure or the broader cultural support to recognise the value of those lives.

If national museums and heritage organisations conserve the past, especially for the pubic, until recently the distinct experience of queer South Asians in Britain has remained a partial or missing story. This absence has meant that despite the long presence of South Asians in Britain, the majority of research and scholarship queering South Asian experience in the diaspora has often come from scholars in North America.[16] Exploring the queer South Asian experience globally through the lens of its diaspora has rerouted some local and very specific coordinates of organising and expression through transnational nodes, favouring a comparative approach anchored in the broader South Asian experience. While this is a vital dimension to the story of queer South Asian lives in Britain, more active connections across queer South Asian diasporas emerge from the late 1980s as identity and community formations shifted, especially in politically black queer spaces in Britain.

In this chapter, our focus is on material that falls outside of the conventional parameters of 'queer South Asian activism', but which is integral to the foundation and development of organisations like Shakti. For anyone starting work on queer South Asian social and cultural experiences in the 1980s, the realities of political life at the time, and the static rigour of cataloguing systems in museums and archives, means finding material can be a challenge. The knowledge of individual archivists can be vital, but in often under-funded community-based or community-held archives, there is no guarantee that well-resourced positions exist. Finding the material involves following the political and cultural trajectories of organising at the time. An example of this can be seen in the Haringey Vanguard Archive (held at Bruce Castle Museum) which documents the history of Black queer and queer of colour activism in the Borough. One of the folders in the archives holds a newsletter from 1984 with the cover slogan 'We Are Here!' accompanied by a picture of three South Asian women in saris.[17] Nothing on the cover refers to them as South Asian women; on the contrary, the reminder is that this newsletter is for 'Black Women Only.' The layered relationship between South Asian women and black feminism can make even more minoritised positions, for example queer South Asians, hard to find as a coherent presence in the archive.

This chapter draws from projects that consciously collected and documented queer community experiences in the 1980s, including queer South Asians (although in all cases queer South Asians are not the explicit subject of the work, or part of the catalogue designation). A large part of our archival research is drawn from the Camden Lesbian Centre and Black Lesbian Group Archive (CLCBLG) at the Glasgow Women's Library (GWL), which was originally part of the highly contested Lesbian

Archive and Information Centre in London (Lesbian Archive), where allegations of structural racism and mismanagement in the Lesbian Archive hastened its demise from the late 1980s.[18] GWL acquired the Lesbian Archive in the mid-1990s and it was catalogued in the 2010s, largely following the original order of the archive.[19] Founded in 1984, the Lesbian Archive was one of the many minorities-focused organisations that were supported by Greater London Council only to lose that funding after the Council's dissolution in 1986.[20]

In 1988, the Lesbian Archive faced a crisis after there were allegations of structural racism from black lesbian feminists. An interim support group was established to help 'ensure greater representation in the working, running and content of the Archive of Black and minority ethnic lesbians, working-class lesbians and lesbians with disabilities', which included Savi Hensman.[21] Linda King was hired as a black worker for the archive as part of what we would no doubt now call a move to 'decolonise' the Lesbian Archive. A white Lesbian Archive worker reflected on what needed to change: 'in the Lesbian Archive, books such as *Zami* by Black lesbian Audre Lorde are rare on the shelves which are sagging with biographies and information about "society" women.'[22] This included challenging stereotypes associated with lesbians which included, 'being white and middle-class and emerging out of white feminism in Western, capitalist societies.'[23] During her four-week post, Linda King bought a Minolta 300 and began taking pictures of, and recording, as many black lesbians as she could find. One of the agreed recommendations at the end of the report was that black lesbians should be the caretakers of resources and material about black lesbian lives.

Archives of black lesbian organising, especially in the early to mid-1980s, offer glimpses into solidarity work across the lines of racialised, gendered and classed difference. In this setting, the work of one community could be the tools used across collectives. For example, we discovered the work of Sisters Against Disablement whose 'access codes' (including information on entry points and types of lighting) are printed and tucked alongside many of the adverts, posters and flyers for black lesbian and feminist events throughout the late 1980s.[24] Another example is the work of the Lesbians and Policing Project, a Gay London Police Monitoring Group project in 1985 designed to tackle lesbophobia in the police. The community activist Kris Black used the project to work across lesbian and migrant communities, demonstrating one of the many ways that lesbian feminist principles informed a sharing of resources that counted women from migrant communities as kin in the face of police violence. An example of this can be seen in the Lespop poster, 'What to do if the police raid' which was translated into several languages, including Punjabi (see Figure 1). Politically black queers were using their funding and resources to support broader racialised and migrant communities in a way white queer communities couldn't or wouldn't.

While forums like the Gay Black Group offered basic access to a community, the politicisation and 'trouble' within black feminist organisations and groups was equipping queer women with practices and vocabularies to name and dismantle what they saw as oppressive (which often turned into dismantling the very organisations they were in). They used these practices to produce research on their lives, and the lives of their sisters. As one South Asian lesbian wrote in *Mukti* in 1985: '"Asian" lesbians have talked publicly about their sexuality. And in conferences.'[25]

Sitting with this archive decades later, in a white-led space, we wonder what was lost during the anti-racist years of the Lesbian Archive in the 1980s, not just in terms of material, but in the consciousness-raising work that questioned whether the work of cataloguing and caretaking of historical work is a neutral act. When we had initially approached the GWL in

2019 to ask about their holdings related to queer South Asians in Britain, their brief response was that they thought they did not have any. Or at least, anything obvious. When lockdowns finally lifted and we were able to access the archive again, one extremely helpful archivist's long and intimate knowledge of the archive's quirks pointed us to a slim unboxed file called 'South Asian Lesbian and Gay Network' that was yet to be catalogued. That was where we were able to find one of the longest runs of newsletters for Shakti, meaning one of the most significant records of queer South Asian community building in the late 1980s to early 1990s was part of an uncatalogued section of a lesbian archive in a museum focused on the history of women's lives. If the visibility of South Asians in queer London scenes was dominated by men, women were more likely to be the caretakers of the memories and materials from those scenes. Working with these newsletters alongside the Camden Lesbian Centre and Black Lesbian Group Archive brought a series of protagonists, plots, conspiracies, action and debate alive across groups, networks and communities which were discretely archived but lived more promiscuous lives.

Alongside this archive, we draw on black lesbian feminist attempts to document the experience of community and belonging during the 1980s, including *Making Black Waves* (1993); *Talking Black: Lesbians of African and Asian Descent Speak Out* (1995); and oral histories and interviews, including work from Haringey Vanguard and Speak Out London. Charting a series of feminist debates, Clare Hemmings argues for the importance of critiquing how we tell the stories of particular social and political movements: 'If Western feminists can be attentive to the political grammar of our storytelling, if we can highlight reasons why that attention might be important, then we can also intervene to change the way we tell stories.'[26] Our aim is to intervene in the stories of queer South Asian life in Britain, often conditioned by narratives of homophobia and familial rejection, and tell another story, one less reliant on conventional plotting.

Studies of queer life have been particularly occupied with the archive, as Jack Halberstam observed almost twenty years ago: 'The archive is not simply a repository; it is also a theory of cultural relevance, a construction of collective memory, and a complex record of queer activity.'[27] The queer archive can be understood as a series of generative affective relationships which replenish the dimensions of queer life. While we focus on queer South Asian life within black lesbian feminism, we are not interested in extracting or isolating this seam. There is no unified or neat history of queer South Asian life, organising or community in Britain. Instead, there are a series of contingent relationships, experiments and encounters between queer forms that begin to unpick what is at stake in claiming a unique queer South Asian identity.

Looking back on her life of activism and archiving, Joan Nestle commented,

> Queer archives of the future perhaps will give evidence that it is harder to live with a history than without one. The traceable arc of the public choices made, the markings of who we left at the border, the futility of thinking such words as "lesbian" or "man" or "woman" have fixed meanings.[28]

As we've suggested earlier, while we use 'South Asian', we have no commitment to its fidelity or accuracy. Rather, we are interested in the way 'South Asian' places subjects in varying relationships to sexual and racial difference. This is primarily explored through the limits and opportunities in discarding the term South Asian (for black) while keeping South Asian cultural specificity, and experience, as part of a black lesbian feminist vernacular. The sections of this chapter are not a discrete part of a successive, progressive or linear narrative of queer South Asian communities, representation or visibility which emerged in British contexts; any singular origin story begins the work of selecting heroes rather than recognizing and naming the distributed labour across political and cultural formations. Rather, these sections can be understood as overlapping parts of a complex network of solidarities where individuals, groups, communities and ideas are strategically and temporarily co-located to answer a specific challenge.

Our methodological approach draws on the legacy of black lesbian feminist archiving and documentation. In this sense, we are informed by 'scavenging' approaches to the archive that look at ex-centric collections and curations of material as fugitive forms of knowledge exploring black queer life. Sophie Marie Niang argues that scavenging 'is wary of the desire to always generate new data, primarily through interviews (when thinking about qualitative enquiry), to the detriment of a meaningful engagement with the wealth of resources already present in the world, created by marginalised people sharing and theorising about their experience.'[29]

Here, Niang was responding to her own experience of asking an activist for an interview, and being turned down, because they had already given one (why not look at the material already there?). We had similar experiences, where some of the prominent activists we approached, who were part of our own imaginary 'heroes' of queer South Asian life in the 1980s, pointed to their body of work as the right place for us to begin. Within the context of the GWL archive, this meant reading through material associated with the black women's movement in London in the 1980s. In the next section we turn to these self-conscious acts of documentation and reflection on queer black feminist life in the 1980s in the context of the black lesbian feminist thinkers whose work was the anchoring and organising principle for their experience. More specifically, we consider the role of solidarity across racialised difference, rather than coherency within racialised forms of difference, as the organising impulse for black lesbian thought and action.

(Politically) black lesbians

> Nineteen eighty-two and nothing much seemed to be happening. Booed out of the OWAAD conference, frozen out of the Black Women's Centre and utterly perplexed by the distant rumblings of the sado-masochism debate as it seethed across the Atlantic like some bubbling boiling mist that no mere mortal lesbian could hope to enter and emerge from unscathed. It seemed to a Blacklesbian that there was nothing but gloom in the air. I mourned the passing of the GLF [Gay Liberation Front] and hated my mother for not having me years earlier in order that I might have been there and seen real struggle and change.[30]

Femi Otitoju's wry observation that 1982 might already be too late for radical black queer action is a reminder of how political nostalgia can either act as an imperative (to re-forge something lost), or as a lament. This section turns to the contested site of black British feminism in the 1980s, especially in terms of queer South Asian women who were at once central to the movement, but who constantly wrestled with the possibility and limitations of black-brown coalitions. The unprecedented funding for voluntary organisations that would flow from Greater London Council in the 1980s would be a double-edged sword: at once funding vital services and work, but also beginning the process of professionalising political collectives through engaging with the hurdles and hoops of funding grants. Otitoju recounted some of the community objections to large-scale local authority funding for lesbian and gay issues at a GLC meeting, including one from a lesbian feminist who argued: '"before you know it the movement will be filled with overpaid unmotivated so-called activists who don't know how to filch a pencil or scavenge a few photocopies. We'll have organisations filled with dead wood drawing hefty pay cheques'".[31] For feminists who criticised the underpinning logic of capitalist economies, especially in the way they conceived of women's labour, the idea of being funded by local authorities was a dangerous path to tokenistic forms of inclusion that used the inertia of bureaucracy to take the heat and urgency out of direct action. These were movements that eschewed leadership in favour of non-hierarchical collectives where debate and dissention were par for the course.

Two important black lesbian feminist-led collections in the early 1990s document this period and include a number of South Asian women. *Making Black Waves* (1993) includes contributions from Savi Hensman, Aqeela Alam (a youth worker and activist of Guyanese and Pakistani heritage) and Ann Khambatta (a community activist with Indian Parsee heritage). As well as piecing together a key timeline for black lesbian activism, *Making Black Waves* reprinted quotes from research and evidence in the 1980s that had become inaccessible, including quotes from the Lesbians from Historically Immigrant Communities report commissioned by Greater London Council in 1985.

Talking Black (1995) features Savi Hensman, Maya Chowdhry (a director of Indian and Scottish-English heritage), Anne Hayfield Black, Seni Seneviratne (an artist with English and Sri Lankan heritage) and Sakthi Suriyaprakasam (who at the time was a worker at the BLGC but would go on to become the Director of the Metro Centre; she arrived in Britain from Sri Lanka in 1982). Maya Chowdhry's chapter included interviews with Mumtaz Karimjee and Tanya Syed (a filmmaker with Welsh and Indian heritage, but who grew up in Scotland). The opening essay in the collection is prescient in identifying the power of a new 'hostile environment',[32] the changing orientations of immigration debates and the dismantling of the Left in the face of new populisms: 'Living in a new and hostile environment, people of African and Asian descent needed to stay together in their own communities for survival, protection and security. The existence of racism, sexism and homophobia in British society has meant that the documented herstory of Black lesbians is brief.'[33]

Making Black Waves and *Talking Black* were politically black-led attempts to document queer and lesbian community-embedded research that took place from the late 1970s to the early 1990s. Cataloguing the types of prejudice and violence faced by Black and South Asian lesbians, *Making Black Waves* included quotes from the Lesbians from Historically Migrant Communities research that documented the experience of racism within the lesbian community that act as a reminder of the gap between the reality of lesbian lives and lesbian feminist ideals:

> During the late 1970s I met this Arab lesbian who was born here... and she had a bruised eye. She had been kicked at a women's bar by some White lesbians who called her a wog and kicked her out. She still has a deaf ear after that, and her spine is still not functioning.[34]

Both collections attempted to challenge stereotypes, whether it was of the inclusive lesbian community or homophobic South Asian communities. Aqeela Alam was a prominent South Asian lesbian feminist whose work included activism in Palestine and who publicly challenged the taboo of sexual abuse within South Asian communities on the television programme Network East. With a reputation for being provocative, her gaze was firmly turned to what 'progress' looked like in second and third generation British South Asian communities: 'I have Come Out to all sorts of people within my own community. One 60-year-old religious Asian woman, on finding out, said: "But daughter, I only got married because I had to." And yet, I've also experienced the most unexpected hostility from young trendy Asians.'[35] While political blackness continued to have value through the 1980s for queer South Asians, related seams of resistance, centred on anti-imperialism and the specificities of heteropatriarchy in South Asian communities, produced new alignments between South Asian feminist community activists and queer feminists whose work fell under the umbrella of political blackness but were frustrated by gender's constant relegation as a secondary or tertiary marker of difference.

Recalling the OWAAD conference of 1978,[36] Valerie Mason-John reflected on the imperative for Black and South Asian women to come together in the face of shared issues and experiences of oppression by the state and within the patriarchal family: 'women of African and Asian descent should stop organising separately around the issues of racist attacks, deportations, Depo-Provera and the question of forced sterilisation of Black women in Britain.'[37] This included feminist solidarity work, for example the formation of Wages Due Lesbians in 1975 by 'Black and white lesbians on the platform of anti-racism' who identified the forces of homophobia and racism as co-conspirers in the economic exploitation of women.[38] By the time of the 1981 OWAAD, and in the midst of race riots across British cities, the imperative for this resistance to state violence was felt more urgently and fuelled the frustration towards causes that were in danger of diluting or diminishing their primary aims:

> Many participants felt that at a time such as this, issues of women's oppression and sexuality should be subordinate to the needs of the wider Black communities. Others were afraid that the accusation of being a lesbian would be thrown at them (Black men had frequently used this as a weapon against vocal Black women). But the lesbians calling for a workshop refused to be silenced. There was uproar. Insults like 'mash 'em up', 'chuck them out' and 'it's disgusting' were hurled

at lesbian participants. Yet despite the hostility and anger, the lesbian workshop went ahead and kept filling up.[39]

Gilli Salvat and Pratibha Parmar were two of the women who faced down this homophobia. The first in a series of Black Lesbian Groups was formed in 1982, with the Camden Lesbian Centre and Black Lesbian Group forming a couple of years later in 1984.[40] In 1984 the 'We are here' conference was the first black feminist conference in Britain where lesbians were explicitly welcome.[41] In the following year, Zami I, the first national Black lesbian conference, was held partly thanks to funding from a working-class lesbian collective, which in turn received funding from a middle-class lesbian group.[42] Amos and Parmar argued for a feminist dismantling of whiteness in the women's movement: 'In describing the women's movement as oppressive we refer to the experiences of Black and working-class women of the movement and the inability of feminist theory to speak to their experience in any meaningful way.'[43] Looking back at her self-identification as black, Savi Hensman points to the fact that before this was a political identity, it was simply a political reality: 'We were most definitely categorised as Black by the state and by the white British people.'[44] But she also acknowledged the ongoing tension in using the term: 'Some lesbians of African descent felt, I think, that their hard-won space was being encroached on, and the uniqueness of their experiences denied.'[45]

Several of our interviewees reflected on the role of political blackness in their lives in the early to mid-1980s, which was invariably tied to their own personal experiences of empire and decolonisation. Reflecting on how she became politicised, Savi Hensman spoke about her parents. They were born in 1920s Sri Lanka (then known as Ceylon) in the midst of socialist and anti-colonial resistance to the British Empire but later left Sri Lanka to escape communal violence. The consciousness-raising that they had experienced, and their belief in grassroots activism's ability to dismantle race and class-based societal inequalities, was passed down to their daughter, Savi, who was born in 1962 in Sri Lanka during a period when the family had returned to try and make a life there. Struggling to find work, they returned to the UK, which was far from an easy choice.

For many Black and South Asian people who lived through '60s and '70s Britain, 'Enoch Powell' was a shorthand for an environment of open hostility that enabled right-wing groups to target migrant neighbourhoods and placed the police in the position of making it known who the streets and public services of Britain were really for. Savi's rising consciousness of structural racism coincided with her own growing awareness of her sexuality. As she put it in the following email correspondence with us,

> on top of my parents' strong Third World identification, for me as an adolescent, as I made strides in overcoming internalised racism as well as taking account of practical risks, identifying as black made sense. And later, coming on to a scene and in a movement which was predominantly white, where racism was sometimes encountered, spending time and sometimes forming friendships with other queer people of colour, with parallel if not identical journeys, made sense, with an identity which reflected this.

One of Savi's earliest encounters with other Black and South Asian queer people was while she was travelling to Bradford in 1981 for a protest. The Bradford 12 were a group of South Asian men from the United Black Youth League[46] who had begun preparations (including assembling petrol bombs) to defend their community against a fascist march. The march never took place, and the petrol bombs were never used, but they were arrested. Savi was one of the many anti-racist campaigners who travelled to Bradford to defend the Bradford 12. On the return journey to London on the bus, Savi clocked some fellow travellers who turned out to be members of the newly formed Gay Black Group. She described the encounter during our interview:

> I saw somebody [...] with, I think, a pink triangle badge and I thought that's brave. And then I saw him after that, and I realised that that was [...] the Gay Black Group. So I think I talked to some of them. And that was probably my first encounter that actually brought together those different sides of my life as somebody had been involved in anti-racist activism and, and at the same time, somebody who was coming to terms with my sexuality.

We also spoke to interviewees whose stories about 'where they came from' carried the legacies of colonisation and indentured labour. Ann (not her real name) was born in the late 1960s to a Trinidadian family. She described her father's heritage as Muslim, South Asian and Guyanese, and her mother's heritage as Christian, Portuguese and South African. After her parents' separation, she was raised in Streatham by her mother and her Black stepfather. Her memories of growing up were defined by racism. From the metal box on their family home's letterbox to stop petrol bombs, to the awareness of the police harassment faced by her brother who was a Rastafari, Ann knew what anti-blackness was, with her commitment to political blackness cementing during the Brixton Riots in 1981 and 1985. But her light skin, and her mother's teasing (for example, asking her if she wanted to wear a sari), meant she never felt like she comfortably belonged.

When she became homeless as a teenager, her love of music drew her into the London Sound System scene (she is still recognised on the street as living legend from the mid-'80s scene). Countercultural music scenes were not immune to the everyday misogyny directed at black women and she found herself ostracised by darker skinned women tired with her racialised elevation in the scene as the closest thing to a white woman. The dimensions of her black experience were challenged and collapsed in different ways. In black lesbian groups, she was not "black" enough:

> I would meet these other black women, who would then have these other meetings about black women, you know, and lesbianism and everything. And I was always the lightest one there. And I remember going to one of them and I remember this woman, doing this talk, this African Caribbean doing this talk [...] she looked at me and then looked around the room. 'We're here to talk about black women's issues. Black women.' And then I looked and I'm like, 'Oh, okay, maybe not.' And then I remember the discussion was all about mixed race relationships, women going out with white women, and that we shouldn't be doing, you know, women shouldn't be doing that.

What the umbrella of political blackness offered Ann were small inroads into the possibility of Afro-Asian unity against a racist state, even when her sense of belonging or identification remained contingent. Queer South Asians were not caught between the binary divide of homophobic South Asian communities and racist queer scenes. The edge-spaces of who was 'South Asian' were always policed through racialised and sexualised difference.

The power of this consciousness-raising was felt in our interviews. We interviewed a couple who had been part of politically black lesbian scenes in the 1980s. Looking back on their twenties in the southeast, they reflected, 'we would both say that we were black lesbian. [...] Because it was a mark of being a politicised person. [...] Nobody said [...] Asian in those days, and certainly not South Asian.' For one of the couple, who had spent her early childhood in Lagos, the Afro-Asian conversation was a way to address the consequences of colonial legacies and their impact in the present: 'Nobody's really talking about the Asian descent, African descent relationship [now]. In those days, we did a lot of that, you know, and it was quite painful and quite difficult, but at least we had the conversation.'

Part of what made this 'difficult' were the socio-economic privileges South Asians experienced in Britain's African colonies. This history was felt in Africanisation policies that led to the expulsion of South Asians from Uganda in 1972 and the steady migration of South Asians from Kenya, Nigeria, Malawi and other former colonies to other parts of the commonwealth. For the politically black-identifying lesbian couple we interviewed, these recent histories were routes into longer critiques of imperialism that informed their understanding of the interlocking operations of oppression. One of the couple described leaving the Midlands to come to London for an art course in the mid-1980s, where 'coming out' meant she 'arrived with one rucksack, one sleeping bag, a certain number of clothes, and all my art equipment, and found a housing cooperative.' In this setting, solidarity against anti-oppression had more fidelity than identity politics: 'you didn't sexualise yourself. So you affiliated, so you will affiliate to the miners, you will affiliate to Greenham Common, you would affiliate to Palestine, you would affiliate to, you know, Northern Ireland.'

In the next section we turn our attention to the affiliations between the marginalised spaces of working-class South Asian women's activism and lesbian feminist action, two groups which at first might seem unlikely bedfellows.

Southall Black Sisters

Reading through the records of Peckham Black Women's Centre, the Black Women's Group, and the newsletter of the Black Lesbian and Gay Centre, we came to a folder for Southall Black Sisters. In the two rounds of cataloguing this archive had gone through, Southall Black Sisters had been organised closer to black lesbian and gay organisations in London than Asian women's groups. In this section, we use this proximal cataloguing to follow how South Asian feminist solidarity work provided space for queer encounters.

South Asian women (straight and otherwise) used the banner of political blackness as the point of entry to sexuality. Southall Black Sisters was founded in 1979 in the midst of organised resistance to right-wing fascist organisations like the National Front. Southall Black Sisters had the specific aim of supporting women on a platform of Afro-Asian unity (although most prominently South Asian women) who found themselves caught between sexism in anti-racist organisations (such as the Indian Workers Association and the Southall Youth Movement) and racism in white-led women's services, particularly in supporting victims of domestic violence. Their work counteracted media stereotypes of South Asian women which saw them as 'sexually erotic creatures, full of Eastern promise' or 'completely dominated by their men, mute and oppressed wives and mothers.'[47] Reflecting on the importance of political blackness to their practice in the 1980s, one of our interviewees saw Southall Black Sisters as an integral part of a network which took distinct but sympathetic approaches to the collective aim of challenging racist heteropatriarchy. This approach brought women experiencing domestic violence in so-called closed and conservative communities into contact with lesbian philosophy and anti-racist creative practice. Keith Khan, the British Indo-Caribbean queer artist, described it as a form of layering:

> The Hounslow Art [...] Cooperative [...]. They were connected to the Southall Black Sisters, you know, so you can kind of see—and then Southall Black Sisters was connected to the black clubs. And so you can kind of see the [...] palimpsests of where all of these things fit together in terms of the layering.[48]

A number of South Asian lesbian feminists collaborated with, or influenced, Southall Black Sisters, from Ritu DJing for Southall Black Sisters at the Dominion Centre in Southall[49] to the feminist anti-imperialist work of Pratibha Parmar, which formed an important part of the collective consciousness-raising in politically black South Asian feminist collectives.

Politically black lesbians were active across a range of women's movements. The 1984 special issue of *Feminist Review* on black women's organising includes a photo-series compiled by Shaheen Haq, Pratibha Parmar and Ingrid Pollard that brings together images from women's activism including the Sari Squad, a South Asian women's group formed in East London, picketing a Conservative Party conference as part of the Afia Begum campaign.[50] None of the images are lesbian-centred but their curation by three lesbians and the stretch across black and South Asian lives documents a black lesbian aesthetic and political practice that would inform aspects of queer South Asian organising.

These connected debates fostered an exploration of women's sexual agency that was informed by black lesbian feminism. Mandana Hendessi (a member of the Southall Black Sisters collective between 1980 and 1982) commented, 'I was introduced to the whole notion of political lesbianism. In those days it was a very radical way of asserting our identity. It was very interesting, very good for us because we hadn't done much on sexuality before that.'[51] These debates, however, did not detract from the practical acts of solidarity within communities experiencing racism. Working with the local gurdwara, Hendessi recalled several times Southall Black Sisters kept rotas to support families targeted by campaigns of racist violence. These were practices that were able to hold different senses of community (communities of women; religious communities; racialised communities) together to tackle the most basic and urgent issue: risk to life.

This work allowed Southall Black Sisters to challenge sexism from within South Asian communities. Women's rights activist Gita Sahgal criticised the tolerance of abuse towards women in order to maintain fragile coalitions on the Left:

> Many socialists accepted these ideas at the expense of their belief in egalitarian politics. They realised they were trading off equal opportunities for girls against multiculturalist ideas which took a non-interventionalist line with regard to Asian families. But few attempted to challenge publicly theories which rapidly became orthodoxies particularly in education and social services. Black women have largely fought that battle on their own.[52]

Ironically describing themselves as one of 'Thatcher's children', the collective formed as changes to benefits, growing evictions, homelessness and violence were having a disproportionate impact on women.[53] Where they broke a taboo was in naming the role of privileged male gatekeepers who often used the interests of 'the community' as a bargaining chip with local authorities. Southall Black Sisters disrupted and disputed these roles: 'by founding a black women's group, we challenged the right of male community leaders to speak for us.'[54] They emerged in the context of increased funding for grassroots organisations working with minoritised communities; as they put it, 'In 1983, GLC (Greater London Council) funding produced a bonanza for the voluntary sector.'[55] This funding supported their campaigning against fundamentalism from within communities, and often led Southall Black Sisters into controversial terrain.

In 1984 they marched in the streets of Southall in support of Krishna Sharma, a woman who had been driven to suicide by her husband and her family. In 1985 they campaigned after the death of Balwant Kaur at Brent Asian Women's Refuge despite frequent warnings being issued to the police about the risk to Kaur's life. The effectiveness of Southall Black Sister's response came through its ability to understanding gendered race–faith pressures in working-class communities.[56] After Kaur's death, her children had been looked after by women in the refuge, and then by a woman called Jasbir, who volunteered at the refuge. Despite Jasbir being from a Punjabi Sikh background (like Kaur), social services decided to award guardianship to a Punjabi family linked to the local gurdwara. During an interview by social services, Jasbir was asked if she had let the children dress inappropriately (presumably by letting them wear Western clothing). When the case went to court, a judge ruled in favour of the children staying with Jasbir and criticised Brent Council's misguided attempts to be 'anti-racist' by placing the children with what they deemed to be the 'ideal' Punjabi Sikh family.[57] Southall Black Sisters were critical of the collusion between white-led councils and influential community gatekeepers in enabling highly patriarchal, and often violent, structures to keep South Asian women, and their issues, sequestered from view:

> White teachers, for instance, worried about Asian girls in their care are usually told to go away and examine their own racism if they raise problems within the family. The message to young girls, meanwhile, is that the real battles they have to fight are against racism in the outside world, while the family is a source of security and shelter.[58]

The site of refuge or shelter for queer South Asian women was a particular issue. Describing the double exile from family and identity, Parmar describes the threat of queer exclusion in near identical terms:

> For many of us, our families are very important, as they give us a base, a refuge, from racism, and give us a sense of our own identity as Indian people. That's what I mean by internal exiles, whether we come out or not, we are exiles within our communities. If we come out, we are more often than not exiled by the community. If we don't come out, we still

> feel that sense of exile because we are unable to share a very real part of ourselves with them.[59]

Where arranged marriage or marriage within the 'culture' was the dominant expectation, queerness was just one aspect of 'deviant' sexuality that women could express. The explosive revelation in this context was the refusal of the prospect of marriage, or the refusal of life within a marriage conditioned by emotional and/or physical violence. When the Indian Worker's Association finally agreed that they should support an anti-dowry campaign, Southall Black Sisters criticised what they saw as the real underlying motivation, namely, that the dowry market had become inflated and it was having a negative economic impact on men, who as fathers would have to pay their daughter's dowries. Their investment in the campaign, according to Hannana Siddiqui, leading member of the Southall Black Sisters, was informed by the misogynistic practices surrounding dowries, namely the equation of women to property (which was somewhat ironic considering they were a trade union).[60] Southall Black Sisters broke unquestioning solidarity with fellow anti-racist organisations in the Black and South Asian community when they felt the pressure to downplay the sexism and violence faced by South Asian communities.

> They [Southall Black Sisters] challenged also, perhaps inadvertently, the 'heroic tradition' of anti-racism, fostered by writers such as Sivanandan who see the crucible of the anti-racist struggle as the breeding ground for the birth of black communities in Britain. Black women were to be celebrated when they came out in their thousands to oppose the presence of fascists in their streets, but not when they tried to create a new movement and consciousness and challenged the notion of a unified community.[61]

This issue was most clearly seen in 1989 during the 'Women Against Fundamentalism' campaign in support of Salman

Rushdie (campaigning for which was included on the pages of *Shakti Khabar*). When Southall Black Sisters joined the Women Against Fundamentalism picket against a national march of Muslim groups through London, they found themselves threatened by the National Front on one side, and South Asian men on another. They had to turn to the police for protection.[62]

Through a circular economy of fundraising, volunteering and shared campaigns, Southall Black Sisters may not have been an organisation for queer women, but its challenges to the silencing of women in anti-racist movements shared a terrain with queer South Asian women who were fighting for space in queer, feminist and anti-racist organisations that claimed the mantle of anti-oppression. Savi Hensman pointed to their influential role in challenging virginity testing,[63] while Valerie Mason-John identified them as part of a network of black feminist organisations that were influential in the Suspect Under Suspicion campaign against the disproportionate police stop and searches experienced in Black and South Asian communities.[64] They are a key example of how solidarities worked in practice through the shared interests which, for a time, could bring groups and individuals into proximal relationships. This opened disruptive discursive intersections that brought lesbian feminism, challenges to religious fundamentalism and direct action against racism and misogyny into a frame that, without constituting singular agreement, gained power through finding shared terrains.

As the affordances of political blackness diminished, some of the characteristics and texture of critiques which squarely targeted the status quo shifted their focus. Reflecting on these failed solidarity projects of the 1980s, activist and writer A. Sivanandan observed a retreating horizon of working-class activism as cultural politics shifted to narrower configurations organised around axes of difference that relegated class to a secondary issue. And so,

'The working class, as a consequence, was stripped of its richest political seams—black, feminist, gay, green.'[65] These were far more than affiliations or identities that were classed; rather, they were ways of articulating the extractive operations of capitalism and its vested interest in undergirding conditions of precarity. In this setting, communities organised around ethno-cultural or religious lines could produce culture, for themselves and others, that could be consumed (turned into a marketable commodity) or codified (and thereby protected). The radical possibilities of political blackness as a collective site of resistance was, for Sivanandan, a deliberate strategy: 'Underlying the whole of the state's project was a divisive culturalism that turned the living, dynamic, progressive aspects of black people's culture into artefact and habit and custom—and began to break up community.'[66] As racial fault lines opened up, perceptions of South Asian 'success' in business and politics, and the historical use of South Asians as a buffer class in colonial projects, all became part of complex series of associations between past and present that made the ongoing efficacy of political blackness dependent on serious accounting within South Asian communities, especially in the context of anti-blackness and Islamophobia.[67]

But these stories of collapse have become part of their own orthodoxy and tend to iron out the contingent and inconsistent ways in which queer black formations continued to forge new kinds of solidarity projects. In the final section, we turn to one of the heroic stories of queer activism in the UK: Section 28. Until now, we have focused on collectivised approaches to understanding the layered connections between black feminism, black lesbian feminism and queer South Asian activism. In the next section, drawing from an interview, we turn to a single life to see how a significant figure in feminist and black lesbian action navigated these politics on a personal level.

Gilli Salvat

Gilli was born in Bombay in World War II. Bombay at the time was used as a rest and recreation base for the Allied forces in the East. She is of Anglo-Indian heritage.

Her mother was born in a tea plantation in Assam and was the child of an Indian plantation worker and a Scottish-Welsh plantation manager. Anglo-Indian children at this time were severely disadvantaged, not being accepted by either the British or Indian society and were often discarded by their mothers who could not bring them up. As a child of mixed heritage, Gilli's mum was rescued by the Christian missionaries to Dr Graham's homes in the Himalayas, which was a Scottish children's home for disadvantaged Anglo-Indian children.

Gilli's father was from an Indian railway family which was a community of Anglo-Indian workers who had been trusted by the British to run the railways, which provided connectivity and vital transportation to the Indian Subcontinent. In World War II, her father was an Indian army officer and served on the border of India with Afghanistan. He was the son of an English sailor who had landed in Calcutta and married an Anglo-Indian woman (who was descended from French settlers that had also colonised India).

The Calcutta of those days was very different from today's Kolkata. It was the biggest port in the British Empire and drew historical migrant communities such as Russians, Jews who had escaped Europe, Muslim communities, Chinese migrants and peoples from the British Empire.

This was before Partition. With Partition, came religious violence between Hindus and Muslims. Calcutta found itself close to a newly created border and country, East Pakistan. The status of the Anglo-Indians was precarious in the wake of Independence and subsequently, Partition. Some who had consciously used passing as European as a route to racial privilege found their status more troubled and troubling, in an emerging democracy, in a state of decolonisation. Talking about her own experience of history of Empire, Gilli reflected:

> you get taught about the Tudors. And then suddenly, you get taught about the Victorians. And all the stuff in the middle of that, when they were going and colonising people, it's not told to you, you know, and when I was at school, they had Empire Day. And then it became Commonwealth Day, and then it got deleted. You know, and I think a lot of us, most of us—not so much nowadays, but—have had that whole thing... Because it's shameful, a lot of it is just downright shameful, you know? And yet, we are here reaping a lot of those benefits, right? Because we're living in the first world now. So we're participants in that in a way. But yeah, we're not taught about that. It's a history that is really disgraceful.

Prompted by her mother, Gilli's father secured passage to Britain in 1950 because he had an English father and had been a British Army Officer. The family permanently migrated. Despite their Anglo-Indian heritage, this was hardly a return home as the family had never been to Britain before. While Britain was dependent on a migrant labour workforce to aid post-war recovery, the reality of racist attitudes flattened the overlapping histories of coloniser and colonised into a generalised suspicion about what else migrants may be bringing with them, whether languages, cultural traditions or perhaps most dangerously an expectation that they would be treated as equals to their white counterparts. The 'deletion' of Empire Day and Commonwealth Day was more than the removal of outdated concepts; it was also the deletion of histories of violence, exploitation, displacement and migration that made telling the true story of British history impossible. This selective historical amnesia came to confront Gilli decades later when, in common with many of the Windrush generation, her citizenship was questioned and she was threatened with deportation back 'home' to India.

Gilli's family experienced downward social mobility in their move to Britain. After arriving in London they lived in a migrant's hostel for a year, and her father struggled moving from a managerial role in India to taking on lower level administrative work in a shipping firm. And for Gilli and her sister, it meant living on a large council estate and arriving at the local state school with sing song Indian accents:

> I soon found out that I had to adapt myself if I was going to get on with these people. Yeah. So I did. Because [...] there's no use speaking like a middle-class person [...] when you're in a council, primary school, in the biggest state, council estate in the whole of London which is Burnt Oak, right?

Gilli became a youth worker in London in the 1970s which, at the time, was a sector dominated by white men. Despite the lack of support to tackle racism and sexism during her training, she undertook a placement in Tower Hamlets, one of the homes of the Bangladeshi community, at a time when the National Front would march down Brick Lane. With South Asian women living in closely protected communities, educational, youth work and social work services that could be delivered in the home and by other South Asian women were a rare commodity. One of the biggest educational challenges was giving women access to English so they could advocate for themselves and access services around them. By the late 1970s, Gilli was working in Manor Gardens, a community centre that had been founded in 1913 to offer free healthcare and education to mothers, where she ran the first feminist young women's project.

She was one of the workers to support the Young Lesbian Group in 1979 emerged at the same time as the London Gay Teenage Group, a group which became notorious for fostering the creative talent of a new, confident generation, including the members of Bronski Beat. Young lesbians and gays went to County Hall and made the case for their own youth club, which no other youth group in the whole of the country ever had to do. Attributing its approval to the liberal bent of the Inner London Education Authority at the time (which the Thatcher government closed in 1986), Gilli was working and living at the intersection of anti-racist and queer-inclusive youth and social work at a time when women workers were in a minority. Her activism was informed in the context of working-class communities and driven by feminist activism: 'the background to all of it was the women's liberation, right. So all of that kind of radicalisation was coming from all around us.'

When Haringey Council advertised for its new Lesbian and Gay Unit, there were over three hundred applicants, including Gilli. She became one of the workers at the unit, thanks to her experience and a deliberate approach by the new equalities units to recruit people with diverse lived experience. Gilli was working at the Lesbian and Gay Unit when another worker sent the letter that sparked the furore that would lead to Section 28 (see our discussion of Haringey Black Action later in the chapter). Speaking about the letter, Gill commented, 'He just sent a letter out [...] He should have gone to our managers and our managers would have said let's hold off for a bit about this. And it blew up—and it blew up all around the country'. The hesitation and deliberation in Gilli's memory of the event touches on a broader shift in politics at the time. The backlash to equalities-driven political manifestos which were leading to targeted funding for minoritised communities was gaining traction.

The closure of the ILEA in 1986, the dismantling of Greater London Council in 1986, and the politicised charge against the council-funded Lesbian and Gay Units (under the guise of protecting the family) was part of a broader movement to undermine and extricate the work of liberation politics within local government. While workers at the Haringey Lesbian and Gay Unit organised against Section 28 in a personal capacity, including through Haringey Black Action, it was a fight that was, until the repeal in 2003, ultimately lost. And while the work of key white figures in Haringey Lesbian and Gay Unit has been recognised, the contribution of the Black and South Asian workers has been de-centred, something Nathaniel Coleman has recently called the 'stonewalling' of queer history.

When we asked Gilli about the founding of Shakti, her answer was incredibly wide-ranging, demonstrating the breadth of identities and communities held together in Shakti's earliest months. Gilli pointed to the mixed cultural heritage of Shiv Khan, while also highlighting how some women found themselves pushed out of the organisation:

> Ritu: It's something that Shiv used to talk about, Shivananda Khan, who founded Shakti—
>
> Gilli: Yeah, but his name was Duncan.
>
> Ritu: That's right.
>
> Gilli: He was a Christian...
>
> Ritu: Duncan Khan. He was a Christian, Muslim bloke. So, Shivanadan Duncan Khan, the founder of Shakti, the South Asian, lesbian, gay organisation that—
>
> Gilli: But listen, listen Ritu, listen to this, I formed that. I formed it with him. I formed it with him. But because it was so male orientated, you know, I didn't stay with it. You know, I might have stayed with it for like three months or something, I pulled out. Not because I was angry, but because it was all about blokes. Right.
>
> [...]
>
> Gilli: And he was Anglo Indian like me. He was from an Indian railway family like me and that was an important connection we shared.

Ritu: You're not acknowledged as a co-founder of Shakti, you—

Gilli: I'm not.

The interview with Gilli demonstrated the difficulty in narratives about pasts and communities too easily read through the recuperative and celebratory impulses of LGBTQ+ historical enquiry today, especially in queer anti-racist activism. Gilli uses her answers to pull in adjacent and antecedent moments. Referencing Khan's Anglo-Indian heritage becomes a moment of identification, but also an entry point into a critique of the interviewer's approach to Shakti's founding. While there is no doubt that Khan was a leading force within Shakti, the fixation on 'founder' status in the vernacular telling of Shakti's history reinforces one of the narrative techniques that undermined parts of Shakti's success in the 1990s: the serial underestimation of the contribution of women to the shaping, driving and success of queer feminist, anti-racist activism in Shakti and beyond.

In the final section, we turn to the black-led fightback against Section 28, which was part of a larger collection of black queer resistance. This is a story that Gilli is intimately tied to, as she mentions above; she was working in the Haringey Lesbian and Gay Unit when the fateful letter to schools would trigger events that would become one of the heroic failures of queer activism in the UK: the queer protest attempting to stop Section 28, the local government legislation that in 1988 banned the 'promotion of homosexuality' by local authorities.[68]

The black queer fightback against Section 28

The folder on black lesbian and gay activism in the Camden Lesbian Centre and Black Lesbian Group Archive contains photocopies advertising the agenda of the Lesbian and Gay Immigration Group (agenda item 1: *what we are and why we exist*), alongside information posters for Lesbian and Gay Employment Rights (LAGER), and Black Lesbians and the Police (the Lesbians and Policing Project: "Lespop").[69] In amongst these local authority funded projects, there is a collection of ephemera from Haringey Black Action, a grassroots organisation which ran Britain's first national black lesbian and gay demonstration in 1987 in response to the emerging proposals for Section 28, which effectively ran as a ban on 'homosexual' content in education (with varying degrees of effectiveness) from 1988 to 2000 in Scotland, and 1988 to 2003 in England and Wales.

In 1984, improving gay rights became part of the campaign manifesto for the Labour Party in Haringey.[70] The 1984 Miner's Strike had demonstrated the powerful potential of Left coalitions resisting a Thatcher-led government whose cuts and disinvestments were targeted at the working classes and socially marginalised communities. The influence of queer and anti-racist organising was felt in local Labour Party organising, especially in London.[71] The community-led responses to poverty and state-sponsored violence were an example of what A. Sivanandan called 'communities of resistance'.[72]

Bernie Grant, one of Britain's first Black council leaders and a Labour Party activist and politician, found himself at the centre of national media attention as he tried to represent the real fears of Black communities in Haringey while responding to escalating tension between Black youth and the police. Grant called for senior resignations in the Metropolitan Police; excess police violence towards Black communities was not a problem isolated to a few police officers, it was racism endemic within policing. In the following years Bernie Grant found himself caricatured as the epitome of the 'loony left', given the moniker 'Barnie Bernie' by popular right-wing media outlets. The experiments in creating an equalities-focused council that took consultation with marginalised communities seriously would provide prime fodder for the Conservative Party, who were invested in characterising the Labour Party as serially unfit to look after spending of any kind.[73]

The Labour Party retained control of Haringey Council in the 1986 election with a campaign that included promoting positive images of gay and lesbian life in education. Under Grant's leadership, the council launched initiatives to target discrimination including the founding of the Haringey Lesbian and Gay Unit, the first of its kind in Britain. Gilli Salvat and Femi Otitoju were both workers in the unit from its early days, and Savi Hensman served on the Haringey Lesbian and Gay Sub-Committee which worked alongside the Unit to embed equalities throughout the borough. What happened over the next two years would become a defining moment in British queer history. Section 28 has become a shorthand for the mundane violence of state-sponsored homophobia and its lasting damaging effects on individual and social psyches. The protests leading up to its introduction in 1988, and its eventual repeal in 2003 (2000 in Scotland), take the failed morality lessons of the right (the defence of the white heterosexual family at all costs) and turn them into morality lessons for a queer Left (even if you lose, keep fighting). The attack on homosexuality as 'pretended family relationships'[74] used a frame that was all too familiar for Black and South Asian communities: your family is a problem for the state. From the policing of 'sham marriages' in South Asian communities to the racist characterisation of Black masculinity, working-class racialised communities knew all too well what the consequences for 'pretended family relationships' might be.

The Positive Images campaign was designed to support schools in Haringey combat negative portrayals of gay and lesbian life, for example through children's books which featured same-sex parents. As right-wing groups increased their targeted activism against Bernie Grant, Haringey found itself in the centre of a moral panic where the work of Positive Image was translated into 'gay sex' lessons by right-leaning media outlets. Looking back, Gilli remembered the routine death threats their office received. While dealing with the backlash, the everyday work of the Unit found itself under the heightened scrutiny of the media and politicians. At the heart of the crisis was a letter sent by a member of the unit, a white gay man and former teacher, to headteachers about increasing gay and lesbian representation. The moral panic around this request became attached to the children's book, *Jenny Lives with Eric and Martin*.

The Parents' Rights Group was formed to represent the interests of local parents but was funded and supported by several organisations including the Conservative Party, especially in press campaigns fuelled by hetero-panic. A newspaper ad featuring a member of the Parents' Group demonstrated the perceived attack on the heteronormative family: 'Hello my name is Betty Sheridan. I live in Haringey. I'm married with two children. And I am scared.'[75] The 'attack' on the family was used to mobilise prominent black organisations, such as the West Indian Leadership Council and the Haringey Black Pressure Group in Education, against the policy. The Haringey Black Pressure Group stated it was a 'racist policy aimed at breaking up the black family', and nothing short of genocide.[76] Haringey Black Action identified this as a conservative strategy to mobilise 'community gatekeepers' with meagre promises of political influence driven by outsized fears: 'Their [right-wing organisers and Conservative Party politicians] strategy was based on the stock racist stereotype that if they could win the support of what they saw as the leadership, the rest of the Black communities would follow'.[77]

Femi Otitoju commented on the traction these views were obtaining across London: 'a visiting friend from Dulwich said he'd heard that Haringey was being denounced by some of his local councillors for introducing racist policies. The gist of it all was that by insisting on equal opportunities for all, and refusing to allow discrimination in service provision and council procedures, the council was alienating the whole of the ethnic minority community.'[78]

As the tension grew through 1986 to 1987, Haringey Black Action[79] and the Positive Images Campaign led a response to growing hostility to Haringey's Council initiatives, which the Labour Party had begun to distance itself from. The Smash the Backlash! demo on 2 May 1987 was Britain's first large-scale politically black-led demonstration against the oppression faced by gays and lesbians (See Figures 2 and 3). While the resistance to what would become Section 28 was a vital context for the march, the organisers were clear that this was far from being a single-issue protest. One of the campaign leaflets for the demo stated: 'The reactionaries are not concerned about what is really happening in schools. They are not concerned about racism in schools, the Tory cuts in education or the low pay of teachers. Instead, they are diverting attention away from these issues by whipping up prejudice.'[80]

The campaigning for Smash the Backlash! was unambiguous: the Conservative government was behind the orchestration and enabling of right-wing coalitions designed to enable moral panics and hysteria towards marginalised communities that could justify their ongoing exclusion from wealth and benefits intended for the white middle classes: 'The local Tories, after launching a racist attack upon young Black youths following the Broadwater Farm rebellion, are now whipping up hatred and bigotry in a climate which is further legitimising violence against lesbians and gays.'[81] The Parents' Group received support from the National Front and the Union of Democratic Mineworkers, which had allied itself with the Conservative Party. On the day of the rally between two to five thousand people came together.

Dolly Kiffin, who had been involved in the Broadwater Farm youth movement, gave one of the keynote speeches to the rally. Through action embedded in place, Haringey developed a black queer left platform that issued a rallying cry: 'State attacks on all working-class people—especially black people—are intensifying. Black resistance to these attacks will continue to increase. That resistance is not separate from fighting attacks on black sisters, or on black lesbians and gays.'[82] Challenging the threat of 'genocide' or the destruction of the black family, Haringey Black Action mobilised political blackness to undo some of the divisive work of cultural nationalisms: 'We cannot allow reactionary cultural nationalism or ethnicity to take root in our communities, or to speak on our behalf.'[83]

In the introduction to the BLGC's 1987–88 annual report, Kris Black reflected on precarious conditions for community and organising, with Section 28 and the Immigration and Nationality Act 1988 marking a double onslaught on the lives of queer people of colour. Black framed these legislative changes in the context of a coordinated approach to undermine the viability and visibility of anti-racist coalitions that could reach beyond conventional lines of identity politics:

> The coming years will definitely be harder for us as Blacklesbians and Blackgays as the strains and stresses of living with aunty homophobia and uncle racism take their toll in lives, suicides, attacks and depression. It is indeed a wonder how some of us survive—yet we do. But are we prepared for what is yet to come?[84]

The work to simultaneously run support services for communities and campaigns against racist and homophobic attacks, whether on the street or in the halls of government power, was taking its toll. The BLGC undertook advocacy, archiving and running events, all of which took basic resources, from financial support to the time of volunteers. Keeping faith in larger projects in constant cycles of precarity required being hopeful for communities that were harder to bring together. Black warned of what this might mean for the 1990s:

> The same sense of community and one-ness that has spurred us onwards through thick, thin and whatever else society has chosen to throw at us should be the way that we continue on into the 1990's. Or we will be just end up burnt out and on the scrap heap having to struggle even harder to survive, as has been the fate of many of our sister and brother projects... LESPOP, FEMINIST LIBRARY, THIRD WORLD ARCHIVES, ASIAN WOMEN'S NETWORK, CAMDEN WOMEN'S BUS, HALL CARPENTER ARCHIVES... to name but a few fallen under the boot of racism and the homophobic knife of funding cuts. Yes, if we are to survive as a project and as a community we need to pull together, instead of pulling apart.[85]

The Smash the Backlash! demo and the events running up to it are an under-rehearsed moment in the telling of British queer history. One of the most infamous forms of resistance to Section 28 was the storming of the BBC Six O'Clock news set by white lesbian feminists in 1988.[86] However, the significance of the collective anti-racist work of the Haringey Lesbian and Gay Unit and Haringey Black Action has been under-recognised by mainstream LGBTQ+ NGOs and scholarship. Bernie Grant was the first Labour MP to speak out in opposition to Section 28 in parliament. A broad coalition of anti-racist and gay and lesbian activists staged the first protest against the hostility to communities pushed out of the lines of acceptable life.

Progressive anti-racist activism was the first line of organising and defence against Section 28. Black queers living in the context of rife state-sponsored racism and homophobia were not just part of a resistance to heterosexism in Britain; they led one of its most important sites of action and consciousness-raising. Gilli Salvat's work in the Haringey Lesbian and Gay Unit, and Savi Hensman's active work to organise the demo, are just two examples of how black-identified South Asian women were at the forefront of challenges to racism and heterosexism that were embedded in local networks emerging from radical responses to police violence in '80s Britain. However, to pull them out as 'exceptional South Asians' any further than this is to undermine the intentions of a broad-based solidarity founded in political blackness. As that term, and movement, lost its meaning, especially in Britain, some of the diversity of those contributions were lost from view. *Making Black Waves* has its own summary of a hard turn from 'dangerous' forms of equality work in local authorities:

> But by the end of the 1980s Clause 28, later Section 2A of the Local Government Act of 1988 forbidding the promotion of homosexuality by local authorities, had been passed by Parliament and many lesbian and gay, women's, disability and race units were being dismantled. It was official—equalities issues were out.[87]

Equality issues were far from out. But the practice, and implementation of equality issues would be fundamentally reworked by neoliberal policies. Haringey Black Action was part of a lineage of Black queer and queer of colour activism in the UK which has been reworked by the shifting tactics of racism. (See for instance the local British Muslim-led response to another debate around the suitability of LGBT lessons in Birmingham schools in 2019.)[88]

Conclusion

In this chapter we have set out to show some of the ways in which individuals and collectives built solidarity platforms across conventional lines of difference, including race and sexuality. These were often aligned with left-wing politics that fought for a redistribution of wealth through challenging the structures underpinning racialised, gendered, sexualised and classed difference. In a decade when local authority equality units were developing, this led to grassroots collectives and local authorities rubbing up against each other in new ways. For example, would the professionalisation of equalities work by local authorities signal the beginning of the end of radical action? If groups didn't take local authority funding, who would pay for the labour, the resources and infrastructure not just to sustain activism today, but conserve the memory and resources produced by that work for the future? Our approach to scavenging the queer South Asian 1980s in this chapter is partly a response to these questions and their consequences. As the chapter touches on, there was an acute awareness of the importance of archiving work within black queer collectives. As various archives were defunded or collectives and politics moved on, some of the hard-won lessons of building black and brown solidarities, and why they matter, were dispersed. We need these lessons and materials now more than ever.

The queer scholar Claire Hemmings has described the 1980s as the 'overburdened decade,'[89] and while it can be tempting to blame the withdrawal of Greater London Council funding for the failure of some community and solidarity projects, the co-operating with, and co-option by, the state was part of the problem.[90] But in a moment when things seem to be going 'backwards', the acts of solidarity here have, at times, more ambitious dimensions and possibilities that we can learn from now.[91] The sociologist Claire Alexander is right in suggesting that, 'while maybe resurrecting "political blackness" may not be possible, or even desirable, there is a need to find some form of expressing solidarity and resistance to racism, even—or especially—in a complex and shifting and contradictory contemporary Britain.'[92]

We end with a letter from an Indian lesbian organisation appealing for queer transnational coalitions.[93] At the beginning of 1994, Sakhi, India's first lesbian organisation, wrote to various lesbian and women's groups to find solidarity. In one particular letter they recounted a conference on alternative sexualities with the Naz Project. Their aim was to collect evidence and material on lesbian lives, and part of their appeal to an international community of lesbian feminists was for resources and to support campaigning for Indian lesbian visibility.

In particular, they wanted help challenging homophobia within the Indian women's movement: 'We are writing to you because of the persistent and suffocating lesbophobia in the denial of open lesbian space by the Indian feminist groups. We have been in existence since 3 years but have not received one letter of acknowledgement or support from any Indian feminist organisation.'[94] Sakhi would receive a reply from the Lesbian Archive which signalled general support, interest and a reference to Shakti (which was redundant as two of the founders of Shakti were also founders of the Naz Project). But the reply also explained, 'In closing I should explain that the Archive is not a campaigning group, but involved in archiving and recording multi-media history (past and present) about lesbians worldwide...'[95] Whatever the achievements of black action at the Lesbian Archive in the late 1980s, by the mid-1990s, this denial of lesbian politics, and the redundancy of lesbian solidarity in the archive, found its way by airmail to India. The queer anti-racist work of the 1980s did not disappear, rather it found itself re-arranged and re-aligned across new types of solidarity projects which enabled queer South Asian community and belonging. It was time for a new set of transnational solidarities that looked beyond Britain to find its roots in the broader queer South Asian diaspora.

2

SHAKTI DISCO TO CLUB KALI

QUEER NIGHTLIFE IN THE BRITISH SOUTH ASIAN DIASPORA

You know, when I see all these Asian lesbians and gay men at the SHAKTI disco, when I see them dancing to Bhangra, or some film sound-track, I just have the most incredible feeling. Here I am, Asian, gay, no longer alone, no longer isolated. What power I feel.[1]

Dancefloors have been the frontline spaces of queer liberation through offering venues for community-making and producing distinct aesthetics. From the right to have a space safe from police harassment and threats of violence to the challenge of creating financially sustainable nights, the right to a dancefloor has always been politicised for queers. Some of our interviewees offered glimpses into queer sub-scenes in the 1960s and 1970s where men, in particular, could access cruising spots and nights if they were willing to risk inevitable exoticisation and the threat of racism. But from the early to mid-1980s a distinct desi queer sound and nightlife emerged at the intersection of the political and cultural consciousness forged by youth-led South Asian anti-racist activism and black queer action. Desi queer nightlife's origins sit in and amongst working-class Black and South Asian-led music scenes that existed outside of commercial spaces, for example house and squat parties and the legendary Sound Systems. For queer South Asians, nightlife was a way to evoke the familiar sounds of home, including folk songs that had travelled with first generation migrants and Bollywood hits, and let it rub shoulders with the fusion of music in black queer nightlife that included influences from house music to pop.

This is a nightlife that persisted through racist and homophobic attacks in the 1980s (spurred on by the negative rhetoric around racialised minorities and the AIDS crisis); the economic pressures of gentrification and the marketisation of queer venues in the 1990s; the sharp rise in Islamophobia in the 2000s; and the full effects of racist government policies, including the Conservative Party's 'hostile environment' through the 2010s. While these dancefloors have offered refuge and joy for generations of queer South Asians, they have not been immune to the politics and conflicts around them. The full weight of people's hopes and dreams for what queer South Asian nightlife could offer played out on the dancefloor. Many of the problems familiar in anti-racist South Asian collectives were felt in queer South Asian nightlife, especially around the role and representation of women, while enduring questions about whether white and/or straight allies could join continued to wear out the seams of queer South Asian community-making.

This chapter revisits the highs and lows of two iconic club nights that inaugurated a desi queer sound embedded in the cultural politics of queer anti-racist resistance in the 1980s and 1990s that offered a lifeline across generations. The work and experiences of DJ Ritu are at the heart of this chapter, from her time DJing across South Asian, feminist and queer spaces in the 1980s to becoming a fixture at Shakti Disco (which opened in 1988), to co-founding Club Kali with Rita Hirani in 1995.[2] Crossing the threshold of the queer club is a rite of passage and part of the familiar plotline of countless coming out stories. This chapter considers the work it took to get there (from securing space to arriving at the club), as well as what those spaces tried to do (from curating new creative spaces to offering frontline support services for public health and housing).

Getting to the club

As the scholar Amin Ghaziani comments in his recent book on London's changing queer nightlife, dancefloors have the potential to act as a through line for bodies that find themselves out of place in normative space: 'Nightlife is transformative for people who are marginalised by multiple vectors of power, as it enables unique ways of seeing and being in the world. And what worlds are they building?'[3] While queer nightlife has the tacit promise of more inclusive world-building in the margins of heteronormative life, it can also reproduce everyday forms of discrimination that continue to stratify the desirability of queer subjects and bodies. From mainstream queer venues that continue to welcome white bodies above all others to the ongoing hostility faced by trans* people within queer communities, the promise of nightlife as an escape from the daytime world of discrimination is cut through with the realities of exclusion. As the scholars Kemi Adeyemi, Kareem Khubchandani and Ramón H. Rivera-Servera argue in their collection on queer nightlife, 'for all the way that queer nightlife spaces can provide refuge and play, they can also be sites of alienation that are circumscribed by normative modes of exclusion.'[4] A striking example of these forms of exclusion was highlighted by one of our interviewees who recalled a daytime 'tea and sympathy' group which met in the mid-1980s in central London:

> We'd have, sometimes after the tea, if they didn't have to rush home, we'd have a little tour of, let's go to a bar together, gather our coats and muster up the courage and then, of course, suddenly twelve Asians would appear somewhere in town and then... they'd never seen this before. [...] So, then there was like a parting of the waves, make space.

Queer South Asians took on the insider/outsider role of what the scholar Nirmal Puwar has called 'space invaders', minoritised bodies which consistently find themselves to be out of place through gendered and racialised difference.[5] Undaunted by the reception, our interviewee described trying to connect to other men he read as South Asian in the bar. He recounted how one 'achha [okay], where are you from?' was met with a resounding, 'I'm from Cardiff and you can fuck off.' Would being close to other South Asian men threaten those able to pass as white? Or would being associated with other South Asian men reorientate the way this man was viewed from being unthreateningly exotic to be being part of a visible community that could threaten the status quo? Lurking behind the 'fuck off' is a fear of how accepting South Asian men might shift the dynamics of who or what queer space is for. While several of our interviewees touched on feeling exoticised within white scene spaces, especially in the 1980s, for one that exoticisation was a dead end when it came to sex: 'That was the main crisis in our little gay lives. Black guys at least supposedly had these huge dicks everybody wanted, but the brown ones had nothing anybody wanted.' Shakti Disco and Club Kali supported queer South Asians to become desirable, and desiring, subjects.

While media portrayals of queer nightlife have tended to focus on the celebration of camp spectacle that critiques gender normativity (one of the seminal examples of this in British television drama was *Queer as Folk* set in late 1990s and early 2000s Manchester), much of this chapter focuses on the less glamorous and more ordinary approaches to the social and cultural functions of queer nightlife in the British South Asian diaspora. Clubbing was not seen as 'respectable' by many first and second-generation South Asians living in Britain, with several of our interviewees describing not being allowed to go out to nightclubs due to parental pressure, not to mention the racism they faced when they did try, from the door to the dancefloor. A rich vein of South Asian club life developed in spite of these pressures.

A generation of South Asians in the 1980s developed an underground music scene with a pragmatic twist: this scene took place during the day. Early South Asian club promoters struggled to secure nights at white-owned clubs, especially at prime times. The South Asian daytime rave scene of the 1980s and 1990s developed across cities like London, Birmingham and Bradford. It filled the commercially 'empty' daytime of the club with desi beats for young South Asians who would not be able to leave home at night. Bhangra fused with hip-hop, jungle, garage, reggae, techno and house to create a sound that spoke to the cultural and political influences that were shaping identities anchored in a different version of what being British meant.[6] These spaces also broke stereotypes about the role of women in South Asian communities. DJ Radical Sister (Rani Kaur) and DJ Ritu were two of the women to be found behind the decks, tapping into the rhythm and desires of a new generation of British South Asians. An article interviewing one of the women who promoted nights in the 1990s captures the thrill of daytime transformations of halls and bodies:

> 'We would go to college in our traditional Salwar Kameez, then at Wednesday lunchtime we would get dressed into Western clothes in the toilets, do our makeup and head to the hall.'

> Sabah [a pseudonym] laughed, 'Our parents thought we had been at the library, it was like a secret club for us all. When we got back home for dinner we were always buzzing! We were on such a high and just prayed our parents wouldn't notice the wiped-off eyeshadow.'[7]

If some women were taking off their salwar kameez to go clubbing, others were deliberately putting theirs on. One of our interviewees described her time in London from the mid-1980s as a 'crazy, wonderful and, like, heady time' when organising was energised by the possibility of change. Dressed in a salwar kameez and a pair of Doc Martens, she described one night at the lesbian bar Rackets in the mid- to late-1980s (the name was designed to disguise what kind of bar it really was) when she arrived with a group of friends and insisted the DJ played a Bhangra track. They took over the dance floor, and eventually two of them ended up dancing on the bar: 'We weren't thrown out, which was a miracle. But that's how we got to do those sorts of things and introduce our own cultural music.' Before Shakti Disco opened in 1988, queer South Asians were an integral part of South Asian and queer club life. Ritu, along with several of our interviewees, recalled their time in some of London's notorious bars and clubs which have long since disappeared, including The Gateways, which had been open since the 1930s. The longer story of queer South Asian nightlife has slipped from view. In some cases those stories and communities have been lost as venues and nights have closed, but in other cases what makes queer South Asian nightlife so unique has fallen between the stools of South Asian club scenes and the history of black queer nightlife in Britain, both of which continue to be under-researched scenes. The rest of this chapter turns to how queer South Asians found their dancefloors.

Queer South Asian organising

Shakti: South Asian Lesbian and Gay Network began with five people, amongst them Shivananda Khan, Poulomi Desai, Pratibha Parmar, and Sunil Gupta—meeting for sandwiches in the Fallen Angel in Islington sometime in 1987–8.[8] The use of Shakti had a twofold significance. By keeping 'lesbian and gay' in the subtitle, English was kept as a necessary but subservient part of the title. The Hindu deity Shakti has often been viewed as the underpinning feminine creative energy and potential in all life. As a generative, life-giving force, the choice of Shakti was part of a queer approach anchored in South Asian antiquity, spiritual philosophy and faith. Despite earlier short-lived collectives, Shakti is generally credited as the first queer South Asian organisation in Britain, and it was certainly one of the longest as it ran until at least the late 1990s.[9] What made the organisation unique was the range of its activities. Shakti Disco (which several of our interviewees described as running like a British South Asian function) featured takeaway food from a family restaurant and decorations including sarees from people's homes, adding colour to the municipal space of the London Lesbian and Gay Centre. Shakti stepped in to support queer South Asians caught between services and forums where they did not fit. And so, a newsletter (discussed in Chapter 3), housing co-operative, HIV/AIDS education and response project, arts group, women's group, and regional helplines became part of its mission. Groups developed by Shakti members (the Naz Project and Club Kali) are still operational at the time of writing and have been recognised as a foundational part of queer of colour creative activism in Britain.

While local authority funding helped to support some of Shakti's work, especially in its HIV/AIDS response, the income from Shakti Disco was key to cross-subsidising activities across the collective. The funding cuts for equalities-focused grassroots work in the aftermath of Greater London Council's dissolution in 1986 made the work of smaller collectives, especially for queer people of colour, harder to sustain. As short-lived collectives and groups formed and closed, unable to sustain the financial and emotional labour involved in keeping communities going, the initial success of Shakti marked a turning tide. For Mayank Joshi (who would go on to found the Gay Indian Network in 2018), Shakti was a lasting source of family:

> I remember I wouldn't let go of people easily so I would really make an effort to make somebody into a friend, although we may argue about some things or disagree about other things, I would always make the effort. Because I think you knew you needed that extra layer of support. Your family wasn't gonna stand by you, you know, your work mate could drop you.

Shakti was an organic outcome of years of queer and feminist politically black activism, combined with a desire to find a queer South Asian community that acknowledged cultural issues, for example family expectations and practices of arranged marriages. As a critical mass of black queer groups grew in the 1980s, the need to balance differences within racialised queer groups meant Shakti was part of the ethnic and cultural turn in organising where being queer and South Asian was seen as distinctly different within larger black queer networks. Sunil Gupta was sceptical of a move away from political blackness to find cultural homes elsewhere: 'If half of us do not accept being black then work being done in our name is not reaching us. The sub-continent can be beckoning but it is not the panacea as we are part of Britain'.[10] The steady move away from a British political blackness orientated towards solidarity in favour of South Asia (predominantly India) as the site of a political and imaginary homeland evened out some of the differences within the diaspora. Regardless of whether you were a Muslim Afro-Caribbean South Asian, a Sikh Ugandan South Asian, or a Hindu Malaysian South Asian, Shakti offered a queer home in the heart of empire: London.

The significant experience of early Shakti members in youth and social work, the creative industries and anti-racist grassroots organising allowed Shakti to leverage experience into action. From its inception, political blackness and anti-imperial lesbian feminism provided a language and social consciousness that initially conditioned who Shakti was for, and what it wanted to achieve, although this would shift over time, reflecting the changing composition of its members. Shakti's immediate success was largely due to the people who were initially involved: intellectuals and creatives in black British arts movements; workers in local authorities (including the Haringey Lesbian and Gay Unit); and experienced organisers from queer and anti-racist grassroots community organisations (for example the Black Lesbian and Gay Centre and Haringey Black Action). Between them, they formed an influential network that had the knowledge and cultural capital to build something new. This was a social collective driven by political imperatives developed from London's left-politics that brought equality experiments in local authorities alongside grassroots movements sceptical of the state.[11] Despite the remarkable achievements and influence of Shakti in the late 1980s and 1990s (which we also discuss in Chapter 3), there is no broader popular memory of its work amongst younger generations of queer South Asians.

While the impact of Shakti has been under-documented in queer histories of British activism and community, the increasing public interest in decolonising approaches to heritage and sexuality, combined with institutional investments in diversity, has created a new interest in Shakti's work. A festival advertised as Britain's first South Asian Queer Pride ran in Croydon in April 2024 and took 'Shakti' as its theme in a nod to the original Shakti.

The organiser, Asifa Lahore (describing herself as 'Britain's first out Muslim drag queen', the topic of a 2015 documentary about her life), framed the event as a point of arrival for the queer South Asian community in Britain:

> I have dreamt, yearned for and advocated for a South Asian Queer Pride for my entire life. To have an event where we can be unapologetically Desi and queer at the same time is my queer Bollywood fantasy come true. The South Asian queer community is arguably the largest queer community of colour in the UK and we are constantly sidelined by the mainstream.
>
> To have an event where we are not there to tick boxes, are simply add ons or have to present western appealing performances is us taking control of our own narratives and destiny. This is our queer Mela. This is South Asian Queer Pride.[12]

South Asian Queer Pride hosted some of Britain's most visible queer South Asian organisations, including the Naz and Matt Foundation; Club Kali; the Naz Project; and the Gay Indian Network. But what did the theme of 'Shakti' evoke in 2024? We want to pause on these two 'firsts' (the founding of Shakti in 1988 and the first South Asian Queer Pride in 2024) to reflect on why we need the story of Shakti now. The South Asian diaspora is marked by sharp divisions and inequalities, from faith and caste-based discrimination entangled with racialised class politics, to the rise of new authoritarian regimes in South Asia supported and funded from within the diaspora. Can the return to the original queer work and practice of Shakti offer a model for reparative work within South Asian diasporas increasingly separated by ethnic and religious politics?

If multiculturalism was instrumentalised as an 'ideology of conservatism,'[13] which became central to what was 'New' in 'New Labour', by the beginning of the new millennium, its efficacy in reflecting social formations was over. Writing in the wake of riots in the north of England in 2001 (which saw South Asian youth clashing with right-wing racists), and 9/11, Arun Kundnani concluded that the liberal promise and politics of multiculturalism, most recently championed by New Labour, was finally dead.

> In January 2002, Sunrise Radio—Britain's 'leading Asian radio station'—took the bizarre step of banning the word 'Asian'. This was the culmination of a long campaign by groups such as the UK branch of the Vishwa Hindu Parishad (World Hindu Council) that want to dissociate themselves from Muslims in the public mind by dropping the secular term 'Asian'.[14]

The influence of religious fundamentalism has always been felt in South Asian diaspora organising, but the relentless forms of Islamophobia (for example, the conspiracies around 'jihadi brides') and other tensions between faith communities unpick a collective frame for imagining South Asian life. At least one which extends beyond hackneyed tropes is based on Bollywood and food. The theme of 'Shakti' for South Asian Queer Pride in 2024 (which the organisers translated as power/force/action) was a renewed attempt to mine South Asian mythology for models of radical queer possibility that resist authoritarian regimes in India that furnish their right-wing homo- and transphobic nationalism with figures from Hindu mythology. But there are other lessons to learn from the original Shakti collective. Like so many grassroots organisations of the period, it struggled to hold the weight of its community's competing interests and investments. Shakti's early years were marked by incredible leaps fuelled by the heroic work of volunteers, especially in expanding across the Midlands and the North; setting up a housing co-op; and running a disco. But they were also marked by some deep-seated divisions and tensions that persist in queer South Asian communities but remain rarely discussed in open forums.

Heroic queer pasts are alluring in two senses. The first is the pleasure in reading earlier versions of your community as deviant and defiant actors in past moments who become heralds of queer possibilities being lived out in the present, fighting the good (progressive) fight. We can enjoy the nostalgia for analogue activism in times where the battlelines appeared simpler because the stakes were so high, and a sense of who the good guys were (the Left), and who the bad guys were (Thatcher and the Conservative Party) seemed less ambiguous. In the second sense, queer pasts are alluring narratives that can become rallying cries for community making which, in turn, can make demands for representation in policy, in media, in museums and other forums where cultural and political visibility coalesce. In their most transactional form, heroic queer pasts are the currency we spend in the present to guarantee our right to be included in the neoliberal identity marketplace. In their most mutable form, they are alive with the possibility of futures that have not arrived.

But what happens when the allure of these pasts is pierced by events or incidents that switch the narrative, that produce undesirable knowledge? Instead of superimposing the identity-based communities of the present onto the past that neglects the 'messiness of commemorative practices,'[15] Jennifer V. Evans, a specialist in queer history, questions what happens when 'we invoke an identity politics that foregrounds identity but leaves the politics behind.'[16] This can be especially difficult when addressing pasts which have, themselves, been marginalised. Here the impulse to tell 'good' stories can be cast as a reparative act (filling in the 'gaps', revealing what's 'hidden').

After dozens of emails, texts and conversations, we were beginning to write our own heroic story of a past that skimmed undesirable moments of trouble and strife in early queer South Asian organising in Britain. This was apparent in the interviews too, where 'I'll fill you in later' or 'I don't remember that' worked to take the edge off old hard feelings where here and now was not the right place and time to revisit difficult or painful memories. This showed the desire from most of our interviewees too, to tell the stories we all wanted to hear because they could be used for progressive purposes (under banners of queering the story of South Asian migrants in Britain or adding to the work of racializing stories of queer movements in Britain). But we got stuck on a moment that loomed large in the archive, which few interviewees could remember, or wanted to talk about (because it did not seem to matter now, or because now it could be of even greater significance than before). As we will explore later in this chapter, as well as providing a supportive and transformative space for queer South Asians, over 1991 to 1992, Shakti banned drag performances at its discos, citing protection and recognition issues for women.[17]

We look back to Shakti to consider how queer sexuality and South Asian identity were sutured in the diaspora. Part of our motivation in this work is to offer a longer view of power dynamics within queer South Asian diasporas which have often aligned 'good' versions of queer life with 'good' versions of South Asian life. British cultural studies and sociology in the late 1980s and 1990s defined the diaspora as a network of relations with historical and geographical specificities tied to different kinds of movement that were not anchored in singular ethnic, religious or national imaginings of 'home.' With the increase of South Asian migration to Britain conditioned by different kinds of arrival (e.g. refugee, working-class economic migrant, exile, student), and from different points of recent origin (e.g. East Africa, the Caribbean, Pakistan), 'the concept of diaspora centres on the *configurations of power which differentiate diasporas internally as well as situates them in relation to one another*.'[18] Experienced through the modalities of gender, race and classed difference, the South Asian diaspora is a '*confluence of narratives* as it is lived and relived, produced, reproduced and transformed through individual as well as collective memory and re-memory.'[19]

Recognising histories of differential racialisation within what we broadly call the South Asian diaspora is one of the routes into identifying the tacit elisions that smooth out the inherent differences within the British South Asian diaspora. If the concept of diaspora relies on marking distinct forms of positionality across a shared imaginary terrain, then the use of words like 'culture', 'heritage' and 'tradition' are its vernaculars. On the transformative potential of diasporas, Paul Gilroy identified their ability to create 'a new topography of loyalty of identity in which the structures and presuppositions of the nation state have been left behind because they are seen to be outmoded.'[20]

If the affective pull of loyalty to a community is a factor in belonging to a diaspora, then what Stuart Hall describes as 'doubleness' is what keeps you situated in the face of cultural difference: 'To return to the Caribbean after any long absence is to experience again the shock of the "doubleness" of similarity and difference.'[21] This sense of 'similarity and difference' was felt within South Asian diasporas, whose family journeys may have been from the Caribbean, East Africa or South East Asia as well as from the subcontinent. A rift between the creative conceptualisations of diaspora that could tap into the productive effects of doubling and the real practices of diasporic nationalism bent on reconciling the double gave a distinct feel to the making of the South Asian diaspora in Britain. From the politics of the separatist movement for Khalistan to the rise of Indian nationalism, there have been a range of South Asian projects that have used diasporas to fund and embellish fictions of ethno-nationalist origins.

Influenced by the earlier work in British cultural studies, Gayatri Gopinath's seminal work on queer diasporas took aim at diaspora projects tied to Indian nationalist projects encoded by heterosexuality: 'A consideration of queerness, in other words, becomes a way to challenge nationalist ideologies by restoring the impure, inauthentic, nonreproductive potential of the notion of diaspora.'[22] Here Shakti acts as a case study of some of the contradictory ways in which the South Asian diaspora has navigated queer activism and community making. Shakti struggled to navigate some of the contradictions between its origin point as a collective founded in (predominantly working class) queer and feminist anti-racist principles forged through political organising in London, and the affective pull of other queer diasporas and homes which shifted the orientation of the collective towards transnational interests that increasingly served mobile, middle-class (and often Indian) masculinities.

DJ Ritu and Shakti Disco

Our return to the opening years of Shakti Disco is another form of queer scavenging. Like so many collectives, and club nights, there is no archive or substantive existing work for us to build on. What we do have are the memories of the people who were there (some of which are collected in our interviews), surviving ephemera and mentions of the club night in the press (held in archives), as well as the insight of the people who designed and set up the nights themselves. While this chapter has been developed through archival research and interviews, this section, and the section on Club Kali, sets Ritu's voice apart, partly to reflect her unique experience and partly to show some of the ways in which our collective work developed through shared discussions and dialogues that slowly unfolded over the past four years.

In the following section we trace the context and influences that defined the early phase of Shakti Disco through the experience of DJ Ritu. Ritu was more than Shakti's first resident DJ; she was part of Shakti's housing co-operative and would serve on the Shakti management committee. With her experience as a youth worker in Haringey, she also helped with some of the research which underpinned *Khush*, the first major community-developed research on queer South Asian life in Britain. As we highlight in Chapter 2, through her DJing work Ritu had connections with a range of queer, anti-racist and feminist collectives, including Southall Black Sisters. The sound and style she developed through her regular work at the monthly Shakti Disco was developed through those experiences from the mid-1980s, and in turn, the sound developing in Shakti would find homes and audiences beyond the queer South Asian diaspora (see Figures 4, 5, and 6 documenting Shakti and its members).

Ritu was an art student in London in the 1980s but started DJing in collaboration with her friend Becky. Becky had a passion for tea dance music, a genre Ritu appreciated but was not deeply immersed in. But they complemented one another, with Becky bringing in tracks from ballroom, while Ritu explored other sounds.

> **Ritu**: It was a learning experience, navigating the equipment together, one of us placing the needle on the record while the other adjusted the volume faders.
>
> But after that night, I realised I wanted to take control of my DJ journey. I craved a fuller picture of the music I played and its sequencing. Already, I could feel the seeds of programming skills taking root within me. I had a vision for the ebb and flow of a set, the highs and lows, the emotional roller coaster I wanted to take my audience on.
>
> What drove me to pursue DJing was a burning desire to share the music I loved with others. Even before stepping into a DJ booth, I was always sharing music, whether it was spinning records for friends or playing tracks from my Walkman. I couldn't bear the thought of hoarding this music for myself—I wanted everyone to experience its brilliance. DJing became the natural next step in that journey of sharing and connection.

When the London Lesbian and Gay Centre (LLGC) opened in Farringdon in 1985 (funded by a major investment from Greater London Council), the six-storey venue had a ground floor café and outdoor beer garden, plus meeting rooms for fledgling support and activist groups and organisations. Nothing like this, or on such a grand scale, had existed in London before. Ritu DJ'd at the LLGC, creating a sound that reflected a range of musical and cultural influences in London's queer scene. 'It took courage to attend Shakti' was how someone described attending Shakti Disco to us. Part of Ritu's work was to create points of recognition and connection through the choice of music, to create those shifts in energy that create a collective moment in the heat and sound of the club.

> **Ritu**: The residency I had at the LLGC required pop music—that's what the crowd wanted to dance to. I had a sizable collection, so I could mix in some soul and disco tracks, even throwing in Motown hits. The setlist spanned from the '50s to the mid-'80s, incorporating rock and chart music, mainly by white artists with some black artists thrown in. But it wasn't until around 1988 that I began to broaden the set and embrace a more eclectic and global sound.
>
> Several factors contributed to this shift. In my full-time job as a youth centre manager, I worked with specialist workers from various communities, exposing me to different musical influences. I frequented record shops in areas like Green Lanes in Haringey, a hub for Greek and Turkish music, as well as shops like Just for the Beat Records in Tottenham, known for its soca, reggae and jungle selections.

Excitement about the new club at the LLGC had been brewing for months and when its doors finally opened, the event exceeded all expectations. It marked one of the first times where the growing community of queer South Asians could embrace and celebrate their cultural heritage and music while openly expressing their queer identities, free from social judgment or risk of censure—a luxury not afforded in family settings. Describing the profound significance of this ground-breaking experience is challenging; it represented far more than a mere social gathering. It was a convergence, not only with each other but with integral facets of their identities—a moment of complete and enriching self-expression, encapsulating a unique British queer South Asian experience. Ritu also describes it as a defining moment in her life as an activist and her career in music.

> **Ritu**: The turning point came in 1988 with Shakti Disco, associated with the newly formed Shakti. I became a founding member and joined the management committee, helping set up the disco as a fundraising initiative. This marked a pivotal moment in broadening my musical horizons and embracing a more diverse and inclusive sound.

Alongside Shakti Disco, Ritu was the resident DJ at the LLGC's popular Saturday women's disco. Her drive to diversify the dancefloor took multiple directions. Amidst predominantly soul, pop and Motown sets, she subtly introduced Greek, Turkish, Arabic and South Asian tracks, beginning the process of decolonizing the music selection.

Shakti and Shakti Disco did more than just provide entertainment and joy. They provided support for South Asians who were going through difficult experiences, being ostracised by their families and experiencing feelings of isolation.

> **Ritu**: There was a significant demand for a space like Shakti Disco to exist—a space within the LGBTQ community that celebrated South Asian identity through music and dance. It quickly became a monthly fixture at LLGC, and I needed to curate the right soundtrack for it. Fortunately, many attendees were eager to contribute, recommending records or even bringing them as gifts, especially those from Southall, where several music shops catered to the South Asian community.

Shakti gained momentum and grew widely through word of mouth (however, bar a few journalists and reporters, the press provided a lukewarm response). The 300-capacity space started to get packed with people from other non-South Asian communities also arriving for the monthly disco. It provided a safe and self-affirming space for South Asian queers and their allies to celebrate their identity. Despite the relative safety of the LLGC, Shakti Disco had to remain vigilant for the safety of its attendees. Ritu recalls one night in the late 1980s when there was a rumour of a planned National Front attack. It ended up being a malicious hoax, but the panicked response reflected reality: South Asian groups and venues were subject to coordinated and planned attacks from right-wing organisations bent on violence.

> **Ritu**: Panic was ensuing because we realised just how exposed and vulnerable we were in every respect. You know, if we're talking about a far-right presence or infiltration, they would literally want to smoke us out and burn us because, you know, we were brown and we were gay, you know. So, I got a friend to just try and cover for me in the booth, and I, me and this other woman that had warned me, we went out, and we stupidly were wandering up and down the staircase through the building, trying to find these National Front people. I don't know what we would have done if we had found them. As it turned out, I think it was a hoax.

Despite these threats, queer nightlife defiantly thrived. The opening of ASIA, the UK's inaugural gay world music club, in June 1989 was another groundbreaking moment for London's queer nightlife. The visionary promoters Don Tyler and Andy Piccos spearheaded this venture, transforming Islington's Paradise Club into a hub of cultural fusion and celebration. DJ Ritu assumed a residency alongside Habib (David McAlmont), Declan Buckley, and favourites like Peter Thomas and The Sleaze Sisters. ASIA not only revolutionised London's club scene but also became a cultural nexus, fostering community and creativity among artists, activists and filmmakers from diverse backgrounds.

> **Ritu**: ASIA was dedicated solely to world music, reflecting the growing interest in diverse musical genres. The term 'world music' had only recently been coined by enthusiasts in 1987, and ASIA represented a new frontier on the gay scene. It was part of a broader trend, with several world music clubs popping up in the straight scene before ASIA made its mark in the LGBTQ community. This period was a time of immense learning and growth for all involved.

ASIA offered a lavish experience across three floors, with one dedicated to techno and punk. However, it was the 'world music' floor that captivated the imagination of a more diverse audience, including open-minded Goan Trance enthusiasts within the gay community and curious newcomers. Bhangra, nestled among Latin, African and Middle Eastern sounds in the 'world mix,' emerged as a focal point, attracting South Asian sub-culture luminaries like Pratibha Parmar, Gurinder Chadha, Poulomi Desai, and Osman Yousefzada. ASIA offered Ritu a route through the music of South Asia that was having the biggest influence in the diaspora, mainly Bhangra. To borrow a phrase from the scholar Gayatri Gopinath, this was part of curating a queer diasporic 'sonic landscape' that was circulating through scenes connected to world music and queer club nights outside the venues dominated by white gay men.[23]

> **Ritu**: Getting involved with ASIA was one of the steepest learning curves I faced at that point in my career. Don Tyler reached out to me, explaining their plans for the club and the need for a Bhangra DJ. Despite my limited experience with Bhangra, I accepted the challenge.
>
> My journey to acquire more Bhangra records led me to Virdee's record shop in Southall. Mrs. Virdee must have found my approach unusual as I only requested tiny snippets of each track to gauge their suitability. I ended up spending a small fortune on a stack of albums,

hastily constructing what I can only describe as the worst demo tape of Bhangra ever made. Bollywood songs like 'Chalte Chalte' from *Pakeezah* and 'Roop Tera Mastana' from *Aradhana* became popular tracks I used again and again, including at Shakti Disco.

To my surprise, Don and Andy loved it, perhaps as clueless about Bhangra as I was. This marked the beginning of my role as the resident South Asian music DJ at ASIA. It was here that I immersed myself in a diverse range of musical genres, learning about Latin, Arabic and African music along the way.

South Asian diasporic music, from Bhangra to Asian reggae, created by many first-generation migrants, challenged the essentialist discourse of South Asian mono-culture. Bhangra was largely a Midlands and Southall reincarnation of Punjabi folk music and this new sound was unleashed in the 1980s. With it came the daytime Bhangra raves and vinyl remixes cutting up Bhangra with hip hop or disco. The music being produced evolved alongside the formation of numerous activist groups in the fight back against racism spurred by some of the horrific racist riots in Birmingham, Southall, Newham and other places against newly arrived South Asian migrant communities. The content of this music was a commentary on racism and migrant experiences and challenged the dominant representation of South Asians. While a contemporary international Bhangra scene has focused on representations of (predominantly masculine) Jatt Sikh Punjabi culture, for Ritu the earlier incarnation of British Bhangra had a broader orientation.

Ritu: If I look at the younger cohort now, there's been a really big and quite obvious, you know, quite blatant steer towards championing Punjabi culture. Back then, I don't know if it was as much about Punjabis, obviously, but now it just seems more marked and with very clear intention. Back then, I think it was people wanting to bring flavours of back home, to be able to feel them and indulge in them here.

> But when we talk about Bhangra, it's really the British form of that music. So it was actually in its British incarnation that this style really took hold. Of course, the influences originally come from Punjabi folk music and instrumentation, but it's really become a British product, one of the chief British exports as well, across the world and across, not just to the South Asian diaspora, but to non-South Asians as well.
>
> And then we know that some of the dance movements traditionally associated or used with Bhangra music are imitations of rural farming, like cutting off corn or hammer and sickle kind of movements. So, the drum was there for harvest time in the Punjab.

Bhangra's folk origins lie in the stylised imitations of everyday practices of arduous labour tied to the seasons, and tied to the subsistence and rare prosperity of small-hold farming (prior to the Green Revolutions that industrialised farming in Punjab from the 1970s). Accompanied by a culture of folk music and stories, particularly *boliyan*, that tied the emotional cycles of everyday family life to the frame of monumental experience, Bhangra was rooted in poetry. How Bhangra evolved in the diaspora is its own testament to the spaces and times many Punjabi migrants in the 1960s and 1970s came from (escaping the precarity of small hold farms), and a British urban life marked by a completely different landscape. For Ritu, music is a powerful way of reconciling the seemingly impossible distance between an imagined sense of loss or nostalgia for worlds left behind and the realities we live in.

Queer diasporic nightlife was genre and border crossing. It was part of the 'queer brown Atlantic' that we discuss in this book. Many performers, musicians and DJs were going between the United States, Canada and the United Kingdom for inspiration, to learn and to distribute their work. Ritu performed at one of the earliest runs of Desh Pardesh [home away from home], a Canada-based queer arts festival founded in 1988 by Ian Iqbal Rashid and enabled by Khush: Gay Men of Toronto. For Ritu, this was not just her first major international recognition as a

DJ, but was also one of the first times she had met queer South Asians from North America where scenes had developed in extremely different contexts.

> **Ritu**: Back in the 1980s, when Shakti was doing what it was doing, and ASIA appeared, we had to work very hard to make any kind of global connections because it was all done by airmail, and maybe telephone. And a bit later down the line, fax as well, you know, phone call. But we were aware, of course, of Trikone in California, an equivalent of Shakti in the UK. We were aware of Khush, which was in Toronto. We were aware of Bombay Dost in India. I think these are about the only places and similar organisations we were aware of. And of course, we forged connections with them.
>
> Our newsletters would always mention what was happening there as we saw it as an important thing to keep growing and connecting with our chosen families across the world because together we are stronger, to use an old cliché. What could we learn from each other as well? And what were the struggles that were going on in those countries in terms of homophobia and racism? And so this idea of Desh Pardesh! This turned out to become my first international gig. I still thought being a DJ was a hobby and had my daytime job. I never thought I would one day be touring internationally. Music, Soca and Chutney music are very big in Canada, as I found out. And of course, I did a lot of record shopping when I was in Toronto, buying up Soca and Chutney, which we really couldn't get, Chutney music, so much in England. And of course, Chutney was this fusion music that was being made by the Indian community in Trinidad.

Black British-led music scenes, especially Sound Systems and house parties, demonstrated how counter-cultural sounds and spaces were political and aesthetic spaces of resistance outside the traditional market forces governing clubs and the distribution of music. While the popularity of hip-hop, Detroit house and RnB eventually created more commercial opportunities for Black

British artists, South Asian musical influences took longer to take hold. The popularity of a distinctly diasporic Bhangra sound eventually coincided with a growing interest in world music.

DJ Ritu was a radio presenter on BBC Three Counties Radio, with one of the very few and very first programmes based on Bhangra music, which was syndicated in Sweden, Germany and Turkey in the early 1990s. A huge audience developed for Bhangra in those countries, particularly in Germany, as a direct result of this programming. Queer diasporic artists started to take a central role in the globalising of British Bhangra and the Asian underground music scene during that time. For example, DJ Ritu co-founded Outcaste Records in 1994 who signed composer and multi-instrumentalist Nitin Sawhney and sourced the first record deal for the then-fledgling band Asian Dub Foundation.

Ritu's contribution to the Asian underground scene has been unevenly recognised. Despite the scene's strong grounding in anti-racism and the issues faced by South Asian communities in 'multicultural' Britain, other forms of prejudice predictably influenced recognition.

> **Ritu**: There was a huge amount of sexism and misogyny, and probably a lot of homophobia. You know, the thing is with the Asian underground scene and the people that operated in it, whether they were in record labels, journalists or other musicians, DJs or club promoters, there was this unspoken street cred liberal rhetoric that used to come out, so you generally wouldn't hear the kind of very stark discriminatory comments or attitudes that you saw on the Bhangra scene. The Asian underground scene was all about embracing everybody and being cool and not being a traditionalist and not being stuck in the old ways of back home. But actually, some of the biggest misogynists and sexist people I ever met were really on the Asian underground scene. It's just they disguised it a lot better. So when we look at some of the very cool people that made things happen and made things happen

successfully on the Asian underground scene it was in reality much more complicated.

DJ Rekha (one of DJ Ritu's contemporaries based in New York) describes how the DJ played a role in holding together the layered expectations of nightlife, as 'people bring their histories to the club, they have their desires. It's the nature of consumer culture. And as a DJ, you're always negotiating what people know and what they don't know and what you wanna tell them, always.'[24] The networking of organisations such as Trikone, Khush and Shakti in the late 1980s and early 1990s brought the different routes and histories of the queer brown Atlantic in touch with one another.

Maya Bhardwaj contends that queer alternative night life represents an important space for challenging white dominance and racial capital: 'queer feminists of colour are embodying queer utopia through parties that centre healing, mental health, ancestral faith practices, queer Black and Brown music and dance traditions, and spaces for activists and cultural workers to gather beyond mainstream bars and nightlife.'[25] Whilst for many people this space is about joy and queer worldmaking, it is useful to note the work of scholars such as Kemi Adeyemi, whose work on Black queer women in Chicago outlines how nightlife is not necessarily a 'utopian outlet' as it comes with frustrations and disaffection. Queer South Asian nightlife was fuelled by a utopian impulse grounded in political realities enmeshed in 'global labour, home, activism, and family as well as mundane embodiments of gender, race, class, and caste.'[26]

As people came to clubs looking for their sound, DJs were instrumental in sampling and mixing music that evoked different kinds of homes: historical homelands (the imaginary 'India' or 'South Asia'), homelands in the diaspora, and queer of colour homes. Shakti Disco offered a space for people to wear South Asian clothes, enjoy food, share music and dance together. Shakti, however, was not immune from the cultural and political issues rippling through queer and South Asian communities. While in its early days it worked hard to create an inclusive environment, some of the broader 'frustrations and disaffection' within Shakti erupted on the dancefloor.

Gender trouble

Drag and other forms of genderqueer performance have become defining features of desi queer nightlife but their acceptance, especially by men, has been uneven. Describing his experiences at *Desilicious* nights in New York between 2002 and 2008, researcher and performance artist Kareem Khubchandani expressed the affection for queens whose queer routes through diasporic belonging felt as familial as they did familiar: 'Like my favourite aunties, they were a source of desi cultural capital, training my ear, eye and body to what nostalgic and contemporary song could be mined for queer potentials: lewd jokes, transgressive femininity, self-exhibition, seduction and innovative intertextualities.'[27] But as Gayatri Reddy has shown in her analysis of queer desi formations in Chicago's scene in the early 2000s, conservative reactions to 'drag-wag' was a put-off for South Asian men whose normative masculinity was invested in being part of the 'model minority' in the US that actively supported the work of homonormativity but with the slight inflection of being South Asian.[28]

Occurring around the same period, Khubchandani describes how drag performances in male-dominated queer scenes became a target for the police raids of house parties in Mumbai in 1999, with bars in Bangalore banning 'cross-dressing' but turning a blind eye to 'cosmopolitan femme-chic fashion,' which itself was held in distinction against historical transfeminine identities and communities which have been aggressively policed by the state.[29] Queer scene-based South Asian drag has been variously positioned through state surveillance (visible/policeable deviance) and cultural distaste (undermining middle-class queer migrant respectability). But as Khubchandani suggests, the enduring possibility of the queen to curate 'innovative intertextualities' means she becomes part of ever-expanding experiments in gendered performances in queer nightlife tied to desire. While there is a rich history of drag in the queer South Asian diaspora, as Reddy shows, undergirding prejudices drawn from classed respectability and normative views of masculine gender (from cis men) policed queer South Asian spaces. At Shakti, this was felt most keenly in the Disco, although here the flashpoint was around the policing of femininity and women's rights in highly patriarchal South Asian communities.

The Shakti Discos had included a regular 'cabaret' section where people were asked to submit ideas. But by 1990, the issue of drag performances became so incendiary in Shakti that it became a contributing factor to the departure of Shivananda Khan, demonstrating the limits of solidarity within the queer South Asian diaspora. There had been some unease about the drag acts in Shakti's early years: 'Should your act require you to cross-dress (wear "drag") then you will need to contact [Piyush] a minimum of six weeks in advance.'[30] This tentative approach to drag was informed by a disquiet about the purpose of the performances, or what the real object of fun may be. In Shakti's newsletter *Shakti Khabar* (which we will further discuss in the next chapter), Shivananda Khan attempted to keep the peace through editorial lines that attempted to give voice to women's concerns:

> So we continue to mock women through our 'drag' shows, in forms of tokenism, in patronising acceptance of 'women's issues', in denying them the right to play other roles beyond that which is deemed appropriate to women, which 'drag' and tokenism sustains. [...] We

> are willing to be 'nice' to our lesbian sisters, but we are not willing to give them space to be free as empowered women co-equal with men, nor empathise with their challenges in confronting the historical disempowerment that they have had to face in whatever culture.[31]

However, this seemed to have little impact on what happened on the dancefloor as an Extraordinary General Meeting was called to address the steady flow of complaints from women about experiences of harassment at the disco: 'It was stated that at almost all of our discos, there have been at least one incident at each disco, of a SHAKTI women [sic] member being harassed. Shakti women felt unsafe attending our discos.'[32] The problem was attributed to the policy of allowing straight friends and family members to attend the disco. This practice had been introduced partly to allow queer South Asians to share an essential part of their identity with their other communities, and partly to help families begin to understand queer life through a South Asian community lens. But in practice, homophobia (directed at South Asian communities, and within the South Asian communities) took precedence. The right to sex was more important than sexism at the disco. Although not explicitly naming Shakti, the following interview from Nasreen Memon from around this period discusses a night at the LLGC with identical issues to those women were raising in *Shakti Khabar*:

> I remember being at the London Lesbian and Gay Centre one night and my friends were at one end of the place. I crossed the dance floor to get some drinks and I was waiting to be served and um, in my head I was thinking 'This guy is just serving the guys—he's not serving me', and I felt like I'd been waiting there a really long time and then this ... this guy standing next to me pinched my bottom! I was so appalled that that could happen in what's meant to be a safe place, and um, an Asian kind of club, an, Asian friendly club. And... and I felt like he was a white racist person who had come in and was tormenting me. And I

> was so angry with him that I picked up um, a dreg... a glass with dregs of beer in it, and I'd done this once before, years before, when someone had done something similar, and I threw it in his face, thinking 'You are not doing that to me!' And er, the next thing... he did the same to me. I was so shocked. I really didn't expect that! And then the next thing, even though I was in these little gold stiletto sling back things, um, we were having a little physical fight.[33]

Memon's reflection exemplifies how the rhetoric of 'safe spaces' can occasionally be parked at the threshold of a club. In her retelling of the incident, she overlays the 'pinch' of sexual harassment with memories of racist torment. The failure of one kind of safety replicates itself across a range of axes which show the multiple ways in which racialised women are made vulnerable to violence in social spaces.

When similar issues were raised in Shakti, the admittance of heterosexual friends and family was characterised as an existential crisis for the organisation: 'The heterosexual debate had become extremely heated with a clear division between many of the men in SHAKTI and almost all of the women in SHAKTI. The issue threatened to become very destructive in terms of what SHAKTI as a whole was trying to achieve.'[34] In the same year Shakti was grappling with the literal problem of the male gaze and patriarchal power, Pratibha Parmar was aesthetically experimenting with de-centring the male gaze in her documentary *Khush* (1991),[35] which creatively documented the lives of queer South Asians and included some scenes from Shakti Disco. Describing the editing process around a dance sequence, Parmar wrote, 'In the original film, the female dancer's act is intercut with a male gaze, but for *Khush* I reedited this sequence and took out the male gaze. I reused this sequence with scenarios of two Asian women watching and enjoying this dance. The gaze and the spectator became inverted.'[36] While Parmar could make the lesbian feminist cut in *Khush*, what would that look like in Shakti Disco? How could drag be as much a site for female visual pleasure as it was for male pleasure? The gap between Parmar's aesthetic experiment and the realities of the Shakti Disco dancefloor demonstrates the tense gap between the possibility of utopian forms of gendered life and the mundane, everyday realities of entrenched misogyny.

The women in Shakti raising objections to sexual harassment, especially from straight men, looked for ways to edit themselves back into the scene. But instead, this became a debate about the inclusion of heterosexual friends and family in the scene:

> It was pointed out that SHAKTI is for women and men, that we also had to recognise that there were four times more men than women in SHAKTI, and should take this proportional issue into account in terms of voting. That SHAKTI Disco is the only social space for asian lesbians and gay men in Europe.[37]

A policy that combined increased security with every fourth disco being open for heterosexual family and friends created a temporary peace. Community solidarity and support (between South Asians, between men and women, between different kinds of queer lives) became distinct from sexualised desire (for and from men). This division rippled through the life of Shakti.

In an issue of *Shakti Khabar* from 1992, the news section began on a low note, 'We have been going through a very quiet period with very little activity and participation in our events by members. Both our discos and regular social meetings have fallen in numbers.'[38] Under a section on the 'drag policy' it was made clear that 'some male members' were uncomfortable with drag performances. But largely this continued to be characterised as a women's issue:

> these cabarets, were offending women, in what is a mixed women and men space. This has created much heated debate and after a great deal of discussion it was decided that there would no longer be any more

> 'drag' shows at our Friday Discos. However, SHAKTI (in consultation with Women in SHAKITI [sic]) would still allow those people who wish to 'drag' up to attend the disco.[39]

If dragging up for the disco could be part of the fun, and part of the queer flexing of normativity, what was so incendiary about a drag performance? One of our interviewees recalled the types of queer South Asian art and performance circulating in the late 1980s and made a passing comment about the drag performers of the time: 'Sometimes they [had] a charm because they were just so dreadful.' While Shivananda Khan would later describe drag as part of a *mujra* tradition—a dance performed by women, which emerged in India—this was never fully articulated or explored in the pages on *Shakti Khabar*, or amongst the interviewees who touched on the issue. Part of what made them 'so dreadful' were different kinds of failure: the perceived failure of femme performance ('dreadful' art), and the failure to locate the performance within a tradition (for example within houses or collectives who worked to fashion an aesthetic and identity for their queens). Whereas earlier in this chapter Khubchandani highlighted how the queen could occupy positions of queer kinship (mother or aunt), these amateur drag performances were less interested in the potential of sisters and daughters in the room as they were fashioned for the pleasure of a male gaze that kept the radical potential of feminine desire, and queered femininities, at a distance. And so, for some women at Shakti Disco, it was hard to avoid the perception that men would rather gain pleasure from viewing a parody of their sexual objectification than look at them.

The debates about drag performances created an increasingly tense situation at Shakti Disco, made all the more significant because the disco was one of the few events people would attend anymore. On one night, there were allegations of an altercation:

> At the July [1991] disco, a drag show was put on, unauthorised. A result of this show was that several women felt extremely hurt and in one case a woman was manhandled because she expressed her feelings of dismay and anger at what she perceived as an offensive statement to asian women.[40]

An early member of Shakti we interviewed recalled the 'infamous time' when, 'I think one of the guys [...] wearing a sari was dancing, kind of throwing money around, pretend money, or people, I think, people would... it was tucking money into a sari and one of the lesbian women there complained and said it was derogatory for women.' What made this incident infamous was what happened next: a woman threw a drink or maybe a glass at the drag performer, and the performer retaliated. Shakti's management committee decided to ban the two from several subsequent discos but also took longer-term action to resolve an issue which had been rumbling for years, something the interviewee recalled hesitantly: 'I think we might have banned drag but I don't think we lost it forever, but I think, yeah, I think we might have... to try, and you know, try and be even-handed, I think we did. Gosh, imagine if you, just tried to do that now.'

In what the interviewee described as 'slips with community,' the Shakti collective weighed the rights of women against the rights of drag performers. The slip 'with' rather than 'from' community touches the heart of this work. An incident on the dancefloor, which was really about everything happening off the dancefloor, changed the feel of the entire collective. Glancing at the programme for South Asian Queer Pride in 2024, and seeing the popularity of drag, might cast what happened at Shakti over twenty years ago as a blip. A minor detour in the progressive work of queer South Asian life. But it touches a nerve that has continued to run through queer South Asian life and organising in Britain: the role of women and the policing of femininity in the South Asian diaspora.

This became the notorious 'incident' that stood in for long-running debates about the role of femininity and women in Shakti. The temporary suspension of the drag performer and the woman involved in the incident did nothing to change or challenge the underlying issues of structural sexism within Shakti. Instead, these real issues found themselves displaced onto drag (which was heavily surveilled and eventually banned) and the figure of angry and problematic women who had to be pacified. *Shakti Khabar* published a letter from a woman who resigned her membership of Shakti and framed her experience through the lens of domestic violence: 'How can women be free in an Indian society which thinks women should be beaten and made to watch something they feel is not in their line of thinking?'[41] Shakti decided to definitively ban drag performances: 'Drag is offensive to women because it demeans women. It sustains stereotypes of women. It places women in the context of mockery, low status, and in some instances, it provides a context to abuse women institutionally and personally. It further demeans men as well.'[42]

A small notice appeared alongside the statement directing anyone interested in drag performances to contact the Shakti Arts group so that they could explore other venues (a clear sign that many saw drag as part of an artistic performance). Drag, genderqueer and other forms of non-normative gender expression were never fully banished from Shakti. But this 'slip with community' was an example of how underpinning tensions could attach themselves to particular bodies and what the cost of these conflicts could be for collectives invested in coalition approaches to challenging oppression. In the final section, we turn to Club Kali which hosted a multi-generational drag house and was the setting for notorious drag battles between queens in London, the Midlands and the North. Club Kali was a bridge between worlds, navigating community support and the need to find a commercially sustainable night that was affordable for as many people as possible, but which could still pay the rent.

Club Kali

As with many queer spaces by the late 1990s, Shakti Disco closed due to a combination of factors, including Shivananda Khan leaving to found Naz Project London and Ritu finding the new Shakti management difficult to navigate and sometimes hostile. This was a difficult moment especially given that the people coming to the disco had become like family but Ritu and her partner at the time, Rita, had saved up some money from their day jobs as a refuge manager and a youth centre manager to set up Club Kali. They chose the Hindu deity Kali to symbolise the destruction of prejudice. That Kali was also a reference to blackness (*kala*) served to show Club Kali's commitments to the anti-racist coalition work of political blackness, one of the traditions that Shakti itself had emerged from.

Shakti Disco and ASIA's musical baton was passed to Club Kali through DJ Ritu and the legacy continued at The Dome in Tufnell Park from 1995 onwards, becoming one of the most legendary queer clubs of all time, renowned internationally, and revered by the many generations that passed through it. For Ritu, Club Kali was an opportunity to offer a redress to some of what she felt went wrong at Shakti Disco.

> **Ritu**: [At Shakti Disco] drag queens had been banned altogether. That's one of the things we did when we opened Club Kali, I wanted my drag queens back. We gave drag queens, the Chutney Queens, free entry. We wanted their colour and their vibrancy and their wonderful costumes, outfits, their dance moves. We wanted them. We wanted to make sure that Kali was inclusive and felt welcoming to everybody, as Shakti had stopped being welcoming. It stopped feeling welcoming to lots of people.

Shakti Disco and Club Kali overlapped in the 1990s, with Shakti Disco recruiting new DJs. Although this was a way of showing the growing diversity of queer South Asian nightlife in London, it also reflected some of the differences within the community. One of the things Ritu worried about was whether anyone would come to Club Kali at all.

> **Ritu**: Well, the first thought was, alright, I mean, it wasn't rammed, you know. It was because the crowd was a bit split. The management committee of Shakti were telling people not to go to this thing called Club Kali. If you go, you're a traitor. All of that. We hadn't managed to spread word about it enough yet. It was still new, you know, and people were still going to Shakti. So now suddenly there were two things they could go to.
>
> So, it was like it was not the most successful opening, and then I know for the next at least six, seven months, it was quite fraught, you know, trying to just get numbers in, spread the word. The gay press were now at a stage whereby they could mention Shakti or Kali, but they didn't know the difference between the two names because they were foreign names. So you know... So sometimes, like we get a mention of our night as Shakti and vice versa.
>
> It was hard. It was hard to find allies. It was hard to find supporters. It was hard to find people. And we just, you know, carried on, pretty much running at a loss. And then we started to break even, and then I would say, maybe nine months into running it, it suddenly kind of really took off, and then it took off more and more and more, then Shakti Disco closed altogether, and Club Kali became this massive thing that even beyond our wildest dreams we never thought it would be.

In some ways Club Kali became integral, serving as a groundbreaking platform for queer South Asian drag in the UK. Club Kali welcomed drag queens and individuals who wanted to express themselves freely, whether through performances or simply by dressing as they pleased. It wasn't just about the performances; it was about creating a supportive and inclusive environment where everyone felt at home.

> **Ritu**: Arriving safely at the club and having a space to get ready was crucial for many. Some folks had the luxury of preparing at their own place, like a group of friends who had a flat in Southall. It's worth noting that dressing up in gender non-conforming clothing and makeup and then taking public transport, especially in certain areas, required immense courage. But for those who attended Club Kali, it provided a sanctuary where they could freely express themselves without fear of judgment or discrimination.
>
> It's incredible to think about the dedication and effort that went into the preparation for Club Kali, especially for the drag queens. While I was caught up in managing various aspects of the club, I didn't fully grasp the extent of their commitment at the time. From selecting the perfect saris to ensuring their wigs were flawless, every detail mattered. The financial investment in costumes and accessories, the time spent perfecting their looks—it all added up to create the dazzling, colourful personas that graced our club nights.
>
> Some of them had ingenious ways of acquiring their attire, whether it was borrowing from family members or scouring charity shops for hidden treasures. Despite the challenges, their passion for self-expression and their dedication to creating an unforgettable experience for themselves and others truly shone through.

The dedication and camaraderie among the drag performers at Club Kali were truly remarkable. As many of the people we interviewed in this book tell us, gathering together after work, they transformed themselves, helping each other with every detail of their appearance—from shaving facial and body hair to applying makeup and adorning themselves with jewellery and accessories. Their transformation process was a labour of love, often lasting for hours before they even arrived at the club. Piled into a small car in true South Asian fashion, they would finally make their grand entrance around midnight, just in time for their performances on stage.

Whilst drag has always been a site of 'performance,' 'humour' and 'unapologetic' expressions of embodiment, it is also a joyful and political reclaiming of space when respectability politics have seeped within queer politics.[43] It would also be useful to point out though that commentators such as Shaka McGlotten do not necessarily see more contemporary forms of drag as subversive or necessarily challenging the status quo. They argue: 'Drag is situated within capitalism, its organisation is highly racialised and classed, it is a commodity of commodities, and its contemporary mainstream success is as tied to the logics of neoliberalism and the global mediascapes as much as any other social phenomena, no matter how liberatory they may seem.'[44] In the context of the South Asian diaspora, drag can be an assertion of alternative embodiment practices and diasporic labour. By taking up space, drag artists are creating space for other people like them to exist, perform and work.[45] The rising commercial success of drag, however, has also begun to influence the look and feel of performances.

While the broader shifting cultural economy of queer spaces had an impact on Club Kali, the effects of global politics and racism were more quickly felt. At Club Kali, the impact of 9/11 and 7/7 resulted in fundamental rifts in the queer South Asian community.

> **Ritu**: We felt the impact of world events very strongly at Club Kali. And you are right that in the absence of Shakti, Club Kali took its place as a support and community organisation, even though we were not a support and community organisation, we were not an organisation. It was meant to be just a monthly club, which then became twice monthly.

But you know, again there was nothing else for people. There was nowhere else for people to go. So this is where their hopes, their dreams, their worries, their fears, their relationships, their friendships, their focus, everything became about Club Kali for a lot of the people that came there.

And with something like 9/11, the impact of 9/11, I think, caused quite a split in our community, maybe in other communities as well. Beyond the gay scene, and probably also beyond the South Asian scene as well. But what we noticed after 9/11 was that this community that Shiv and then myself had been so keen to make, without faith, divisions and regional divisions, started to get challenging.

Club Kali was trying to heal these divisions by celebrating Diwali, Eid, Navratri. Despite Shivananda Khan not really wanting to organise on religious grounds it was imperative to not let religion divide the South Asian queer community that had been built.

As Ritu, and others interviewed for this book point out, there was a lot of hostility within the queer South Asian community. Given that it was quite small, it was important to galvanise people into fighting racism together rather than becoming divided by these events that made them even more vulnerable. Soon after this, groups like Imaan, which is a queer Muslim charity, and Hindu and Sikh queer groups quickly started to set up to talk about issues which were impacting their own communities which others would not necessarily understand.

Ritu: Thinking back on the time around 9/11, it's tough to recall everything clearly because it feels like such a long time ago. But we do remember not feeling a sense of unity or solidarity within the community. Instead, what I observed was a lot of Islamophobia and a sort of 'us vs. them' mentality, with some people portraying Muslims as the 'bad ones' and themselves as the 'good ones.' These tensions were palpable and manifested in various forms of discrimination and prejudice. This atmosphere brought a lot of anger, hurt and unresolved emotions into the club. People were carrying these burdens with them,

> and it definitely affected the overall vibe and dynamics within the community.
>
> It's true that within the club, I personally didn't witness much Islamophobia, and I believe it's because we were united enough to not let it infiltrate our space. However, it's entirely possible that some individuals were experiencing or harbouring Islamophobic sentiments privately, and they may not have shared them with me.
>
> Outside of the club, particularly in interactions with other South Asians, I did see Islamophobia. It was disheartening to witness people thinking they were somehow immune to discrimination because they weren't Muslim themselves. But discrimination doesn't work that way—it's not like racists check your religious affiliation before targeting you.
>
> It's a frustrating reality, but unfortunately, it's one we've seen time and time again, even to this day. People often believe they're safe from bigotry until they're directly affected by it, which is a dangerous assumption to make.

The pressure on queer South Asian nightlife to provide spaces of belonging places outsized expectations on venues and nights struggling with the basics of keeping the lights on and paying staff. Especially in London, gentrification and rising property prices have made it increasingly difficult for independent queer venues to survive. Many iconic LGBTQ+ spaces have been forced to close due to financial constraints or redevelopment projects, leading to a loss of vital community hubs. The proliferation of online social networks and dating apps has changed the way people interact and meet one another. While these platforms offer new opportunities for connection, they can also contribute to the decline of physical spaces where queer individuals can gather. Overall, the changing landscape of queer nightlife reflects broader shifts in society and technology but there is still a need for inclusive spaces where people can celebrate their identities and connect with others who share similar experiences.

> **Ritu**: Some of the fizz has gone out of clubbing, and therefore nightclubs. It was a worldwide trend, not just in the UK. The events leading to the slow decline of clubbing were many. Pre-pandemic, we started to see the closure of major queer clubs that had been successful for decades, like Popstarz, for example, which started around the time Club Kali began. Duckie was also dying a death, and they started just after Club Kali had begun. There were quite a number of significant closures.
>
> I don't know why that is; it's been attributed to lots of reasons. Some say it's because queer people are happy to be in a mixed environment now and don't need queer clubs anymore. That's absolute bullshit. There are plenty of people who did and do still need a separate and safer space to be in.

The material history of queer nightlife has, in some cases, literally been demolished or repurposed through gentrification. Venues and communities not captured in archives, or whose histories and memories are not conserved or passed down through communities, can easily disappear from view. In several ways, digital media has been an unwitting co-conspirer in the erasure of queer South Asian histories.

> **Ritu**: Social media is very paramount in this conversation, actually, because, on the one hand, we don't have those social media references and the visual imagery or the soundtrack to what we were doing. We don't have that because we did not have social media. And we also had strict policies, even stricter policies than we have now, about what could be recorded, what could be displayed outside of that safe space. So we don't have videos from Club Kali, you know, even now, really... We can't put them on Instagram as reels for people to see.
>
> So it's easier for younger promoters and wannabes to make up their own history, to rewrite history in a way that places them centre stage and centre frame. And it's very hard for people to dispute what they're saying. And I think there is also pressure amongst them, or a culture amongst them, to say that they were the first to do this, or they're

> the first to do that, to make out that they are pioneers, and that they are innovators because it feels important for them to do that. But you know, some of the more honest people I come across, they just don't make those kinds of claims because they know it not to be true, to be not true.
>
> And they're quite content with saying, I am doing this. It's new, it's fresh, it's exciting. It's got different aspects to it. Different tangents. But I'm not the first to do this. And actually, I look back to people before me for inspiration as well. You know, for me, when I came out in the 1980s, Pratibha Parmar was, you know, and others were already there. They were already writers and filmmakers and activists and powerful activists, and far braver than my generation was because they had to do it earlier. And we looked up to these people. We didn't, we didn't want to be better than them. We didn't want to steal their thunder and claim to be the pioneers that they were. We wanted to learn from them.

The labour of staging South Asian-ness and queerness within an otherwise hostile environment was in many ways pioneering. For many South Asian queer migrants, it was one of their first encounters with other queer South Asians. As one interviewee told us, when he first moved to London, he took out the London A–Z guide to map his way to Club Kali; the idea of dancing to South Asian music with others who looked like him, and where he wouldn't be judged for his accent, clothes and gestures, was one of many ways he was claiming his stake in the diaspora. These were never pristine, ready-made spaces for queer life. They have been, and continue to be, freighted and hard-fought rights to joy and survival.

3

SHAKTI KHABAR

NETWORKS AND NEWSLETTERS FOR QUEER SOUTH ASIANS

We dedicate this to all those isolated lesbians and gay men in our Asian communities. And if one statement can be made with any assurance to you, it is this:
'YOU ARE NOT ALONE'.[1]

During our research for this book, we spoke to people who mentioned the material they had from the 1980s and 1990s, from photos of meetings and parties to digital files stored on old floppy discs. Some people described not being sure what they had filed away, and what may have been lost in various moves. One time's junk is another time's history. Even where there was material that people recognised had value, it was hard to know how to deposit it with an archive or make it openly accessible. Some material had been informally passed on in networks where there was no formal organisation that 'owned' everything. Sometimes sensitive material was informally passed to queer networks to protect them; this was especially true in the case of people worried about what would happen to that material after they died. Would it be destroyed by family who had a legal right to inheritance? In these situations, it can be difficult for individuals to know whether they are able to complete the information and sign the forms that libraries, museums and archives need when they hold material.

For many of the archives we visited (often focusing on queer and women's history), there was a gap between what was listed in catalogues and what was available in boxes. While lots of material from queer South Asian activism in the 1980s and early 1990s has made it into archives, the material itself can sometimes be hard to find. In the rest of this chapter, we turn to a small but significant body of print material that does exist from the late 1980s to early 1990s: issues of *Shakti Khabar*, the print newsletter of Shakti (longer runs can be found in the Bishopsgate Institute in London, and Glasgow Women's Library). These issues often ended up being collected by individuals, or by collectives (like the Lesbian Archive and Information Centre). Through the pages of *Shakti Khabar* we catch glimpses of the burning issues of the day for queer South Asians, not to mention the curation of self-conscious efforts to fashion a queer South Asian diasporic identity.

Shakti Khabar: *A queer network in print*

Shakti launched their newsletter *Shakti Khabar* (Shakti News) in 1989 (see Figure 7). We draw on the seventeen issues of the newsletter published between 1989 and 1992, at the height of Shakti's activity and activism. With a combined page count of well over two hundred pages (and well over three hundred when combined with accompanying reports), Shakti's publications contradict the myth that there is little or no material documenting the full range of political and cultural life and activism of queer South Asians in Britain in the 1980s. Collectively, the issues we looked at are held in the Camden Lesbian Centre and Black Lesbian Group (CLCBLG) Archive at Glasgow Women's Library; Bishopsgate Institute (London) and the Bruce Castle Museum (Haringey Council, London).

We read *Shakti Khabar* in two ways: firstly, as Shakti's own narrative act to fashion a queer South Asian identity from its location in Britain; and secondly, as part of a network of contradictory flows and transnational connections that contested what being queer and South Asian means. Despite the substantial interest in queer print culture, we were not able to find scholarly material that included considerations of *Shakti Khabar*.[2] The return to black feminist print culture, especially from the 1980s, has offered new productive routes, from the reprint of classic collections such as *The Heart of Race* to new collections reprinting work from the Brixton Black Women's Group, and new overviews of feminist print culture from black perspectives;[3] however, Shakti and *Shakti Khabar* fall short in the different identity formations used to group and catalogue queer print culture.

This was queer organising that followed the map of working-class South Asian communities.[4] The Shakti Development Report for 1989–1990 documented remarkable progress in a short period of time.[5] In their first year, they claimed to have reached over 600 South Asian lesbians and gay men. Their regular weekly meetings grew to 50–60 members, and the regular Shakti discos attracted over 200 attendees while generating vital revenue, which Shakti would continue to be dependent on alongside its membership and the sale of *Shakti Khabar*. Within its first two years, Shakti had a steering group to develop an HIV/AIDS response (SHARE) as well as a housing co-op for homeless South Asian lesbians and gay men (Shakti Ghar).[6] Shakti also opened the first of several branches across Britain (starting with Leicester, and later expanding to Bradford, Birmingham and Manchester). Where there was a lack of research to advocate for policy changes within local authorities, Shakti responded to the issues within the community, producing evidence for longer term change through doing the work. This was a motivating factor for creating Shakti Ghar: 'Although there are nor [sic] proper statistics available at present to show the extent of homelessness within the Asian lesbian and gay community, our experience in SHAKTI shows that there is a great need for housing and that no agency at present meets those needs.'[7] Shakti Ghar's work articulated what everyone in the queer South Asian community knew, but which remained a minor or under-researched area for housing associations: 'Homeless Asian lesbians and gays are ostracised or isolated from their communities which expose[s] them to the dual threat of racism and homophobia.'[8]

As artists and activists who already had experience with the mainstream media, it is no surprise that Shakti had a significant media impact for a new organisation. Network East, a British South Asian news and cultural affairs programme aired on the BBC, featured Shakti in 1989. In 1990, Shakti was part of a Channel 4 programme called 'On The Other Hand' which carried a segment on a South Asian gay man coming out to his mother. In 1990, Shakti members also led a discussion on gay and lesbian lives on Sunrise Radio, the London-based British South Asian radio station. In June 1990 Shakti marched for the first time in the Strength and Pride rally alongside Orientations (a Chinese and Southeast Asian group), the Black Lesbian and Gay Centre Project, and the Lesbian and Gay Black Group.

Shakti was not a minor part of queer organising in London, nor was it invisible within South Asian diasporas in Britain. Democratically organised with a rotating elected committee and a series of sub-groups, it was designed to respond to the interest and needs of its members. As Parmar reflected in 1993: 'When I first came out twelve years ago, there were very few South Asian lesbians and gay around. We knew we are around and would travel hundreds of miles to meet. Now, twelve years later, we have Shakti, a very strong, over 1,000-member gay and lesbian group with a newsletter, regular meetings, and socials.'[9] For some of the members, Shakti could rewrite the script of traditional South Asian family values by harnessing a collective energy bent towards the creation of a queer South Asian community. As one interviewee commented, 'just in terms of sharing about Shakti, I guess, it was like finding a family. It was very much like finding a family, and you know, and it was exciting, we were doing new things, we're working together.'

While Khan remained the most prominent face of Shakti in its formative years, the labour of prominent social activists was felt on the pages of its newsletter. Even though there is evidence for gay newsletters in India prior to the publication of *Trikone* and *Shakti Khabar*,[10] desi diaspora newsletters and publications were a forum for connecting largely lesbian- and gay-identifying readers of South Asian heritage. For those born in the diaspora, letters and dispatches from India, Pakistan or Sri Lanka were queer glimpses into a world that may have only ever been relayed to them through those two loaded terms: *our culture* and *our home*, which seemingly placed queer life at an impossible distance when refracted through conservative and faith-driven conceptions of what being South Asian meant in Britain. For readers in Calcutta or Karachi, newsletters such as *Shakti Khabar* gave an insight into queer organising in Britain, as well as a practical means to spread the news about local meet-ups and new groups. More than once the pages of *Shakti Khabar* record readers from other parts of the diaspora arriving in India, details of a meet-up in hand, and coming along to a group.

Within two years, *Shakti Khabar* was printing a sixteen-page newsletter six times a year and had a circulation of 500 (with 100 copies being sent to South Asia and North America).[11] *Shakti Khabar* was distributed for free in South Asia, via select university campus groups and personal networks, leading to a predominantly middle-class educated audience (which did not mirror the UK readership). Like many collective-based newsletters of the period, *Shakti Khabar*'s content was varied, although Khan was scrupulous in using his editorial privilege to challenge views which pathologised homosexuality. The newsletter's advertisement page, and its media coverage, give a glimpse into Shakti's impact in late '80s Britain. Stonewall advertised roles for workers; Lesbian Line looked for volunteers; OnlyWomen Press (later Women's Press) looked for contributions from South Asian lesbians; and a hotel in Scarborough announced its doors firmly open and welcome to Shakti members. Although its early issues did not include helplines for UK-based Black lesbian and gay organisations, they did include numbers for Trikone (the US-based queer South Asian group), Khush (the Canada-based queer South Asian group), and Paz y Liberacion (a US-based queer organisation for Latin America, Africa, the Middle East and Asia), demonstrating Shakti's changing orientation from queer politically black organising in the UK to transnational queer South Asian and brown networks.[12]

Although based in London, *Shakti Khabar*'s reporting and content spent more time in India than Bradford or Birmingham.[13] The 'networking' section of the newsletter was dominated by men in India, and the broader South Asian continent, seeking to connect to one another, or establish friendships with others (mostly men) in the diaspora. On the one hand, this showed the importance of *Shakti Khabar* as a point of access to a global queer South Asian network that could facilitate the circulation of ideas, material, sex and routes to community-making.[14] What gave Shakti its power was also the disturbance to its harmony: South Asian experiences of queer and trans* sexualities in the subcontinent and Britain ran contrapuntally. Although Khan would sometimes intervene with an editorial gloss to link some of the contributions from South Asia with the social and cultural issues unfolding in Britain, the distance between these debates and observations was an accurate measure of how class, caste, faith, gender and geography created 'impossible' conditions for a transnational queer South Asian collective identity.[15]

Could gay liberation be something that changed and adapted as it moved across the world or were its only stable frameworks for identity incommensurate with social life in South Asia? *Shakti Khabar*'s first feature article captures the issues that Shakti would continue to grapple with: to what extent was it meaningful to discuss a global 'gay liberation' movement when that term was so redolent with white saviourism? Issue 1 of *Shakti Khabar* (April/May 1989) featured an article by Sunil Gupta on nascent social groups for gay men in Delhi that organised along lines very distinct from Shakti. Speaking to an architect in Mumbai, Gupta touches on the segregation between access to sex and the literal and figurative spaces that desire needs: 'He developed a more balanced sex life by sleeping with foreigners who had access to that all important and rare commodity, private space. Since then he has been able to develop his own circle of Indian lesbian and gay friends, but the social scene whilst providing warmth and reassurance does not provide him with a framework to develop his gay identity.'[16]

Shakti tried to build this framework through its work, but ultimately it would be unable to stretch across the queer valences of South Asian experience. The aims and objectives of Shakti included networking across queer South Asian diasporas, encouraging self-awareness, providing resources and support for queer South Asians, as well as creating new social spaces.[17] But creating a balance between activists who had come of age through working-class anti-racist activism and people out to cruise for friends and lovers was almost impossible. This was a question mirrored in the formation of Trikone chapters in the US. In an article from Trikone-LA reflecting on their emergence, the author asks, 'In the beginning there was the dilemma of self-definition. Were we to be a social club? Should we stay away from politics and activism? (This was a moot question, since our mere existence is a political statement and our membership in a gay group brands us as activists. Yet this point was cause for discussion then and continues to be so today).'[18] Part of the difference in London was the political and cultural environment for Shakti's emergence. What was not different was how sex had the potential to re-arrange social relations, especially between men.

While *Shakti Khabar* deliberately used the term 'South Asia', the contents of its pages often focused on India and Indian issues, with part of the traffic of air mail between 'here' and 'home' carrying news, appeals and information for desi queers. The pages of *Shakti Khabar* would be used to help recruit for meet-ups in Delhi, especially of the Red Roses group, which became a type of queer *gup-shup* (a South Asian term used to describe informal conversations between friends, often focused on gossip and community news) for people who recognised themselves in the language of gay and lesbian identities. A letter from the group would be sent to the PO Box for Shakti. Later, the letter would be printed in an edition of *Shakti Khabar* and with any luck the meeting spot and the details would not have changed in the intervening months. It was a painfully slow, precarious and high stakes investment, an appeal sent through the post without a promise of reply.

In another case of slow activism across the desi diaspora, *Shakti Khabar* published an appeal for a reader in Bangalore who came out and found himself jobless and homeless.[19] In another, there was an appeal to crowdsource alternative terms for desi queer life.[20] Some South Asian readers asked for Shakti badges to help identify each other in public, others appealed for gay guides to South Asia (primarily for active cruising spots) and resources for what could be a queer reference library, or atlas, to South Asian lives, past and present. However, the most popular form of transnational exchange on the pages of *Shakti Khabar* was more intimate.

The personal ads in *Shakti Khabar* offer a glimpse into the (sexual) desires of its readership. Its June/July 1990 edition marked Shakti's second birthday with a celebratory article and a picture of an all-male selection of Shakti members. The dominance of men in Shakti and the pages of *Shakti Khabar* is most acutely seen in the personal ads, which included calls for pen-pals and friendship as well as relationships. Out of twenty-four ads in the June/July 1990 edition, there were only two ads from women looking to connect with other women. There were two appeals from men for women who would be interested in entering into a relationship or marriage of convenience. A few ads were less discriminating about gender, and were more concerned with connecting with like-minded or culturally similar South Asians (for example, a call for gay and lesbian Sindhis). But the vast majority were gay-identifying men seeking men, presumably for sex or relationships. We say presumably, as a significant minority of people explicitly asked for advice around migration (to the Middle East, Europe and the US) and employment, predominantly from South Asia (including Assam, Bangalore and Chennai).

The pages of *Shakti Khabar* facilitated queer migration through finding educational or economic routes directly into existing or emerging desi queer diasporas. Although all the ads are in English, the geographic, linguistic, ethnic and national spread of the requests demonstrated that a significant part of *Shakti Khabar*'s appeal was its provisional ability to foster and imagine a relationship between South Asia and its diasporas that barely existed beyond the journeys of the individual letters to the Shakti PO Box. One area where the potential of this transnational network to create a collective response across South Asia and its diasporas was realised was in HIV/AIDS activism and the work of SHARE, Shakti's HIV/AIDS directed collective.

In August 1990, SHARE ran the first HIV/AIDS seminar for South Asians in Britain. It received local authority funding which resourced a range of activities, from translating educational materials to providing counselling.[21] In collaboration with the Terrence Higgins Trust, they produced training packs around AIDS specifically for South Asian communities which included information around bereavement, sexuality and religion, and women and young people.[22] Building on the feminist principles that originally informed Shakti, the HIV/AIDS epidemic was an issue that cut across gender, and where solidarity was part of a politics of collective radical anti-racist queer care. The potential promise of this approach was laid out in *Talking Safe Sex*, co-authored by Parmar:

> It would recognise the different ways the epidemic is affecting a range of groups and would consign to the rubbish heap the notion that different groups asserting their need of AIDS resources take away from other groups. The idea that gay men are competing with women, are competing with drug users, are competing with Africans, are competing with Asians for resources fits very nicely into a divide-and-rule perspective.[23]

Shakti's increasingly visible work in this area brought relief to people who could not find help elsewhere. Nazim was a closeted married Pakistani man in Britain who was HIV positive. When his status became public knowledge, he was rejected by the close-knit Pakistani Muslim community he lived in. Shivananda Khan relayed this story as part of the inspiration for setting up the Naz Project in 1991 to support people from South Asian and Muslim communities (which included, for example, the Turkish community in the UK).

With the same energy as the opening year of Shakti, they quickly expanded with a helpline in Punjabi, Urdu, Hindi, Gujarati and Sylheti, and actively sought Turkish and Arabic speakers. The need to reach men who did not belong to self-identifying queer communities led to a shift in some of the political activism to focus on men who have sex with men.[24] The close links between the Naz Project and AIDS Bhedbhav Virodhi Anolan (AIDS Anti-Discrimination Movement) led to key reports such as *Less Than Gay* which gathered evidence from academics, doctors, lawyers and politicians.[25] The urgent need for this research was exemplified when the researchers for the report in India tried to access Delhi Public Library's copy of the Kamasutra, only to find that it had been on loan to the Union Health Ministry for four years.[26] The Naz Project was part of this queer South Asian transnational movement to lay claim to the texts, resources and materials needed to support its community.[27]

The success of the transnational work around HIV/AIDS was an exception for Shakti. As the pages of *Shakti Khabar* demonstrate, there was a political, social and economic gulf between the lives of Shakti members in Britain and the lives of its readers in South Asia. In one letter, a reader admonished South Asians in Britain for lacking class:

> Asian lesbians and gays are still far behind the West, at least in India in gay attitudes, sophistication, enlightenment, etc. [...] you are in a position to absorb so much from your white counterparts—and can give them so much of your culture. Asian immigrants to the West do have a habit of hanging together and forming ghettos, e.g. Southall and

> Brixton, rather than trying to assimilate themselves into the country (if they are so keen on their ethnic roots, customs, cultures, why the fuck do they not come back to the country of their origin and contribute to its welfare?)[28]

Khan added a response to this letter that pointed to anti-imperial and anti-racist activism as one of the key foundations of a global South Asian imaginary that had the subcontinent as one of its many homes. While Khan remained consistent in his editorial commitment to a political foundation for a desi queer diaspora, the differences within this imagined community continually fractured any stable paradigms, especially around the role of political blackness and patriarchal dominance in South Asian cultures. More activist-minded members of the collective recognised the tension between issues that needed to be addressed within South Asian communities and the work done by mostly white researchers, policy makers and local authorities on South Asian communities. Shakti decided it was time for queer South Asians to lead the research on their experience.

Khush: The first research report on the lives of queer South Asians in the UK

The London Borough of Camden's Gay and Lesbian Unit helped to fund the first large-scale community research project on queer South Asians in Britain (which produced the *Khush* report in 1991),[29] designed and led by members of Shakti alongside crowdsourcing existing relevant published material by queer South Asians through its international networks, including *Shakti Khabar*, *Trikone*, *Bombay Dost* and *Shamakami*. The Khush Report advocated for a turn to reference points within queer South Asian history and culture to tackle homophobia in South Asian communities and combat racism. Until this point much of the work of Shakti had been through the voluntary efforts of its members, several of whom had jobs in equalities-facing roles in local authorities, and limited funding generated through membership fees and revenue from the disco. The financial support for the Khush Report supported the first sustained study of queer South Asian life outside formal research institutions, like universities, where scholars of colour were more likely to be in precarious roles and where queer research was too often being led by white staff.

Over thirty years have passed since the report's publication, but much of its content remains startlingly relevant. The report drew on fifty members of the queer South Asian community in the UK (with an even binary gender split and an attention to diversity of faiths and nationalities), fifty members of the LLGC (the implication was they were predominantly or exclusively white); and ten community organisations within the South Asian community. The report found that while there was a strong denial that queer South Asians existed amongst first generation South Asian migrants, in the second generation, 'Asians seem to be split between two extremes.'[30] This cleavage in the community was also gendered, with the research finding that younger South Asian women were more likely to be accepting of gay and lesbian sexualities than men. What made this a slightly surprising outcome was other research carried out in colleges in London and the Home Counties with a high proportion of South Asian students, where over a third of South Asian men admitted to having had a homosexual experience (much higher than other population averages in surveys).

What was evident throughout their work was the importance of the role of open secrets as a mechanism by which the strictures of *izzat* and the desire for South Asian community belonging could accommodate the reality of non-normative desire. As discussed through the pages of *Shakti Khabar*, while some men felt able to continue their heterosexual marriages and maintain sexual and emotional intimacy with other men (as long as it remained in the closet of white-centred queer scenes), women were more likely to have to leave the family home, which, if they were unmarried, could also mean leaving behind their respectability in the community. There were no accounts of women coming out to their husbands as lesbians, let alone accounts of long-standing accommodations of queer lesbian sexualities within heterosexual marriages. A quote from a South Asian woman captured the paradox of survival in some of the most extreme scenarios, where the choice to emotionally survive was pitted against the impossibility of your survival outside the family network:

> I ran away from home on the night before my wedding. I was nineteen. My parents had chosen this man from India, who I hardly knew at all. I just couldn't go through with it. I know I was a lesbian. I ran off to live with my girlfriend. She was Asian and had also separated from her family. It was good to be with her, sharing the same background so to speak.
>
> My family found out where I was staying a couple of months later. I don't know how. Somebody must have told them they saw me and then they must have watched me and followed me around. Anyway, they turn up to where we were staying at 1.00am. Four car loads of them. Smashed the door down, screaming and yelling at me, slapping me around and my girlfriend [...] They began dragging me out of the flat towards the car. Luckily a neighbour had called the police when she heard the noise.[31]

This account is similar to countless testimonies from women who refused arranged marriages or left highly conservative South Asian families. While women were characterised as bearers of *izzat*, sexuality as a personal choice rather than a public contract was an unacceptable threat. Stories such as this were seen to compound common-sense assumptions within white queer participants in the study that queer South Asians had to leave their culture behind in order to come out. These impossible binary positions had a profound impact on queer South Asians, some of whom reported that they would not seek relationships with other South Asians (because the connections to that cultural background were too painful), while others reported the challenge of dealing with reductive and harmful prejudice towards the families and communities who, despite these problems, had also been a source of strength and love in the racially hostile environment of the UK. This posed a particular in inter-racial relationships where white partners pressuring their South Asian partners to come out to their family (which could culturally isolate them), accompanied by their disinterest in South Asian culture, helped to reinforce a view that South Asian cultural life had nothing to sustain or enrich queer possibilities.

This was a particular problem in Muslim communities, who found themselves particularly vilified as intransigent and dangerous extremists in popular media. The furore around the publication of Salman Rushdie's *The Satanic Verses* in 1988, followed by the Gulf War in 1990, distilled negative stereotypes of Muslim communities and, as a result, Muslim communities formed closer and tighter networks to gird themselves against the rising tide of Islamophobia. Community respondents to the research from Muslim communities had a stronger negative reaction to queer South Asian life. When read in the political context of the time, this correlation aligns to the weaponisation of liberal Western values to continually demonise Islam as a faith. The material consequences of this were stark, from violence on the street to racist immigration policies that took aim at practices of marriage migration. Attitudes which denied queer South Asian life filtered across politicised communities of colour, with the report finding a correlation between South

Asian community organisations involved in anti-racist activism and a refusal to believe that queer South Asians actually existed in any kind of significant number.

If many South Asian community organisations refused to believe queers existed in their community, white gay and lesbian organisations had no hesitation in reproducing racist attitudes. As Khan points out in the report,

> We are constantly asked as to why we don't 'integrate' within the lesbian and gay community or in society in general. We are told that we have to 'integrate' because we live in this country, that 'we must change our ways', 'become English.'
>
> Another term used by many lesbian and gay organisations is 'multiculturalism' and like other terms such as 'ethnic minority', 'minority ethnic', or 'black', are rarely understood in their specific contexts, and end up being hidden terms of tokenism and abuse.[32]

Part of what made the report unique was the range of expertise behind its production. Khan had been on the sharp end of raising awareness of queer South Asian lives in the media and through a community activism that was able to activate queer of colour networks across local authority equality units and third sector organisations. The report highlights the strain on Shakti, who were constantly asked to send representatives to committees and groups to represent South Asians in performative gestures of inclusion.

Pratibha Parmar (listed as a consultant on the report) had connections with leading figures in anti-racist scholarship, including Stuart Hall and Paul Gilroy, meaning the report was connected to, and informed by, ongoing debates about the promise and failures of multicultural Britain. This combination of experience and expertise illuminated the mundane, day to day operation of diversity optics that superficially worked to support minoritised communities, but always remained invested in ensuring that those communities remained minoritised. The importance of integration led to a common ground amongst white respondents: 'Strangely, in doing the research to present this document [...] we found very little difference between the respondents irrespective of political ideology. Conservative, Labour, Radical Left, Liberal Democrat, Anarchist, whatever the label, the general state of unknowing was pervasive.'[33]

Rejecting the Merchant-Ivory imagining of India and Orientalist stereotypes, Khan's ire towards the serial denigration of South Asian culture is barely veiled: 'Our clothing is smiled at, our food is ground into "smells", our colour based upon desires for "suntans". We are perceived through a miasma of Tandoori restaurants, the "Raj Quartet", "The Kama Sutra", and "arranged marriages."'[34] By pointing to evidence from ancient South Asian culture, the Mughal Court, and the British Indian Penal Code 377, Khan points to South Asia as a key site for contesting gender and sexual norms. By taking this decolonial approach to the history of sexuality, Khan, through the report, advocates for the queer South Asians let down by the services that are meant to be there to support them. Shakti navigated the contradiction between the plentiful cultural templates for queer South Asian life in history and religion and the extreme precarity in visibility and support for the reality of queer South Asians in Britain: poor access to HIV/AIDS support (through the assumption that they do not exist or by providing access to services in local pharmacies and GP surgeries where they could be identified); poor access to counselling support (through a lack of understanding of their social environment and the over-use of psychiatric institutionalisation); and poor access to emergency housing for queer South Asians suddenly rendered homeless and in highly vulnerable situations. Through its circulation to local authorities and the creation of educational resources for South Asian communities and LGBTQ+ NGOs, the *Khush* report was a major step in providing evidence on queer South Asian life in the UK.

Debating the marriage question

This section brings to light stories of desi queer family trouble from the pages of *Shakti Khabar* alongside the reflections of our interviewees. Looking back on the 2000s, one of our interviewees referenced the 'goodbye parties' queer men hosted at Club Kali just before getting married, a last hurrah before slipping into good desi heterosexuality. While it was accepted at the time, looking back now, he commented, 'Which is so bizarre when you think about it, it's like why are we celebrating this shit?' What took the edge off the goodbye was its insincerity; everyone knew they would be back in a few weeks. But the case was entirely different for the queer women who entered heterosexual marriages. A more common exit strategy for women was to wait proposals out—'a woman can bat off a proposal then sort of get to a certain age where people stop asking and say she's getting married, and there's quite a few people who are actually in my community like that.'

The worst-case scenarios of expulsion and death have helped to characterise South Asian communities as a key locus of violent homophobia. As one woman reflected on the consequences of coming out in the 1990s:

> If I told my parents, they would ask, 'how would I have babies.' Then they would say it's against the religion of Islam, and therefore homosexuality will make me unsuitable for a husband. They would call me dirty, a pervert, prostitute, a corrupting influence on my younger sister and her friends, and accuse me of being HIV positive. They would accuse all my friends of being gay, before trying to murder me.[35]

Figure 1: Lespop (Lesbians and Policing Project), 'What to do if the police raid' poster [Punjabi Translation], Kris Black.

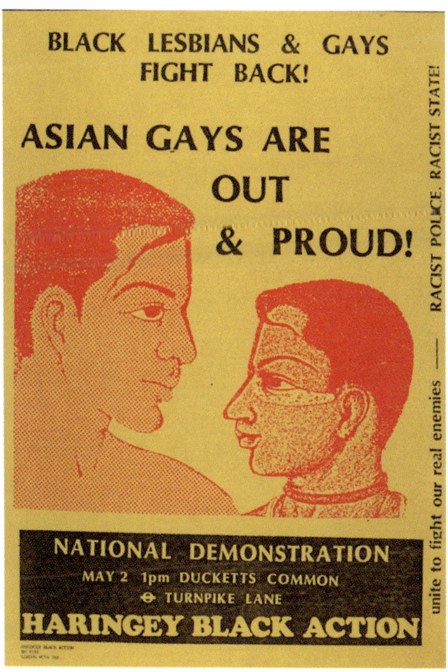

Figure 2: Haringey Black Action, 'Asian gays are out and proud' poster.

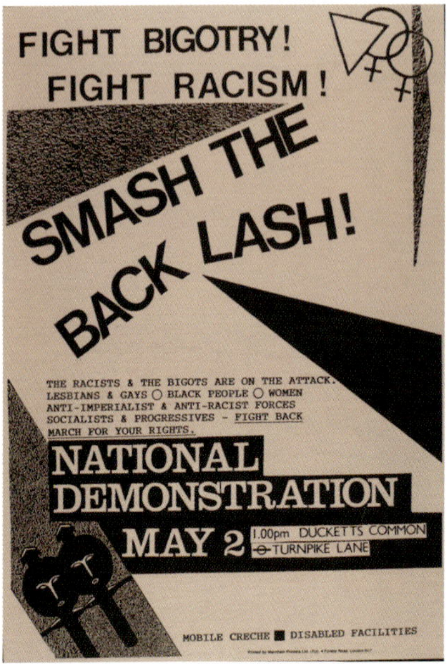

Figure 3: Haringey Black Action, 'Smash the backlash' poster.

Figure 4: Shakti Management Committee, Gordon Rainsford.

Figure 5: Women at Shakti, Gordon Rainsford.

Figure 6: Shakti's birthday, Gordon Rainsford

SHAKTI

dates of meetings

May 14	Meeting/Social	London Friend
May 28	Meeting/Social	London Friend
June 10	Meeting/Social	London Friend
	Party	London Lesbian and Gay Centre
June 16	Disco	London Lesbian and Gay Centre
June 25	Meeting/Social	London Friend
July 9	Meeting/Social	London Friend
July 23	Meeting/Social	London Friend

Meetings between 3.00pm-6.00pm. Afterwards we usually go to LLGC for a drink.

London Friend, 86 Caledonian Road, London N1 9DN. (Kings Cross tube)
LLGC, 67-69 Cowcross Street, London EC1 (Farringdon tube)

NETWORKING

32 year old gay man wishes to write/meet others. Age, caste, religion not important for friendship either in Calcutta, India, or anywhere in the world. I am also interested in meeting anyone visiting Calcutta. Write to Y. Kumar, Post Box 7815, Calcutta 700012, India.

I am Goan and I welcome friends anywhere in the world. If you visit Goa, I can show you around. I love travelling, writing, making new friends, massage and being gay. Write to Fred Britto, Rua Toma Riberia E280, Panaji, Goa 403 001, India.

40 year old gay man in Bombay, computer buff and owner of a Specturm 128+ would like to contact any other gay computer buff who owns a Spectrum 128+ also. Caste, creed, colour no bar as long as the person is genuine in his intentions. Write to T. Sundram, Post Box 6101, Colaba, Bombay 400 005, India.

WE UNDERSTAND YOUR NEEDS

If you wish to subscribe to SHAKTI KHABAR then please fill the form below:

Name:
Address:

telephone number:

Send to SHAKTI KHABAR, c/o London Friend, 86 Caledonian Road, London N1 9DN.

This newsletter is free to all readers. However donations towards production costs and distribution are most welcome. Should you wish to make a donation then please write cheques/postal orders to SHAKTI and send to the above address.

SHAKTI HELPLINES

For advice, information and/or counselling, you can call the following numbers:

837 2782 (office hours)
885 3543 (office hours)
802 8981 (office hours)
993 9001 (evenings after 9.00pm and weekends)

In all cases ask for SHAKTI. All calls will be treated with the utmost confidentiality.

SHAKTI KHABAR

shakti — south asian lesbian and gay network

April/May 1989 — No.1

Conversations with Gay Men in India

by Sunil Gupta

Delhi. Viju, a radical activist from Karnataka, talked about the need to make gay issues relevant to India. It is impossible to simply "import" Gay Liberation from the West. He spoke about his experiences within the Left scene in various parts of the country. "A Politics of Deprivation", appears to be the guiding principle of conducting one's life as an activist here. This covers the whole gamut of material needs including sex. Not only is this oppressive to women in general but it stifles any articulation of lesbian or gay experiences. Without this articulation it is not possible to generate a movement.

Bombay. Parag, a self-employed architect from Maharashtra, analyzed his experiences of growing up gay in Bombay. He knew he was definitely gay by the time he was at college and was able to identify at least five other gay men in his class. Information was limited to occasional literature from the West. Although sex was always available, he found that the context that it was taking place with other Indians was too limited by space and time. He developed a more balanced sex life by sleeping with foreigners who had access to that all important and rare commodity, private space. Since then he has been able to develop his own circle of Indian lesbian and gay friends, but the social scene whilst providing warmth and reassurance does not provide him with a framework to develop his gay identity. A disastrous love affair has discouraged him emotionally and he has decided to devote his energies towards his career. Since he is resisting any pressure to marry him off he reckons that he will have to provide for himself later in life.

Delhi. A group of gay men gathered together in a South Delhi flat to discuss gay life. The participants as unmarried men reflected the growing resistance to pressurised marriages. To of the men, originally from Calcutta, had been together as a couple for seven years. A consensus emerged that more discussions should ordinarily take place and that some kind of publication should circulate as a forum for generating debate. Everyone reiterated the two main drawbacks of the Indian gay scene: invisibility and the lack of a private space for people to meet. Although some articles have appeared in the last few years in the limited circulation of the English language press, these were mainly done by journalists "about" gays. The relevance of 'Trikone' was discussed. Although produced on the other side of the world with an apolitical tone it had encouraged at least one person present to come out. For comic relief, conventional wisdom on regional differences were debated - "Biharis, Muslims and Sikhs do it", collapsing eventually into the wishful thinking that "any Indian man would do it, given the right approach."

The final impression one gets is that there is a younger generation of gay men who are both confident and rebellious, and who are dissatisfied with merely a social scene and years for both cultural expression and organisation.

Figure 7: *Shakti Khabar*'s first issue in 1989 (front and back cover).

Figure 8: 'Khush boys...', Parminder Sekhon, The Naz Project (1995–2000).

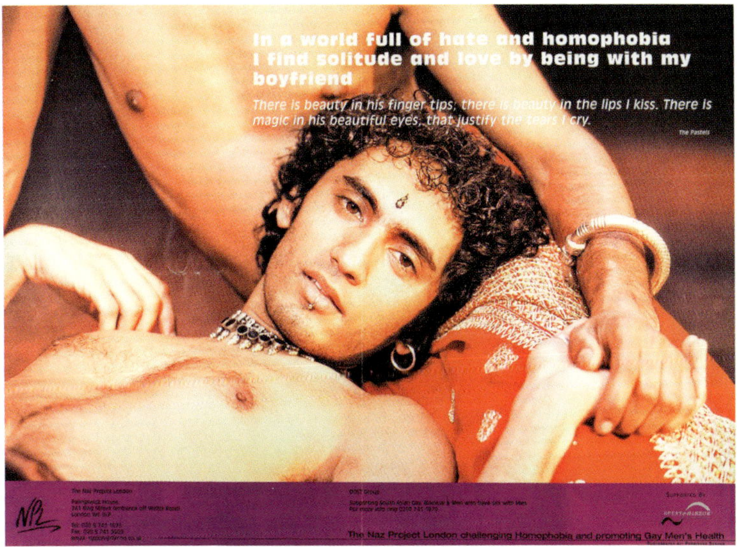

Figure 9: 'In a world full of hate and homophobia I find solitude and love by being with my boyfriend...', Parminder Sekhon, The Naz Project (1995–2000).

Figure 10: *Pretended Family Relationships*, Sunil Gupta, 1988.

Figure 11: *Pretended Family Relationships*, Sunil Gupta, 1988.

Figure 12: *Sita*, 2013. 35mm C41 photomontages by Raisa Kabir from *In/Visible Spaces* series.

Figure 13: *Girl in Hijab*, 2013. 35mm C41 photomontages by Raisa Kabir from *In/Visible Spaces* series.

Figure 14: नील *Nil. Nargis. Blue. Bring in the tide with your moon*, 2019. Film by Raisa Kabir.

Figure 15: *Gather your spools, let your hair down for me. Gently. Here. Undo*, 2021. Film by Raisa Kabir.

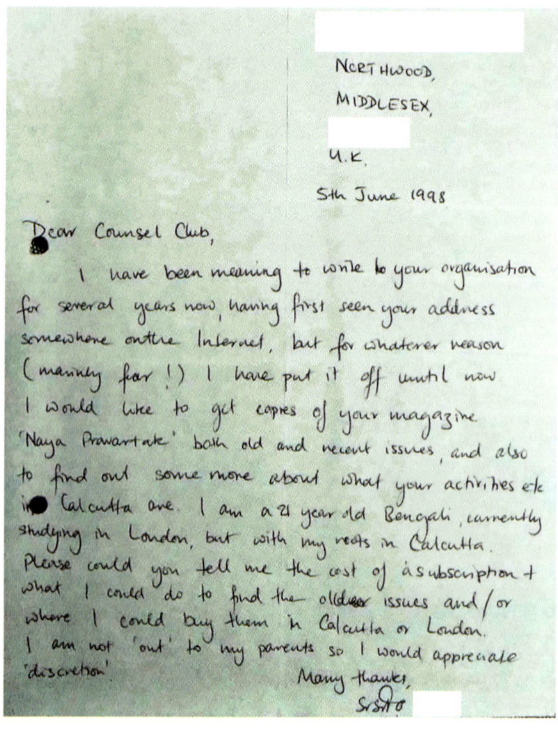

NORTHWOOD,
MIDDLESEX,
U.K.

5th June 1998

Dear Counsel Club,

I have been meaning to write to your organisation for several years now, having first seen your address somewhere on the Internet, but for whatever reason (mainly fear!) I have put it off until now. I would like to get copies of your magazine 'Naya Prawartak' both old and recent issues, and also to find out some more about what your activities etc in Calcutta are. I am a 21 year old Bengali, currently studying in London, but with my roots in Calcutta. Please could you tell me the cost of a subscription + what I could do to find the older issues and/or where I could buy them in Calcutta or London. I am not 'out' to my parents so I would appreciate 'discretion'.

Many thanks,
[illegible]

Figure 16: Letter from 'Samir' in London to Counsel Club, 1998.

The parsing of homophobia's operations in the South Asian diaspora shows the slippage between different types of fear in South Asian migrant communities that found their strongest expression in the reproduction of family as realised through highly regulated approaches to marriage.

Marriage was one of the most contested topics in Shakti. On the one hand, South Asian marriage practices were a site of state scrutiny and regulation. The 'Primary Purpose Rule' (1983–1997) was introduced by the Thatcher government to control South Asian immigration by asking for proof that the marriage would be on the basis of a romantic relationship (which is not part of the legal requirement for a wedding in the UK). Through anchoring the ideal marriage in love, immigration policies cast romantic love at the heart of the legal and social contract of marriage. 'Sham marriages' became a catchall to characterise particular practices, for example arranged marriage, as antithetical to the inherent values of a liberal democracy, primarily expressed through the perceived threat to women's rights.[36] Fears around the lack of consent and possible coercion cemented perceptions that arranged marriages were dangerous to civil liberties and prevented social integration.[37] The double-standard for South Asian communities had less to do with protecting women and more to do with regulating working-class economic migration and perceptions that South Asian communities were failing to properly integrate into British values and structures.

A harder topic for Shakti was where they stood in relation to racist immigration policies and challenging heteropatriarchal kinship structures in the South Asian community. While immigration policies remained a peripheral topic in the pages of *Shakti Khabar*, the moral and ethical dimensions of marriage were a recurring issue, and featured among the reasons that Khan felt he had to leave:

> The issue of marriage was also causing some problems. My opinion was that the social space and the support space was open to any person whose identity had something around lesbian and gay issues or who were men having sex with men or women having sex with women. So the space should be accessible to people, whatever their marital status, and maybe we could use the space to educate them.
>
> But all that became quite heavy, and in April 1991 I resigned from Shakti. I was also exhausted.[38]

The emphasis on marriage as a social tool for the reproduction of 'good' South Asian communities organised between families meant that the question of sexual agency, and whose interests heteronormativity served, was high on the agenda of social issues for feminists in Shakti. Queer marriages of convenience in the diaspora were debated in Shakti in terms of their efficacy (can they be a good hack to heteronormative institutions?) and coercion and deception (queer South Asians are being forced into the closet of heterosexual marriage to keep their culture). Unsurprisingly, marriage, or how to perform queer hacks of the marriage question through more ethical approaches to 'marriages of convenience', was a popular question in *Shakti Khabar*.[39]

Shakti Khabar's February/March 1990 edition carried the story of a Bangladeshi man (S.A.) who had moved to the Middle East. He described his upbringing in a strict middle-class Muslim family, which had not prevented him from having a series of active relationships with other men and an active social life within a gay and lesbian community. His biggest fear, however, was whether he would age out of this queer sexuality:

> I dread to think of the future. I know gays have a lonely life when they get old. I visualise myself as being all alone and deserted. I feel that I will get married so as not to be alone. I know many gays who are married, and they've managed quite well. All that is required is discretion. I don't think that this will be very unfair to the woman. I feel I can make a

> success of my marriage. I'll be honest with her. Maybe I'll let her know the factual story of my past and hope for an amicable solution. Maybe I will give up my gay life completely, but with absolutely no regrets of my colourful past gay life. Perhaps this is the only way ahead to avoid what appears to be certain loneliness as I get older.[40]

While the ethics and efficacy of this as a way to live remained debated, the difficulty in imagining life beyond the structure of intergenerational families and their responsibilities persisted. The attitude towards women in this article, caught somewhere between paternalism ('I don't think that this will be very unfair') and an impulse to live openly ('I'll be honest with her') reflects the desire for queer South Asian men to live queer public lives and to access the possibilities of more romantic and longer-term connections with other men, without any serious considerations of what that may mean for the women they were married to. Shivananda Khan continued a series of articles focused on ancient and indigenous forms of non-heteronormative culture and practice in South Asia, while many of the South Asian contributors to *Shakti Khabar* used the orientation to the West in a deliberate experimentation of what (predominantly) gay life and futures might look like for men outside of South Asian family life. The practice of sex between men being accommodated within heterosexual marriages remained a widely commented on phenomenon within the pages of *Shakti Khabar* and was generally discussed under the banner of 'marriages of convenience.'[41] These marriages were often opened, by one party, to a life facilitated by cruising spots, classified ads and personal networks, in South Asia as well as Britain.

One contributor's frustration was an oft-repeated refrain for men who had paid the price to pave the way for a new world where openly romantic relationships between men could be accommodated because there was no alternative: 'Give them the opportunity of staying away from the family (they won't). Living and making it alone (they can't). Standing on your own feet and making your own decisions (not preferable). They would rather live in daddy's house, mummy's shadow (as their wives) or run to grandpa for support and advice.'[42]

The necessity to be 'out', to be visibly queer, was hotly debated in the early pages of *Shakti Khabar*. For some readers and contributors, Shakti was held up as an accessible entry into a Eurocentric equation of social visibility with the moral dimensions of honesty and 'authenticity'. As a contributor from Nagpur wrote, 'Being gay, practicing it, and then reading *Trikone*, *Khush Kayal* and *Shakti Khabar* without admitting your sexuality in public is not being a hypocrite according to the Indian male. The achievement gays acquire in the West is irrelevant unless we on our part firstly accept our sexuality, and secondly do something if possible for the gay community.'[43]

While the most active discussions of marriages of convenience were from South Asia, it was a visible issue in the diaspora. For many members of Shakti and readers of *Shakti Khabar*, there was a red line for queer sexualities that made them incompatible with existing South Asian heteronormative arranged marriages. Savi Hensman pointed out that the 'convenience' experienced by gay men was not experienced by lesbians, who often found that as wives their movements and expectations around children curtailed their freedom: 'Gay husbands may try to force themselves into a mould they do not fit. Or they may shamelessly exploit their wives; gays can have fun with their male companions, knowing that someone else will do their cooking and washing and provide them with a "cover" for their sexuality.'[44]

What connected South Asian women, queer and otherwise, was the expectation of unpaid domestic labour that literally and figuratively tied them to the site of home. With her signature pragmatism, Hensman proposed that couples draw up contracts pertaining to conduct and expectations that could effectively regulate marriages of convenience. Needless to say, the world Hensman imagined did not come to pass (at least at the time). The question of personal choice led Hensman to question the efficacy of marriages of convenience: 'do you think that such a strategy is a "cop-out", that what we should be about is to fight our families for our own individual freedom to make personal choices. Should lesbians and gay men have such types of marriages?'[45]

While the desirability of marriages of convenience from the perspective of men was a visible thread in *Shakti Khabur*, a few articles pointed to what was at risk when the strict lines of family-sanctioned traditional marriage practices failed. *Shakti Khabar* reprinted a news story covering a heterosexual inter-caste marriage which led to the couple being hanged. It was published with no comment.[46] They also reprinted a notorious news story related to a lesbian couple who committed suicide when they were forced to marry men: 'On 30 November, 1979, in Ahmedabad, unable to live in separation after their marriages less than a year before, two childhood friends, Jyotsna and Jayashree, ended their lives together jumping in front of running train [...] A joint letter by the two showed that they had entered a suicide pact.'[47]

As the scholar and community activist Ruth Vanita, co-founder of Indian feminist magazine *Manushi*, has noted, many of these accounts of suicide involved women from lower socio-economic backgrounds and so diverged from the interests and concerns of educated male middle-class *Shakti Khabar* readers and contributors, but converged with the interests and politics of some of the queer women in the diaspora.[48] For women, romantic love outside the family led to very different narratives. For some it involved reaching for accounts of matriarchal influence in South Asian history. In the words of Gita Thadani, reprinted from *Lesbia* magazine, 'I neither felt comfortable in India because it's very difficult to assume a lesbian identity there—nor in Europe (where the women have a vision of the world limited to the West). So I decided, 7 years ago now, to teach myself sanskrit. And I set out to read the ancient texts, looking for traces of visions of a feminine world which pre-dated patriarchal society.'[49] Another reprinted article, from a 1982 edition of *Connexions*, pointed to the inherently queer nature of middle-class women's social life: 'women live their lives in a community of women. Until a certain age, young women remain segregated from men. Lesbian relationships are not infrequent among schoolgirls and at university, although they are not commonly mentioned.'[50] The article in *Connexions* drew on research from Shakuntala Devi's *World of Homosexuals* (1978) published in a 1980 edition of *Gay Scene*, and a 1982 edition of *Manushi*.

The network of reprinted articles and sources gave queer material long afterlives. *Shakti Khabar*'s approach to scavenging and crowd-sourcing queer material related to South Asian life recycled articles and ephemera as part of a deliberate curation bent towards creating a tradition and archive. After Khan left, this process would, itself, fall into abeyance. And so too would the popular memory of *Shakti Khabar* within larger queer networks. While there would be resurrections of Shakti publications (for example, the newsletter *Awaz* around 1997), none would have the range of content or geographical reach of *Shakti Khabar* in its opening years.

In the next section, we turn to one of the most divisive issues in the early years of Shakti which we read as emblematic of the stress fractures which curbed some of the more utopian impulses of the collective's work.

Desi killjoys: Feminists writing back

The October/November 1989 edition of *Shakti Khabar* included an ad for a premium call telephone support service from the

Punjabi agony aunt Kailash Puri (infamous for her advice on sex and intimate anatomy). Alongside eliciting calls on the menopause and vaginal infections, there was a specific highlight for lesbians and gays. She also worked to support Shakti Parivaar, a group designed to support the families of queer South Asians. Despite the prejudice many queer South Asians were facing, Puri is one example of how progressive views of gender and sexuality were far from alien in South Asian communities. Figures like Puri and the Hindu priest Chanda Vyas used their academic and religious knowledge to create new routes of belonging for queer South Asians in the diaspora who equated coming out to losing a vital piece of the cultural world that had made them who they were.

Shakti Khabar made it clear that queer life in South Asia was entirely distinct from queer life in the diaspora. In an article titled 'Homosexual: An Indian View' the author stated, 'The perception of homosexuality in India is vastly different than in the West. (When I say India, I mean the Indian sub-continent.) Here in India the attitude is one of tolerance. Nobody talks about it. In fact sex itself is not talked about.'[51] The tension between the plentiful evidence of queer life in South Asia and a visible social framework for naming and identifying queer life was felt in the pages of *Shakti Khabar*. In 1991 Gita Thadani delivered three presentations to Shakti members on gender and sexuality in ancient India. Khan's write-up of the sessions identified the potential in excavating queer pasts:

> As we, living toward the end of the twentieth century, fight for our rights to be lesbian or gay, we need to reclaim our historical antecedents, to reconstruct our history, to reinvent the social and philosophical basis that preceded our historical times. If we are to reclaim our invisible history... then we need to explore our temples, our religious sites, reread our Sanskrit texts, truly explore our history with open eyes

> and go out here and record our history. We must not leave it to the dominant heterosexuals to construct our own history for us.[52]

This was more than simply naming and claiming evidence of queer life. The strategic and selective use of material from ancient India was an attempt to tap into a pre-colonial and matriarchal mythology to form the basis of a collective queer South Asian identity that could avoid the trap of identity or communal tensions. This was most evident in the name of the organisation itself: Shakti.[53] Although their use of Shakti was never defined, its allusion to feminine creative power was part of the organisation's enduring aesthetic: ancient (Indian) and transcendental routes to queer becoming. This section addresses the history and experience of queer South Asian women in Shakti.

It can be hard to resist taking contemporary positions (which may be positioned as evolved or corrected knowledge) on past moments. In the present, that could cast the 'woman issue' in Shakti as the recalcitrant transphobic lesbian other of trans* lives, performances and aesthetics. But neither of these roles, of villain or hero, capture what was at stake when drag was temporarily banned at Shakti Disco, as discussed in Chapter 2. If drag queens were framed as a site of male pleasure, then they found themselves open to the contestation of who or what femme, queer and women's pleasure and performance was really for.

Drawing on the work of Sara Ahmed, we read the 'women's issue' in Shakti through the lens of the lesbian feminist killjoy.[54] Ahmed deliberately uses the negative connotations of the lesbian (undesirable, miserable, out of step) to position 'lesbian' as a location from which to refuse heteropatriarchy. The lesbian is undesirable because she is undesirable to men; the lesbian who turns away from the promise of a 'happy' life turns towards a less valued and less valuable life in liberal modernity:

> She is without question a killjoy figure; so often coming up as being anti, antisex, antifun; antilife. The investment in her misery needs to be understood as just that: an investment. To live out a lesbian life is to become willingly estranged from the causes of happiness. No wonder she causes unhappiness.[55]

By refusing to be defined in relation to men, some of the women in Shakti occupied positions of revolt that turned them into a problem for the collective. As Ahmed argues: 'Lesbian feminism: how revolting! We are revolting against the requirement to be in relation to men; we are revolting against the demand to be female relatives.'[56] Here, we are not invested in reading the 'good' and 'bad' side of the debates in Shakti. Instead, our approach is to try and contextualise some of the sources of conflict within the collective to understand the ways in which concerns (for example, sexism) found themselves refracted and deflected in a series of encounters that cast women as minority stakeholders in Shakti. Although Shivananda Khan is recalled as the primary founder of Shakti, he was part of a collaborative effort which he came to lead, especially in the work of *Shakti Khabar*. Gilli Salvat (whose work we discuss in Chapter 1) was just one of the people to give examples of how some women felt side-lined from the work of Shakti, despite supporting its foundation.[57]

One of the most enduring and public tensions on the pages of *Shakti Khabar* was the problem of sexism within South Asian communities in general, and the role of women within Shakti more specifically. If many of the founders and organisers of Shakti had been inducted into community organising through political blackness (as discussed in Chapter 1), then some of the now well-rehearsed debates of sexism within anti-racist movements would track into Shakti and be ready for deployment.

As Chapter 1 showed, there were active links between queer South Asian women and Southall Black Sisters, which was most evident in the Women against Fundamentalism campaign set up in May 1989 in response to the furore around the publication of *The Satanic Verses* in 1988. The pages of *Shakti Khabar* warned that the place that had fostered Southall Black Sisters was now becoming the site of a new ethno-nationalism which was threatening over a decade's worth of work to tackle sexism within South Asian communities: 'we have seen young men and women nurtured in the ideology of anti-racism beginning to wear the symbols of Khalistan [...] It's often these men, young men, not just their conservative elders, who harness religious revivalism in their attempt to control women's sexuality and limit their freedom.'[58] For some of the women in Shakti, the egalitarian and anti-caste principles of Sikhism as a faith veiled the everyday practice of caste and patriarchy-invested communities.

For the Shakti members involved in Women Against Fundamentalism, the rise of multiculturalism, accompanied by its emphasis on ethno-religious differences, undermined the cause of women, who were rendered a sub-issue where 'any challenge to the right of an orthodox religious leadership to speak for the whole community is deemed racist or leading to racial hatred.'[59] For these campaigners, the tension between communities who felt their religious and cultural practices were not being respected by the state (for example, through casting arranged marriages as out of step with British society) and emerging equalities frameworks in government and local authorities led to the failure of coordinated work to support women who were most at risk of experiencing domestic violence. Women Against Fundamentalism was much more than standing in solidarity with Salman Rushdie; it was a protest against endemic misogyny in South Asian communities that used women's bodies as the double guarantor of *izzat* (honour) and the appropriate practice of faith.

In his editorial comment on one of the articles, Shivananda Khan showed his own solidarity by extending the threat of fundamentalism to queer life: 'as lesbians, gay men and bisexual[s], fundamentalist arguments are also arrayed against sexuality and sexual choice. [...] All fundamentalist approaches to human sexuality deny categorically the right to be lesbian or gay, and often extremist language is used against us.'[60] What was named less explicitly was the benefit men accrued in maintaining the status quo of heteropatriarchy. In the documentary about the Gay Black Group (which we mention in Chapter 1), one of the gay South Asian interviewees described arranging his sisters' weddings before he could leave home to live his own queer life. While he described how being connected to his family after coming out would be important, he assumed his sisters would take on the work of tending to, and reproducing, his imagined ideal of the South Asian family home.

Apart from tireless editorial positions from Shivananda Khan supporting the cause of women, the pages of *Shakti Khabar* were relatively silent when it came to men's voices connecting the social issues women were raising in Shakti to the lives of their mothers and sisters. This seeped into a vein of barely veiled resentment that saw open calls in the pages of Shakti for contributions under the series 'sexism and Asian men'[61] that was tacitly connected to allegations of everyday sexism within Shakti. While there had been a women's group in Shakti when the collective began (at one time coordinated by Gilli Salvat and Savi Hensman), the group had become defunct by 1990. In an article by two members of Shakti, Meena and Harbinder, they observed:

> Over 70 women have been in contact with SHAKTI over the last year. Some have come to the discos, some to the Sunday meetings and some have attended special events. But only a small minority have actually become involved in the running of SHAKTI and few attend either the

> discos or the Sunday meetings regularly. We know that many have come to SHAKTI once or twice and have felt that it offers little to women.[62]

This was followed up by appeals from women to women for ideas about how to address the isolation and underrepresentation of women in Shakti, and calls for more women in leadership roles. This led to an increasingly siloed debate about the role of women in Shakti on the pages of the newsletter which was largely confined to women, with support from Shivananda Khan.[63] After Meena and Harbinder's call, a meeting to discuss the role of women in Shakti took place in Camden Lesbian Centre with sixteen attendees. They agreed an action plan including having a female co-editor for *Shakti Khabar*. Shakti's potential to tackle intersectional approaches to queer justice were swiftly and finally derailed by the incident at Shakti Disco, discussed in the previous chapter, which took the complexities around the complementary aims of Shakti (building community, offering support and campaigning) and turned them into a polarising debate about women's rights.

In an interview with Sandip Roy in *Trikone* in 1995, Khan reflected on why he felt he had to leave a collective he had been so instrumental to setting up:

> Mujras were very popular at the disco but some women found it very offensive, so we decided to stop it. This brought about a major conflict between some women and some of the men. It was resolved physically, but not emotionally because there hadn't been built into that decision-making process a process of educating the men partly because some men refused to be educated.[64]

The role and responsibility of men in Shakti remained peripheral throughout the debate, somewhat surprisingly as they were the dominant presence at the disco. While some men disliking the presence of drag performances was mentioned in passing, it was rarely explained or explored apart from in the quote from *Shakti Khabar* that described drag as 'demeaning to men'. Underlining all the dissent was the refusal of some men to see Shakti as a collective that could have the power to dismantle dominant forms of discrimination through critique, solidarity and community-focused action. All the aspects of community building that had characterised Shakti's opening years of energetic activism were slowly dismantled to leave behind a disco, which would eventually fold too. Looking back now, our interviewees who remembered the incident tied it to trouble between individuals. But as Khan suggested in his interview with Sandip Roy, it touched on a deeper hurt that turned into forms of betrayal for which there was no mechanism of forgiveness.

Drawing on the connection between wounding and resistance in the work of Gloria Anzaldúa and Audre Lorde, Xine Yao considers the different senses of callous feeling: 'Their images of thick skin and stone indicate that the callousness of insensitivity may be a development of an affective callus, a protective hardening of the sensitive psyche against the wear and tear of everyday life and the repetitive tasks of racialised and gendered emotional labour.'[65] In the re-telling of the incident, women in Shakti can be read as callously indifferent to the desires of drag performers. The slow layering of this affective callus was a hardening towards attitudes and gestures that were seen to undermine, marginalise or diminish women. With so many of the women activists at Shakti finding a voice and orientation through black lesbianism and South Asian feminism (in Britain), the woman issue at Shakti was an extension of debates about entrenched sexism in South Asian communities. In this context, two types of gendered and marginalised life and expression found their interests pitted against one another.

In the final sections of this chapter, we touch on two important figures in queer South Asian life, activism and representation who came of age through the broader cultural practice and politics nurturing Shakti's most influential work (they also both contributed to, and attended, Shakti). Through them, we touch on how the legacy of Shakti's work continues to shape and influence queer South Asian life now.

Keith Khan

Keith Khan is a multidisciplinary artist who created the innovative multicultural arts organisation Motiroti in 1989, was the Head of Culture of the London Olympic and Paralympic Games in 2012, worked as the Chief Executive of Rich Mix in London, and currently serves as the Creative Director of Hackney Empire. Keith was born in London in 1963 to parents who migrated from Trinidad in the wake of Windrush. He grew up in Wimbledon, which at the time was a predominantly white neighbourhood. Migration and racism came hand in hand for his family; he readily recalled, via his family's collective memories, the slogan 'no blacks, no Irish, no travellers'.

Like many people we spoke to for this book, the experience of racism was tied up with the experience of being, or living in, Britain. For those who had their schooling in the '70s and '80s in particular, racist language and violence was normalised in mixed and predominantly white schools.

> Actually, that was interesting, because I think probably both my race and my sexuality were pretty much examined by people at school before I examined them myself. But yeah, 'Paki poof' was a pretty common name that I was used to... And it used to really annoy me because I just wanted to explain to people that I was from Trinidad.

For Keith, though, the racism he experienced later in his professional role for the Olympics was far worse than that of the playground: 'I have experienced more direct racism in that position than I ever had during school. I got more shots across the broad side then than I'd ever had before. It was fascinating and that's part of the reason I couldn't sustain it, because it was so blatant.'

Keith's entry into a queer identity wasn't through white or brown men, but black feminism:

> But I guess I remember the people, because in answer to your question, [...] I first aligned myself to being non-white and gay [...] with black women. And I guess this is the story of my life, actually, more so than with Asians. The Asian stuff came more professionally with my own company, and the stuff we did then. So I think in terms of my gay identity, I think I was educated a lot by the black women's movement.

For Keith the broader ecosystem of politically black feminist action fostered a series of creative spaces that were remaking social worlds in connected micro-climates orientated by anti-oppression. This opened the way for groups from the Hounslow Art Cooperative (co-founded in 1980 by a fourteen-year-old Poulomi Desai) to the Southall Black Sisters, who themselves were connected to politically black clubs.

As we discuss in Chapter 1, Greater London Council funding helped to seed small-scale grassroots experiments embedded in creative resistance. For Keith, these small pots of funding, combined with his own work sewing and selling clothes at Kensington market, and the availability of squats (for housing), made all the difference:

> I was doing education work, or we would take education work, we would take a commercial gig to do something for television, and we'd get public money to do projects. And I don't... I think that that money side of things gave us a level of security. Plus, housing was a lot cheaper.

> You know, I think the other thing I can remember is... squatting. I wasn't probably squatting by then. I would have been renting by then. But you know, that really did help.

Part of what enabled and sustained this creative environment was what Keith called a 'mixed economy' of commercial, educational, and public work which, combined with low rents in London, gave the fine balance of financial security and made the spaces, networks and resources for more experimental anti-racist grassroots projects possible.

> And as we said, things were much more interconnected. So I mean, the connection between that and things like Southall Black Sisters, to work that you were doing setting up Club Kali, all these things kind of coincided at a point that meant that the sum of the parts was greater than them individually. It crossed into feminism, it crossed into gender politics and identity politics.
>
> And it was the first time there was visibility in that way. And it was much more outrageous to me—don't forget, we had just been through a period where it was very scary to walk along the street. You know, I don't know if it has changed or not, but the idea of being egged or being shouted out, be that gay or be that homosexual or be that gender or racial, politically, you know, that was always the risk. I don't know. I mean, that I hope has changed.
>
> But that was a very real threat. So I think the early adopters of Club Kali or even things like Naz were a lot more frightened. [...] I mean, you were incredibly brave to set that up. Because, you know, there were a lot of people that were very scared to even come to that event. [...] I think all of this other stuff gave people the power to want to be visible. Thank goodness for that, because as we can see, now, you know, it's worked.

And while for some activists such as Savi Hensman the 1990s marked the beginning of a downturn, for those able to ride the waves of the creative industries and navigate the cultural politics of NGOs and their funding, the 1990s heralded a new wave of conversations about identity politics and transnational solidarities, something Keith experienced with the early days of the Naz Project: 'I think I was at the first meeting, which was a really interesting conversation [...] about identity because the original Naz was going to be quote unquote, "Indian". And I was sitting there going, "But I'm from Trinidad?"'

As 'Indian' and 'South Asia' took over from the politically black orientations of the 1980s, some of the key points of contestation and routes into political blackness were deprioritised in favour of more flattened 'South Asian' identities. Keith reflected on this when he considered the make-up of who went to Club Kali in the 1990s:

> If you look at the immigration to London, particularly in the people that went to Club Kali, we were a mixed bag of people who came from refugees from Idi Amin's Uganda, I mean that's the same generation as us, through to people who were Indian professionals who are working in the medical profession, or likewise, families like mine, who came to work with the teaching and civil service and nursing. So there was a mixture, I think, of social class, that was great, that now is more [...] layered and more complicated.

Club Kali's dancefloor became a leveller for different queer South Asian diasporic identities. But that queer levelling is a temporary sleight of hand that disguises how classed and stratified the experience of the South Asian diaspora in Britain has become.

Keith has been a pioneer in British theatre. In 1992 he opened *Moti Roti* at the Theatre Royal Stratford which he described as 'Bollywood on stage'. Keith used his success in theatre to support other queer South Asian artists and performers. Here, he speaks about casting some amateur queer South Asian drag artists in his show *Ma* at the Royal Court in the early 1990s, possibly the first performance of its kind in mainstream British theatre:

> [T]hey [the drag artists who volunteered to join] were the ones that were happy to be visible enough, because we were like going, well, it's a show at the Royal Court... your identity is not going to be compromised because no one that you know is going to come and see that show. So yeah, they were game for it.
>
> It was great, because they were all dressed up and they were integrated into a show, [we] sort of worked out a way to pay them [...] And they were mixed with professional dancers... but it was an absolute car crash of a show, I have to say.
>
> But it was a lot of fun making it although the actual show itself was really all over the shop. But I guess it had such an energy, I mean, if you could imagine, you know, five drag queens coming on every ten minutes to do a star turn in between the kind of narrative and projections and costumes and set—it was that, yeah, it was that—just kind of the sort of work I used to make.

Keith hacked the traditional registers of theatre performance to create space for the unpredictable and evolving grammar of desi queer performance in the diaspora. His commitment to art's potential for educational and community-embedded transformation led him to the senior echelons of the culture industry, somewhere it was difficult to feel at home, especially when it came to his work on the Olympics: 'And I think the truth is that I feel a little let down because I realised that it's so controlled by the middle class, be they of colour or not, but they still have strong elbows to push out other voices.'

Reflecting on what has changed in the queer South Asian scene since the days of Shakti and the early days of Club Kali, Keith reflected on the changing economic, aesthetic and cultural flows between South Asia and its diasporas:

> [I]t was a joy actually seeing, you know, somebody dressed up at a night in Club Kali. People really made an effort and it was very, you know, it was spectacular. To a period where, that, you know, people

> look the same now, you can't tell class or race because everyone pretty much looks the same. And it's become very globalised. You know, if you go to Mumbai, it's pretty much rich people in Mumbai dress the same as they do in London. So a lot of the dynamic of what inspired us is diminished.

As accented classed difference has been smoothed out by more complex flows of migrants in recent times, the working-class anti-racist story of queer South Asian activism has become less relevant and more subservient to transnational debates on queer South Asian life. These, in many ways, have worked to loosen some of the binds of solidarity within queer racialised communities in the UK.

Parminder Sekhon

Parminder Sekhon is the CEO of the Naz Project, the highly influential HIV/AIDS organisation that emerged from the work within Shakti. As a prominent figure in South Asian queer cultural production, she personally identifies more as an activist than just an artist. Embracing a multifaceted identity, Parminder defines herself as 'South Asian, Indian, lesbian, queer and activist.' She is deeply engaged in advocacy and community work and her upbringing in Southall, West London, where she resided until the age of eighteen, shapes her perspective and activism.

Her parents, who were originally from Lahore, were displaced by the Partition of India and subsequently resettled in Patiala and Amritsar before moving to one of the many diasporic spaces of Punjab, Southall. Southall had played a pivotal role in anti-racist movements against the National Front during the 1970s and 1980s. In our interview with Parminder, she recalled her parents' challenging experiences during their migration to Britain amidst the hostile environment at that time.

Her first in-person queer experience was as what she called 'a learner lesbian' in Peacocks in Birmingham when she was twenty. But she quickly learnt from the snickering and looks of the white women around her that finding a community here wouldn't be easy.

> I didn't have queer friends. I was submerged in a very heteronormative environment. And yet there was this yearning to connect. So luckily, you know, there was the London Lesbian and Gay Switchboard and they directed me to this club and I went, and I sat on my own and had a drink. And I was the only South Asian person there... I had my drink, and I left. The only thing that I remembered was that there was a group of white lesbians sat quite close... completely eyeballing me to say this little South Asian girl has clearly got lost.
>
> But interestingly, what they didn't do was reach out and speak to me... there was just a bit of tittering, smirking, nothing to make me feel that I'd want to stay. And so that sense of being in the minority, you know, maybe not fitting in, was my first experience of being in a mainstream [queer] space. And so after that, it was a huge comfort to find South Asian, lesbian and gay men finding spaces where you really could be as Indian as you were in Southall, but this time, you know, you could be your full queer self.

Experiences of isolation and fear (whether of reactions from family, or the reaction of other people in queer scenes) have become defining characteristics of queer South Asian life. While the Naz Project has been key to providing a space for a visible and culturally distinct queer South Asian community in Britain since the early 1990s, there is little available material from the early phase of its work, especially in India.

Parminder was one of many creatives working at the intersection of art, activism and community support. From the late 1980s onwards, she had experience working in a women's refuge; produced photographic series of queer South Asians in

Britain for exhibitions and anti-racist public health campaigns; set up Kiss (a highly successful group for queer South Asian women); helped to lead the Naz Project; and produced one of the few documentary accounts of a distinctly British queer South Asian sub-culture in the landmark volume *Red Threads* (2003) produced with Poulomi Desai.

Parminder highlights a significant challenge she faced growing up: the absence of South Asian queer representation. This dearth of representation not only hindered her own sense of identity but also posed obstacles for young people seeking points of reference and awareness regarding sexuality within the South Asian community. The lack of visibility and representation contributed to a broader cultural silence surrounding queer identities, making it difficult for individuals like Parminder to navigate their own experiences and forge connections with others who shared similar identities and struggles.

> I didn't see any queer images of people growing up. I didn't see any images of LGBT people. I wasn't aware of my own sexual identity until I was about nineteen—eighteen or nineteen. And the only images I did see, I think the first queer film I saw was *Another Country*. And then *Maurice* by E.M. Forster and then the American lesbian film, *Desert Hearts*. And so those were my reference points, really, for queer culture... and *My Beautiful Laundrette* which I think was probably an iconic moment in a lot of young, gay people's lives at that age. I think it was 1985 and I had the... I was a resourceful seventeen-year-old so I somehow blagged an interview with Hanif Kureishi whilst I was studying for my A levels, and went into town, blagged free tickets, went to see *My Beautiful Laundrette*. And even then, I wasn't aware of my own sexual identity. But of course, subconsciously, I must have been and that's why I was drawn to the films and culture and books that I was drawn to.

My Beautiful Launderette emerges as a significant touchstone for many South Asian queers, as noted in conversations with various artists, including Parminder. The book and film, set in Thatcherite Britain, offer complex portrayals of 'home'. Rahul Gairola astutely observes that while some depictions of South Asian characters in the narrative are framed within classist, heteronormative and neoliberal capitalist frameworks, the story also resists these norms through its queer politics, forging new spaces of belonging.[66]

Parminder identifies what she thinks is the quintessential factor in coming out as queer in the South Asian diaspora, especially for women:

> the pivotal moment is saying, 'I'm not going to get married' and I think that is what really distinguishes between the LGBT coming out process I think sometimes for particularly South Asian women [...] Having a baby, having three children out of wedlock with a gay man, and coming out to my parents about that, that was easy. Compared to... I mean it wasn't easy. It was difficult of course, it was fraught with difficulty, but it was easier than saying I'm not getting married.

This partly explains why women were more active in sustaining social groups than men as there was a ready network of South Asian women's organisations dealing with the consequences of stepping out of line with traditional community values and expectations. The intricate interplay between belonging and the diaspora is a prominent theme in Parminder's work, which prompts crucial inquiries about identity and the establishment of queer-inclusive spaces. This is particularly significant given the challenging circumstances under which safe spaces for South Asian individuals within the queer community have historically been established. Writing about Shakti, Parminder says:

> I didn't have a support system around my sexual orientation. I didn't come out to any family members. I didn't have any LGBT friends until I was in my early twenties, so it was quite isolating. I think Shakti was a big moment in my life, where I began to see and meet other brown,

> queer people. And so it became a life-defining, life-affirming moment. And that's why I'm a real believer of creating as many different diverse spaces, even if they're only made up of a handful of people at a time.

At Naz in the 1990s, Parminder worked on anti-homophobia and sexual health campaigns, where she used photography to shed light on the challenges encountered by South Asian queer individuals (see Figures 8 and 9). She emphasises the importance of the camera and documenting queer lives as essential components of her own self-identification and empowerment:

> I first picked up the camera in 1989. I was twenty years old then. I think the camera has always been a real friend and ally to me. I think it was a really essential part of my coming out. It was my friend, it was my safe space, it was my way of identifying my place in the world because I was a little bit adrift, in terms of my sexual orientation and how I identified and who I could connect with. So, developing an identity as a photographer, as a portrait photographer, really, really helped me get over my anxieties and loneliness. In terms of my photography, I started taking images that could be used for HIV awareness campaigns, because I wanted to do something to generate awareness and the only things that I could see were white images. So I decided I wanted to create some of my own.

One striking image, depicting two gay men of South Asian origin, challenges the myth of queer relationships being transient and short-lived. The caption reads, 'They said gay relationships never last, they always end in tears. 5 years later we're still together and very much in love' (see Figures 8 and 9). Parminder recognises the potency of visual messaging and utilises standard advertising tropes to create a powerful image of two young men expressing affection for each other. Given the discourse surrounding the lack of South Asian visual representation, images like these were instrumental in confronting homophobia and providing support to South Asian queer individuals.

In another public service poster for Naz, we see two bare-chested South Asian gay men adorned with visual markers of marital adornment—bangles, a red sari and earrings—positioned intimately, with one person gazing at the camera while the second person sits upright with their face hidden away. The poster reads: 'In a world full of hate and homophobia, I find solitude and love by being with my boyfriend. There is beauty in his fingertips, there is beauty in the lips I kiss. There is magic in his beautiful eyes that justify the tears I cry' (see Figures 8 and 9). Queer South Asian bodies are seldom seen, and what Parminder does with this poster is evoke love and intimacy between two men, inserting it into public spaces as a way to challenge the often-inhospitable geographies that South Asian queer people have to face. Cultural outputs such as these can be literally lifesaving.

Parminder uses cultural outputs as forms of documentation to ask key questions about South Asian queer lives:

> I think cultural output is really important—any initiative and intervention that has the potential to be lifesaving is really critical in terms of documentation because we need to know, how did people cope? Where did people go to survive? How did people nourish themselves whilst facing racism, whilst feeling as though they were invisiblised, or they were being erased? How did they maintain two, three different identities that were all siloed and stay safe? What was the impact of doing that? What is the trauma or the distress that they compartmentalised, how did that play out in their life choices? I think it is incumbent on us to share our stories, and for those who are able to have the lives that they want and deserve, that we are all able to look over our shoulders and to think, Well, what can we do?

Parminder's work, both as a community activist and artist, constructs an alternate South Asian diaspora that embraces queerness and female subjectivity. In 1999, Parminder set up the Kiss group for queer South Asian women, which ran until the early 2010s and was based at the Glass Bar near Euston Station. This was a pivotal year for queer, South Asian and Black communities in Britain as a white supremacist targeted Brixton Market, Brick Lane and the Admiral Duncan pub with nail bombs. The nail bombings were a reminder of how derided racialised and sexualised minorities were by the extreme right. What had changed from the 1980s were the range of skills, knowledge, and resources to set up more specific support networks that could speak to varying vectors of intersectional difference. For example, some of the women who used to come to Kiss, went to Imaan. Or they set up their own organisations. The power of anti-racist, working-class or queer platforms to form broader anti-oppression coalitions had, subtly, shifted.

For Parminder, the loss of umbrella spaces is also a sign of strength: 'I feel sad about the loss of people coming together and more spaces that are available, where people can bring all of their identities. But I like the fact that there are more spaces for people to access.'

The absence of an umbrella organisation that inevitably fosters debate, combined with the changing migration flows of South Asians to Britain, has changed the dimensions of political organising, with older community allegiances to the Left, particularly the Labour Party, waning:

> But I think that as a community, we could be more politicised. I think there is a sense, but it's not just unique to South Asians. I think there is a sense that we have arrived and there are rainbow coloured roses around the door because we can marry and... and there is less appetite, that's my sense [...] less of an appetite to protest and more of an appetite to celebrate. And this is what part of the whole Pride issue has been. I mean, I've always considered Pride to be a march. Pride has always been a protest. It's never been a parade, in my eyes.

Parminder expressed this failure most strongly in terms of transnational organising, especially around trans* rights and a renewed need to define what queer allyship means in a context where our rights have supposedly been 'won': 'I think we as a community not only need to educate ourselves more, but we need to politicise ourselves more.'

Conclusion

In one of Shivananda Khan's editorials, he reflected on the difficulty of building communities committed to challenging interlocking forms of oppression: 'There is a natural coalition. But to form such a coalition for the struggle for human rights is to recognise that the struggle is broad, planetary in scope, but personal in nature. A global vision with a local input.'[67] The pages of *Shakti Khabar* materialised this vision to an extent: it produced unlikely forms of dialogue on its pages through a practice of recycling and reproduction (of letters and content from across the diaspora) that acted as an index to the lives, loves and hopes of queer South Asians globally. The pages of *Shakti Khabar* became their own eccentric attempts to capture, and hold, an archive of desi queer experience. We end the chapter with a quote from Parminder remembering the best of Shakti, but also reflecting on the inevitability of its redundancy as an organisation:

> Shakti was very much an umbrella and it was an umbrella for people of all faiths. And it was very inclusive, and you would dance the night away with people of Muslim faith, Sikh, Hindu, and have no faith and that were not Asian. Because there were no other spaces. So I think part of the splintering, the way that I process that is that, the more established communities become, the more space and freedom people have to look at their individual identities and feed and nourish

> their different identities. And so people may come together because they are attracted to people of the same gender, but there are many, many differences as well. And they may be drawing together with their universal experience of racism. But there are many different aspects to people's identities and people want different parts of their identities fed in different ways.

Even though Shakti would slowly dissolve from the late 1990s, its members would go on to create other collectives. These would, however, reflect the changing cultural politics of queer organising within the South Asian diaspora. The rise of Hindu nationalism and Islamophobia have been just some of the stress fractures that have pushed apart the solidarity within brown queer communities. The return to Shakti, and the pages of *Shakti Khabar*, allows us to revive the potential of older failed utopias. From researching our own experience to building the queer historical and mythological imaginaries to sustain different models for kinship, Shakti offered templates for a world of brown queer reciprocity and care across the diaspora. In the next two chapters, we focus on the distinct activist-aesthetic lexicons of desi queers in Britain from the 1980s to the present day.

4

QUEER ART AND VISUAL CULTURE IN THE DESI DIASPORA

This chapter explores the role of culture and art since the late 1980s in the creation of the distinct visuals and aesthetics of queer South Asians. It delves into how art has been utilised to visualise and articulate the experiences of queer South Asians, while also examining its role in fostering community building and 'creative resistance.' Although the artworks discussed in this section span nearly forty years, the analysis presented is not an exhaustive annotated guide to the rich archive that emerged during this time. Rather, the chapter brings together oral histories and illustrative examples to examine the interplay between art and its documentation of migration, queer subjectivity formation and politics. At its core, this chapter poses the question: How do experiences of South Asian migration and queerness manifest in artistic and cultural expressions?

At the outset, it is pertinent to explore the concept of creative resistance and its relevance to this study. Malik et al. elucidate how, in an increasingly hostile societal landscape, various forms of artistic expression such as banners, slogans, poetry, visual art and film have emerged as powerful tools to confront everyday racism and racist violence.[1] They posit that artistic creativity plays a pivotal role in challenging, resisting and disrupting structures of inequality while fostering radical hope. Similarly, our utilisation of the term creative resistance presents the manifestation of queer art and performance by South Asian queer artists in Britain not merely as a means of visibility but also as acts of assertion and resistance.

Taking our cue from Gopinath's exploration of alternative forms of visuality, wherein queer and feminist reconceptualisations of the diaspora engender new possibilities and aesthetics,[2] we seek to investigate how visuality, expressed through mediums such as photography, film and video art, can interrogate queerness and South Asian identity.

Creating a queer visual archive

Ranajit Guha in his brief but seminal essay 'The Migrant's Time' poignantly writes: 'To belong to a diaspora... I wrote down those words and stopped. For I was not sure one could belong to a diaspora.'[3] Building upon this foundation, Guha prompts an examination of the essence of diaspora, questioning whether it is solely defined by physical space. Delving deeper, he probes into the notion of who is included within the diaspora. Extending this inquiry, we endeavour to discern the composition of a South Asian queer diaspora and the aesthetic practices inherent in its formation.

An early trailblazer in this realm was the artist Mumtaz Karimjee. Her seminal essay on the intersection of Black and Asian identities, and the assertion of a distinct identity, was featured in the feminist publication *Mukti* in 1987. This issue notably showcased Karimjee's photograph of a tree on its cover, a self-referential piece encompassing various facets of her identity—as a woman, lesbian and Muslim. Karimjee's work courageously engaged with the legacies of the British Empire and challenged prevailing Indian attitudes towards queerness. Sunil Gupta lauded it as a significant and historic milestone, marking one of the earliest published pieces by an openly lesbian Muslim woman.[4]

Mumtaz Karimjee's *In Search of An Image* (1988) brings together self-portraits with lesbian-focused extracts from Gloria Anzaldúa's *Borderlands* and the racist fantasies in Richard Francis Burton's 'An Eastern Disease?' (a part of his 1885 translation of *Arabian Nights*). In the first part of the series, Karimjee prints extracts from Burton's Orientalist fantasies that fix queer sexualities as obdurately other, literally foreign bodies, primed to infect the racial and sexual hygiene of the West, alongside portraits of herself.[5] In the second part of the series, she refers to the notorious case of two Edinburgh schoolteachers who in 1810 were accused of having a sexual relationship by Jane Cummings, one of their pupils. Cummings's birth in India, to an Indian mother, contributed to the credibility of her account being brought into question. Ultimately, the accusations brought against the two teachers were 'not proven' (a distinct term in Scots Law). In these works, Karimjee assembles text and portraits as evidence of longer histories of queer South Asian life that through her work literally break the confines of discursive attempts to fix and categorise racialised and sexualised difference.

Like Karimjee's, Pratibha Parmar's works are snapshots into the lineage of desi queer art in Britain that critiques oppression within the South Asian diaspora, and at the same time, places it in longer histories and legacies of imperialism. Born in Nairobi and relocating to the UK in the 1960s, Parmar, as a queer migrant of South Asian descent, draws upon her background in feminist and anti-racist activism to delve into the everyday experiences of South Asian queer women. Her four-minute short *Bhangra Jig*

(1990) follows a young South Asian woman walking through the streets of Glasgow, the second city of Empire. As she walks past the imposing grandeur of statues and buildings largely funded by wealth derived from slavery, scenes and sounds of a DJ (Ritu) and South Asian dancers form the soundscape and backdrop for the woman's journey through the material presence of imperial pasts. *Bhangra Jig* demonstrates the power and vulnerability of queer racialised subjects who seek the resources and contexts to decode the literal and figurative dimensions of oppression.

Parmar's film *Khush* (1991) is a pivotal entry point for delving into the broader implications of the politics surrounding the South Asian queer diaspora in Britain. The title 'Khush,' an Urdu word signifying 'happy,' meticulously traces the roots of homophobia within the Indian diaspora back to the colonial era. This groundbreaking work is emblematic of Parmar's commitment to exploring and unravelling the complexities of identity and marginalisation within diasporic communities. Parmar notes: 'I do not speak from a position of marginalisation but more crucially from the resistance to that marginalisation.' *Khush* was a breakthrough film as one of the first queer works to be shown on Channel Four and went on to win several awards.

Using a documentary style, Parmar includes interviews, performance and archival footage juxtaposed with Indian iconography. The interviews directly deal with the issue of hybrid identities. Several interviewees talk about the influence of their South Asian cultural heritage but also living in Britain, a legacy of colonialism which displaced so many people across the former empire. These oral histories are powerful and for many of the interviewees it was also the first time they were coming out. Parmar, in an interview with Kaplan, notes that several of them found the experience of being able to talk about their sexuality and racial identity on prime television empowering. She notes that the film was intended as a dialogue that didn't pathologise queer people or have to explain their existence to the audience. The film is unapologetic in celebrating the sensuality and pleasure of the female body. Parmar argues that just because lesbians have been fetishised does not mean that she, as a feminist film maker, cannot enter that space and provide a different way of 'seeing and experiencing the female body.'[6]

Parmar's cinematic approach offers a unique lens through which to explore forms of sexual subjectivity and desire that may remain invisible within mainstream queer art. Through repeated shots of adornment, Parmar not only situates these items culturally but also critiques their heteronormative function within matrimony and heteronormative constructs. Another compelling sequence in the film involves the imagery of Goddess Kali, a figure worshipped primarily in the Hindu tantric tradition, symbolizing death, destruction and liberation—a figure with inherent queerness. The significance of Goddess Kali would have been readily understood by Indian viewers, adding layers to the film's multifaceted narrative. Parmar's interviewees frequently reference the role of colonialism and its enduring trauma, highlighting the film's nuanced exploration of the intersections between racism and the South Asian experience in the United Kingdom. This nuanced approach underscores the complexity of queer identity, which, for Parmar's subjects, involves not only challenging homophobia but also confronting the intersections of homophobia with racism and class discrimination. In one sequence of the film, interviewee Punam Khosla says:

> For me, being a lesbian is not only a fight against homophobia and the kind of homophobia we face everyday, but it's also a fight against the system that creates that [...] a class system as a system that it is imperialist. It's a system that's responsible for the incidences of racism that all of my family and all of the people I know of Asian and African descent have had to go through...

Gayatri Gopinath notes how the film *Khush* traces an emerging movement of the queer South Asian diaspora; Parmar uses Bollywood tropes to allow the diaspora to 'lay claim to the home space of the nation.'[7] As we have discussed, the work of artists such as Parmar is especially important to disrupt the erasure of racialised and indigenous histories from white queer archives that create narratives of resistance that begin and end with whiteness. Films such as *Khush* play an important role in documenting the diverse ways in which South Asian queer communities used creative ways to form support structures, resistance movements and celebrate South Asian queerness.

Indeed, it is essential to acknowledge the emotional labour underlying works like Parmar's in the '90s, which were frequently unfunded or underfunded, driven primarily by the desire to tell stories and enact social change. This aspect of artistic endeavour is often overlooked but plays a crucial role in shaping the narratives and representations within cultural works. This was highlighted by Sunil Gupta in his interview with us about the significance of progressive bodies such as the Greater London Council and Channel 4, which provided support for queer artists of colour to develop work exploring the intersections of race and sexuality. Their contributions were instrumental in fostering greater visibility and representation for marginalised voices within the artistic landscape.

Parmar noted in an interview that:

> funding came from Channel Four Television. This channel was set up in the early '80s as a channel to cater for the needs of so-called minority audiences—women, lesbians and gay people, and people from ethnic minorities. That was its original remit and it's changed considerably now. Within Channel Four there is a department for independent film and video which at the time was headed by Alan Fountain and his assistant, Caroline Spry, who's been responsible for initiating women's and lesbian/gay programming. So I approached them with the idea.[8]

Her earlier film *Sari Red* is a profoundly political cinematic piece, borne out of Parmar's creativity and resourcefulness. Initially funded with a modest grant of £200 from a video collective in Brighton, Parmar seized the opportunity to craft a short film addressing a subject close to her heart: the tragic killing of Kalbinder Kaur Hayre by three white individuals on 7 November 1985. Kaur's defiance against racial slurs led to her untimely demise, a defiance celebrated by Parmar in the film. A video poem and a poetic tribute to Kaur, as described by Parmar, the film examines the pervasive threat of violence that South Asian women faced both in private and public spaces. The title alludes to the colour of spilled blood, symbolizing the violence inflicted upon marginalised communities and the enduring memory of Kaur's tragic death.

The opening sequences of *Sari Red* immediately plunge viewers into a realm of intense and unsettling imagery. Containers filled with crimson liquid are hurled and shattered against a wall, a red sari flutters in the wind, and the British flag is engulfed in flames. Images of a brick wall splattered with blood are interspersed with words such as 'Blood red, cherry red, plum red, sari red'. As the tension mounts, rapid flashes of light illuminate a dancing figurine, casting eerie reflections against a backdrop of red and silver hues. Amidst this visual cacophony, a narrator's voice solemnly intones, 'She shouted back, of course she shouted back,' recounting the pivotal moment that led to Kaur's tragic fate.

Despite its non-documentary nature, the film skilfully employs a juxtaposition of Indian iconography, featuring goddesses and a young woman draped in a sari, alongside glimpses of London streets. The recurring motif of red, symbolizing both bloodshed and resistance, serves to heighten the audience's emotional response to the violence depicted. This contrasts sharply with subsequent scenes portraying serene moments of

South Asian women and children going about their daily lives in Britain: kneading dough, tending to gardens and interacting within their community. Through these juxtapositions, *Sari Red* poignantly captures the resilience and everyday struggles of South Asian communities amidst the backdrop of racial hostility and discrimination. In another sequence of the film the voiceover constantly chants 'PAKI, WOG, PAKI, WOG.' The chants are a jarring and disconcerting reminder of the violence that South Asians living in Britain faced on an almost daily basis.

Parmar's distinctive approach, accompanied by a poignant voiceover, yields a profoundly emotional work of art. Reflecting on the creative process behind her video art, Parmar illuminates the late 1980s and 1990s as a period witnessing a significant surge in Black and Asian artists emerging and interconnected within the UK. She underscores the collaborative nature of artistic practice during this time, highlighting the mutual support that queer artists of colour extended to one another. This collaborative ethos fostered a vibrant artistic community, enabling marginalised people to amplify their voices and challenge prevailing social norms and injustices through their creative expressions.

> Isaac Julien was a good friend and we were very supportive of each other because at that point, there were not that many Black, Asian or gay artists. Both of us were gay and we were out and we were very open about our sexuality. So, we occupied quite an interesting position within the Black Arts Movement, where we were also bringing our queer identity to bear on the work that we were doing at the time.[9]

Indeed, Parmar's film *Reframing AIDS* (1987), funded by the London Borough of Lambeth, exemplifies this collaborative ethos. The film features familiar faces such as Isaac Julien, Sunil Gupta, Kobena Mercer, Simon Watney and other artists and cultural activists, showcasing the interconnectedness and mutual support within the artistic community during that period.

Parmar herself is featured in the works of Gupta and Julien. This collective participation underscores the shared commitment to addressing pressing social issues, such as the AIDS crisis, through artistic expression and cultural activism.

Through interviews with prominent British AIDS campaigners and cultural theorists, Parmar's film sheds light on the conservative attitudes and homophobia that contributed to the government's delayed response to the pandemic. In her exploration of the AIDS crisis in the late 1980s, Parmar delves into the political and media context surrounding the disease, highlighting its impact on gay and lesbian communities. By shifting the focus away from harmful and dehumanizing media narratives, Parmar amplifies the voices and experiences of lesbian and gay individuals, providing a more nuanced understanding of the social and emotional dimensions of the epidemic.

Love, sex and politics

Sunil Gupta needs little introduction. He has been a stalwart in the South Asian queer cultural scene for decades. In 2020, The Photographer's Gallery in London showcased 'From Here to Eternity,' a retrospective exhibition commemorating his distinctive photographic oeuvre spanning three continents. This marked one of the first significant exhibitions to consolidate Gupta's political and often provocative body of work amassed over several decades. In an interview, Gupta expressed his view of his work as part of broader cultural activism aimed at enhancing the visibility of the South Asian queer community.

Originally from India, he migrated with his family to Canada where, in his own words, he 'had the good fortune of arriving straight after Stonewall.' However, Sunil found Canada back then to be a much more exclusionary place, making migrants like him feel very unwelcome. Following a brief period in New

York where he abandoned a degree in business management for photography, he made his way to London in late 1977 to join the West Surrey College of Art and Design (now UCA Farnham) on a full-time photography course.

> In Canada and the United States, I could pass for various things—Puerto Rican or something—because there weren't many Indians. It was only when I came here [to London] that I also encountered the 'Indian problem.' For the first time, I heard about 'Paki bashing' and was told 'Paki go home.' I had never experienced that before. Even getting on the tube felt difficult. The 'gay stuff' here wasn't that great, and then there was this...

Sunil's account of London during that time serves as a stark reminder that South Asian gay men were not only navigating homophobia but also facing violent racism fuelled by Enoch Powell's infamous 'rivers of blood' speech and Thatcherite policies. These policies reversed social welfare measures and ushered in an era of social conservatism, exemplified by legislation like Section 28. This legislation limited government funding for LGBTQ+ social groups, censored what could be taught in schools, and contributed to a rising tide of homophobia. The purpose of such laws was to curtail the support provided by local authorities and bodies like the Greater London Council to racially marginalised communities and LGBTQ+ support groups. Despite these challenges, intergenerational knowledge sharing and interethnic solidarity played crucial roles in the early organising phase, although they were not without their difficulties. Sunil says:

> By 1983, I had discovered the GLC [Greater London Council], which supported ethnic artists and 'radical' work, and I got... well, I became politically black. After this, I became much more involved in gay and black arts and similar activities. However, there was a problem with this kind of organising because half of the desis I was meeting did

> not want to identify as black. Immediately, we encountered a problem there.

Sunil's time at Farnham and later at the Royal College of Art, where he obtained a photography degree in 1983, was also fraught with challenges. Presenting 'gay work' was often frowned upon, and the gay art he had encountered in New York was largely ignored or omitted from the curriculum. However, during this period, he connected with other Black and Asian artists and became involved in community organising efforts. These connections led to introductions with the Greater London Council (GLC) and other local authority bodies that were among the first to fund minority initiatives, marking the beginnings of the Black Arts Movement.[10]

Sunil Gupta's body of work documents significant moments in LGBT history, including the gay liberation movement in New York, the HIV/AIDS crisis, the enactment of Section 28 in the UK, and queer activism in India. In their introduction to the exhibition and book project *Ecstatic Antibodies: Resisting the AIDS Mythology* (1990), Sunil Gupta and Tessa Boffin articulated the necessity for artists and cultural producers to intervene in the cultural sphere. Their aim was not only to maintain the visibility of AIDS in the face of a homophobic backlash but also to scrutinise the politics of representation, particularly concerning the visibility or invisibility of certain communities, notably Black and Asian. Through actively promoting diverse forms of cultural expression, including video, photography and installation, artist-activists sought to address questions of sexual difference and race, shifting them from cursory acknowledgment to the forefront of the discourse.

At a time when the British media often depicted people living with HIV/AIDS in a negative light, the artists and contributors to this exhibition and book affirmed the persistence of love and desire, advocating for alternative forms of cultural representation to address the challenges posed by the epidemic. Gupta's work delves into the biopolitical and necropolitical dimensions of the state, which determine the liveability and survival of queer bodies, especially those of colour. According to Gupta, there has been minimal progress in the past thirty years. He noted a lack of discussion about the historical context and legacies left by queer artists of South Asian origin. Instead, each generation seems to be attempting to 'reinvent the wheel.'

Gupta's photography has documented the numerous challenges encountered by British South Asian queers as they navigate racial and homophobic hostility. His photo series *Pretended Family Relationships* (1988) served as a response to the infamous Section 28. Each work in this series consisted of three components: a large colour photograph featuring a same-sex couple, a text panel containing excerpts from poetry written by Gupta's partner at the time, Stephen Dodd, and a segment of an image captured during protests and demonstrations against Section 28 in London.

The title of the work is a reference to the clause's provocative lines which prohibited 'the teaching in any maintained school of the acceptability of homosexuality as a pretended family relationship.' The images in this series, which include portraits of interracial gay couples of diverse heritage in familiar settings of home, work and public places, attempts to bring to the forefront relationships and lives which were forced to the margins as 'pretended' due to their delegitimisation by the state. 'Seeing you, seeing me, it all becomes so clear' reads the text excerpt which accompanies a photo of a couple relaxing in their home and a photo of a protestor holding the sign 'fight.' Photographing couples in their home environment seeks to highlight novel kinds of care and chosen family as well as the importance of a safe haven, where people can express their gender identity and sexual orientation without fear of violence or persecution.

Gupta highlights queer intimacy as a political act, a theme that resonates throughout much of his work from this period. In Gupta's photographs, queer bodies are not mere passive subjects; instead, they actively challenge societal norms. By capturing moments of intimacy and connection alongside scenes of protest and activism, Gupta's work emphasises the agency and presence of queer individuals within the broader social and political landscape.

In another photograph from the series, two South Asian figures are depicted exchanging an affectionate glance, possibly in their living room adorned with a couch and a bookshelf. The accompanying text reads, 'What you got tell me the lines of your pretty black hair,' evoking a sense of tenderness and intimacy. Meanwhile, the third panel features a protester carrying a placard advocating to 'stop the clause and fight for lesbian and gay rights.' These images of queer brown bodies embracing love and intimacy convey a profound sense of connection and mutual care, deriving their political power from the ordinary, everyday nature of the scene.

Sexual freedom and liberation are enduring themes in Gupta's body of work. His early series *Exiles* (1986) was commissioned by The Photographer's Gallery in London to document the experiences of gay men in Delhi. Despite its documentary style, the subjects remain anonymous, reflecting the challenges posed by Section 377, the colonial-era law criminalizing same-sex activity in India. Against this backdrop, Gupta captures scenes of gay life in Delhi, set against familiar landmarks like the Jama Masjid, Hauz Khas and India Gate—symbolic sites of national identity where gay desire persists, albeit in marginal and often clandestine ways.

In one of the photographs, in Hauz Khas, a man leans against a monument with his back turned to the viewer, his intentions ambiguous—whether he's cruising or waiting for someone remains uncertain. Accompanying the image is the text: 'It must be marvellous for you in the West with your bars, clubs, gay liberation and all that.' This text, while not necessarily expressing envy, reflects Gupta's own positionality and experiences in the West, imbuing the scene with a sense of irony. Despite the hyper-visibility of 'gay culture' in the West, Gupta's series highlights how queer intimacies and sexual freedom thrive beneath the public radar in Delhi.

Natasha Bissonauth, writing about the series, observes that the relationship between text and image in 'Exiles' fosters intimacies between site and citation.[11] This not only sheds light on the queer dimensions of well-known landmarks but also queers the landscape of the nation's capital, revealing hidden realities despite the highly censored nature of such expressions.

In both *Exiles* and Gupta's later series *Homelands* (2004), set in parts of India, photographs rarely depict families or scenes of coming out. Similarly, *Delhi: Communities of Belonging* (2016), produced by Sunil Gupta and Charan Singh, presents powerful testimonies and photographs of LGBTQ lives in contemporary India, yet seldom features family portraits. Gupta himself has described his complicated relationship with his mother, particularly during her visits to London when he lived with his partner. He also describes the tension that South Asian queer men might have to face even in the West, having to navigate family obligations alongside non-traditional queer relationships.

> She would come, and she would weep. We lived in a small flat in Brixton, a little terrace conversion. She stayed in the adjoining bedroom, so we could hear her crying. We'd ask her, 'Mother, why are you crying?' She'd respond, 'Because you're having homosexual sex...' These showdowns would happen at 3 a.m. Then my boyfriend would say, 'It's either your mom or me. You have to decide.' But you can't say that to a South Asian because I'll just choose my mum. That's a given, isn't it? So you always lose.

In the first image of Gupta's *Sun City* (2012) series, the (absent) figure of the mother is symbolically present as the Indian protagonist arrives in Paris and is greeted by his French male lover, who receives him with an approving look reminiscent of a mother or guardian angel. According to Gupta, this figure could represent a bystander or passerby, symbolizing the protective gaze of a mother. The images in the series oscillate between tender domestic scenes between the man and his lover—on the couch, in a shopping mall—and highly sexual imagery depicting his exploration of gay bathhouses and encounters with multiple lovers. The protagonist's expression reflects a sense of uncertainty and innocence as he navigates between reading Victor Hugo and engaging in sexual activities in extravagant, exotic settings.

The exhibition of *Sun City* opened in India in 2012 with support from Alliance Française, the French cultural institution promoting language and cultural exchange. However, within days of the show's opening, it was violently shut down by Hindutva fundamentalists who demanded its closure. In response, queer activists criticised Alliance Française for giving in to communal pressure and censoring artistic freedom. This event significantly influenced Gupta's decision to move back to Britain and continue his work there.

> We initially planned to return to Delhi. However, with the rise of Modi, things escalated quickly. Everyone is warning us not to come back, emphasizing how dire the situation has become. His supporters have a strong presence everywhere, and undoing the damage they've caused will be an immense challenge. They control the museums and are rewriting history, among other things. Part of us also feels a responsibility to be there during this difficult time. We left feeling like we're abandoning a sinking ship, but at the same time, we wonder if we should be there to offer assistance and support...

Sunil Gupta spent a significant amount of time in India before this period, during which he continued to create artwork and engage in community organising. Drawing from his extensive experience with organisations like Autograph and other progressive groups in the UK, Gupta quickly became involved in various queer political campaigns in India. One notable example is his involvement with Nigah, a group dedicated to establishing safe spaces for Delhi's LGBT population and organising cultural and educational activities, including the annual Nigah QueerFest. Gupta also conducted photography workshops at events such as QueerFest, aiming to empower queer individuals through artistic expression and visual storytelling. Through these engagements, Gupta contributed to the visibility and advocacy efforts of the queer community in India.

In Sunil Gupta's *Sun City*, the central figure can be interpreted as a racialised object of desire. By situating an Indian/South Asian body within the context of a gay bathhouse in Paris, Gupta challenges conventional notions of desirability, power dynamics and ownership of space. Natasha Bissonauth suggests that the camp Orientalism present in 'Sun City' employs aesthetic techniques to critique and dismantle racial fetishisation in sexual desire.

Gupta's work in *Sun City* also reflects influences from Bollywood and Indian cinema, evident in the framing and aesthetic choices. Despite the absence of openly queer figures in Bollywood during Gupta's upbringing, the camp aesthetics of Indian cinema played a significant role in shaping his own queer identity. This incorporation of Bollywood aesthetics into *Sun City* adds layers of complexity to the representation of desire, identity and cultural influences within Gupta's photographic narrative.

> No, they weren't openly queer figures, but they conveyed something deeply profound, you know? Most people resonated with the female

> characters. In my time, these women were figures like Meena Kumari and Asha Parekh. Then, the male lead would come along, seduce them, and sing a song, and so on. It wasn't about wanting to be him. Instead, he desired to be the centre of attention, the one receiving all the affection.

Indeed, the erotic gaze of the Indian figure in Gupta's photographs can serve multiple purposes. Beyond being objects of desire, these images may provide a sense of healing and connection for viewers. By depicting brown gay bodies expressing love and intimacy without fear of scrutiny, Gupta's work creates a space where viewers can feel seen and understood, free from the pressures of societal judgment. The depiction of queer intimacy in everyday contexts becomes a powerful political practice in Gupta's series of photographs. Through these images, the boundaries between private and public, as well as between home and foreign land, are blurred. The everydayness of queer intimacy is highlighted, emphasizing its significance and normalcy in diverse contexts. In this way, Gupta's photographs challenge normative narratives and assert the validity and beauty of queer love and desire.

Gupta's video art, although less discussed than his curatorial and photographic work, includes two notable pieces: *India Postcard*, produced in 1988 and screened by Channel 4 in 1989, and *London Gay Switchboard*, first exhibited in 2013 as part of the Birmingham Slide/Tape exhibition. *London Gay Switchboard* is based on fragments of a slide tape projection that Gupta initially created in 1980, although the original audio files are missing. Gupta photographed the London Gay Switchboard and its volunteers over the course of a year, documenting their pioneering efforts in a cramped office setting. Glyn Davis, historian of queer visual culture, observes that race and ethnicity are not prominent topics of exploration in *London Gay Switchboard*. Instead, the piece offers a deep and thorough engagement with the lesbian and gay culture and politics of its time. Despite the absence of a focus on race and ethnicity, *London Gay Switchboard* provides valuable insights into the dynamics and activism within the LGBTQ+ community during that period.[12] Davis further notes that this work received quite a poor reception when it was first exhibited, leading to its neglect and only being resurrected more recently.

In contrast, Gupta's short film *India Postcard* serves as a kind of greeting from gay men in India to the queer community in the United Kingdom. The film begins with two characters unconsciously meeting, accompanied by the song 'Chalte Chalte' from the camp classic film *Pakeezah.* Gupta chose this well-known cultural device to convey queerness in India to British audiences without feeling the need for explicit explanation. Additionally, he recognised the potential for 'queer pleasure' that South Asian queer audiences in the diaspora could derive from such cultural references. Defending his aesthetic choice, Gupta emphasises:

> One of the most limiting aspects of trying to make work within a foreign dominant culture is constantly having to explain one's references. In short pieces, that means using up most of the duration of the film or tape simply explaining away what it's like to be a double minority with very little room left for pleasure or developing particular stories.[13]

Indeed, Gupta's work serves to centre the experiences and narratives of queer South Asians within a global context, particularly in the face of colonial-era homophobic legislation. By incorporating cultural references that may not be immediately understandable to a eurocentric audience, Gupta reaffirms the right of queer South Asians to assert their identities and stories on their own terms. This approach challenges the dominant narratives that often overlook or marginalise non-Western perspectives within discussions of queer identities and experiences.

Gupta's 2021 exhibition *Black Experience* at Hales Gallery in Bethnal Green, served as a retrospective of ten works originally commissioned for the significant 1986 exhibition *Reflections of the Black Experience* in Brixton. Reflecting on the social and political landscape of Britain during the Thatcher era, Gupta's collection of works includes photographs capturing various aspects of life, such as South Asian families, anti-racist activists, newly arrived migrants and scenes from South Asian corner shops. Additionally, the exhibition features a self-portrait of Gupta with his lover in front of a theatre screening *My Beautiful Launderette* (1985), further emphasizing themes of identity, belonging and representation within the context of British society at that time.

For Gupta, placing his queer self within the wider context of the South Asian diaspora was not just challenging the 'impossibility' of queer desire within the South Asian diasporic imagery but, to borrow Gopinath's words, 'installing it at the very heart of the home'.[14] In another piece, *Love Undetectable*, Gupta uses his artwork to document his own queer body and the impact of HIV/AIDS, particularly focusing on his HIV diagnosis in 1995 and its profound effects on his personal life and community as he witnessed the loss of numerous friends and partners to the disease. At first glance, *Love Undetectable* may not lend itself to a straightforward interpretation. It comprises a diverse collection of photographs featuring face portraits, bare and nude body parts of individuals and couples, and depictions of gay and lesbian couples in various indoor and outdoor settings. However, the initial challenge in interpreting the series' purpose ultimately leads the viewer to a deeper understanding of the theme implied by its title. *Love Undetectable* addresses the complexities of love in the context of HIV/AIDS. The title itself carries multiple meanings: it can refer to one's HIV status being undetectable, as well as the challenges faced by HIV-positive individuals in detecting or experiencing love amidst societal stigma and discrimination.

Through his artwork, Gupta highlights the presence of love even in the face of adversity, emphasizing that while love may seem elusive to some, it remains tangible and visible to those who are open to experiencing it.

Gupta is one of the very few openly positive South Asian queer artists who uses his art as a form of disclosure and bringing South Asian queer art into the necropolitical. Queer necropolitics 'refer to regimes of attribution of liveliness and deadliness of subjects, bodies, communities and populations and their instantiation through performatives of gender, sexuality and kinship, as well as through processes of confinement, removal and exhaustion.'[15] Gupta, in his interview, discusses how thinking about his own body and mortality helped him reimagine new forms of intimacy and question the reactionary nature of global gay assimilation politics which situates certain voices as worthy of celebration and veneration whilst others are confined to isolation and 'slow death'.[16]

Constructing transnational desi queerness

The construction of 'desi queerness' is indeed a transnational process that reflects the complex migration routes and historical legacies of British colonialism. The experiences of desi queers are shaped by various migration patterns, including indentured labour in the Caribbean, migrations after the Second World War and independence to Britain and the United States, and movements to East Africa and the Middle East, among others. These migrations are interconnected, reflecting the broader historical and material conditions of postcoloniality and globalisation.

Jigna Desai's concept of the Brown Atlantic captures the tension between similar and overlapping historical and material conditions that characterise postcoloniality and globalisation, leading to migration. This concept highlights the interconnectedness of

South Asian diasporic experiences across different regions, emphasizing the shared struggles and experiences of diasporic communities.[17] Sunil Gupta and Pratibha Parmar were part of this creative resistance and construction of the Brown Atlantic.

In this section we move on to another artist, Ian Iqbal Rashid, to discuss the inseparability of queer brown subjectivity and art practice. Rashid was born in Tanzania into an Ismaili Muslim family of Indian descent. Following an unsuccessful bid for asylum in the United Kingdom, Rashid subsequently relocated to Canada before ultimately settling in London in 1991.

> My ancestors migrated to East Africa around the time of World War Two, working as indentured labourers for many generations. When conditions became challenging for Asians in East Africa, my father made the decision for us to leave. We hastily packed our belongings one night, obtained tourist visas to the UK, and embarked on the journey with just one suitcase. We sought asylum upon arrival, but unfortunately, it was before the upheaval under Idi Amin in Uganda. Sensing the worsening situation, my father decided to relocate us to the UK. Despite holding British passports at the time, we faced rejection. However, Canada was welcoming immigrants, so we eventually settled there.

Rashid's journey as a creative artist began as a poet. His debut collection *Black Markets White Boyfriends and Other Acts of Elision* was published in 1991 and was concerned with the twin issues of queerness and racialisation, particularly interrogating power and how it was used to discipline non-heteronormative and racialised bodies. Concepts of belonging have been key in his literary and cinematic work. Rashid begins his story of creative activism with the organising of the festival Desh Pardesh:

> The inaugural Desh Pardesh took place in 1990... or was it early 1991? It was a relatively small event that I organised mostly on my own, using the Euclid, a cinema event space in Toronto where I used to work. It

> was an event I arranged both for the cinema and for the community. Initially, it wasn't intended to be a big deal; it spanned a weekend and aimed to introduce queerness to the broader South Asian community in a creative, cultural manner. It served as a form of subtle activism, while also presenting South Asian culture in a contemporary, non-nostalgic light, reflecting life in the West. At that time, things were just starting to unfold in Canada... Then, unexpectedly, it became a huge success. Meanwhile, I had made the decision to move to London. Despite my relocation, Canadian funding agencies expressed interest in supporting and expanding Desh Pardesh into a more formalised event. I remained involved for a few years from the UK.

Desh Pardesh is deeply intertwined with the migration narrative by many queer South Asians looking for acceptance and community. This sentiment finds resonance in the festival's name, Desh Pardesh, signifying 'home away from home' in Hindi. Through the convergence of a South Asian diaspora from across the globe, the festival harnessed art and activism to challenge prevailing stereotypes and misconceptions. In her analysis of Desh Pardesh, Sharon Fernandez underscores its emergence as a countermeasure to the prevailing socio-historical backdrop, characterised by entrenched concerns over the institutional marginalisation encountered by communities of colour in the creative sphere during the late 1980s. Opportunities for participation within the broader mainstream cultural milieu were notably limited for queer communities of colour during this time, and their artistic contributions were frequently met with apathy, thereby rendering their visibility conspicuously obscured.[18]

Numerous artists interviewed in this book reflect upon their positive experiences traveling to Toronto from the United Kingdom, with one individual describing it as a 'South Asian diasporic family of queers'. These accounts often include comparisons between the South Asian communities in Toronto and those in the United Kingdom. For instance, a British artist notes the relatively dispersed nature of the Toronto South Asian community compared to the more segregated communities in Britain, where racist housing policies and safety concerns have contributed to the formation of distinct groups—such as Punjabis in Southall, Bengalis in Brick Lane and Gujaratis in Wembley, among others. In our interview, Rashid observed that the South Asian identity in Toronto during that period seemed to transcend linguistic, national and religious differences, potentially indicating a stronger sense of cohesion within the community compared to counterparts in the United Kingdom.

> We formed a tight-knit community in many ways. While circumstances evolved over time, simply identifying as South Asian sufficed. We found common ground politically and within our families through this identity. It was significant, and even being South Asian alone was considered distinctive... There was a palpable sense of unity among us. Perhaps I'm idealising it, but that's how it felt to me. When my family arrived in Canada in the early '70s, immigration was still relatively new... Racism was prevalent, naturally... [However,] Canada was actively seeking immigrants. The initial decade proved challenging; it was a difficult time. But by the late '80s, there was a shift towards greater acceptance of non-white individuals... at least in urban areas... in contrast to London, where I've resided for thirty years now. Regrettably, I've never felt as secure as I did in Toronto, which is disheartening.

Rashid's feature film *Touch of Pink* (2004) serves as an artistic exploration of the complexities surrounding transnational queer brown spaces and how they are contested and shaped by racialisation dynamics. The film depicts Alim (played by Jimi Mistry), a young gay immigrant from Toronto, who resides with his partner Giles in an upscale area of London. Giles and Alim are portrayed as upwardly mobile individuals within the queer community, belonging to the middle class. Alim's emotional landscape primarily revolves around his relationship with Giles and his idealised friend, Cary Grant, portrayed by Kyle MacLachlan, until his mother arrives from Canada with the intention of convincing him to marry a woman. Alim's ostensibly 'joyful' queer existence is disrupted as his mother, a devout Muslim, begins to question his adherence to a 'gora' (white) lifestyle.

The historical backdrop of imperialism, colonialism and the transcontinental migration of South Asian immigrants profoundly influences Alim's sense of displacement. His family, originally from Mombasa, Kenya, experienced forced relocation following Kenya's independence from British rule. Alim himself moved from Toronto to London in search of a gay community, while his extended family remained in Canada. Against the backdrop of the British Empire's historical legacy, which involved sending Indian labourers to Kenya for railroad construction, Alim's narrative reflects the aftermath of colonialism and imperialism. Indian immigrants in Kenya were required to obtain Kenyan citizenship post-independence, with the risk of deportation for those who did not comply. Consequently, many migrated to Canada, the United States and the United Kingdom.

Alim's feelings of displacement are further underscored by references to the film *Gunga Din* (1939), adapted from Rudyard Kipling's poem, which perpetuates imperialist racial narratives. In *Touch of Pink*, Cary Grant's character symbolises nostalgia for the British Empire and its bygone eras, reinforcing Alim's complex relationship with his brown and Muslim identity across three continents. The film portrays Alim's struggle to reconcile his ethnic and religious heritage with the liberal promises of London, positioning him on the margins of liberal modernity. Alim and his mother Nuru are depicted grappling with conflicting desires and societal expectations, navigating the tensions between their personal aspirations and the constraints imposed by their heteronormative, religious and immigrant communities. This portrayal reflects a racialised process linked to broader histories of colonialism and imperialism, wherein Muslim migrants are relegated to the periphery of 'liberal' London. The film is a means to critique the notion that brown queers are perpetually 'out of place,' challenging essentialist narratives of belonging and displacement within the context of transnational migration and racialised identity formation.[19]

The idea of being 'out of place' is also reflected in many of Rashid's early poems. For example, in 'Knowing Your Place' (1994) Rashid describes a scenic nature scene in Alberta, Canada, and not feeling like a brown queer body could claim belonging. He writes:

> On the other hand—trapped brown against
> glassy purple-grey of sky purple-green of
> trees—this nature reminds me holds pleases
> me unables me to claim this. Brown skin on
> hand paints my nature urban, *pakis live in
> suburbs pakis live in ghettoes* Brown hand on
> glass makes an invisible visible, reveals an
> adulterous duality.[20]

Rashid's exploration of the Ismaili community in his cinematic oeuvre emerges following his initial independent production, *Surviving Sabu* (1997), which narrates a father-son tale. The film depicts Amin crafting a documentary about his father Sadru's admiration for the Indian Hollywood actor Sabu. Both Sadru and Amin grapple with the legacies of colonialism and exile: Sadru was compelled to depart from Uganda to Britain during the expulsion of the Indian minority in 1972, while Amin, a gay man, grew up in Britain amidst pervasive racism and discrimination.

Surviving Sabu interweaves fragments of original Sabu films, which Amin critiques as embodying the 'coloniser's gaze'. As

Amin endeavours to coax his father into sharing his personal narrative on camera, the documentary evolves into a deeply intimate endeavour for Sadru, prompting him to confront the dissonance between his pre-migration aspirations and the realities he encountered upon arriving in England. The tension between Amin and his Muslim father, mediated through the figure of Sabu, becomes a poignant reflection of their shared experiences as individuals of South Asian descent navigating the complexities of identity and belonging within the framework of the British Empire. Gopinath invokes the concept of the 'Brown Atlantic' in relation to the film, arguing: 'Such a mapping of South Asian diasporic movement suggests the divergences and similarities between the experiences of racialisation of South Asian immigrants in North America and the UK.'[21]

The film, despite its London setting, incorporates various historical colonial frames of reference that constitute the South Asian diasporic experience. Gopinath argues that the film's Brown Atlantic framework necessitates situating the South Asian diasporic experience within the context of British colonial legacies. Rashid's personal experience in the British arts and culture sector sheds light on how he has been perceived by British producers when pitching his work, as well as his own subjectivity as a participant in the Brown Atlantic. He tells us:

> ...nobody wanted to tell the stories that I wanted to tell, but also, my North Americanness. You know, I was a foreigner in many ways. I remember I was pitching a show to ITV about a British Asian family, and they basically said to me, 'Well, but you're not British.' I said, well, I've been living here for twenty-five years, you know. I've probably lived here longer than I've lived anywhere else. I was born under Britain in a British colony. My parents were, you know, came of age... I understand Britain more than I understand any other cultures, don't let the accent fool you. You know, it's the mothership...

Rashid acknowledges Pratibha Parmar and Sunil Gupta as influential mentors during his initial transition to Britain, emphasizing their invaluable support in offering contacts and sharing resources, a generosity he found lacking among other artists. In the context of limited funding, particularly for artists of colour, the environment was hyper-competitive, and Rashid observed a scarcity of the collaboration and solidarity that other artists had described.

> In the UK, there was only space for one person like Gurinder or Isaac Julien. And if you weren't like them, you had to compete to become the next big thing. It might have been when I arrived a few years ago, during the Channel Four workshop movement. Maybe there was more of a sense of community politics back then. But by the '90s, it felt like everyone was focused on themselves. I think it was because the GLC had just closed down. Funding was decreasing, and there were other challenges too. Before that, funding was plentiful, and there were many opportunities. The GLC was a great supporter of equality.

The artists discussed in this chapter thus far invoke Sara Ahmed's concept of the 'melancholic migrant,' referring to the challenge queer immigrants face in navigating racism in their environments to align with liberal modernity espoused by mainstream queer communities. Ahmed highlights how the state's acknowledgment and legal safeguards for queer individuals can sometimes obscure and camouflage the racial and socioeconomic inequalities experienced by diverse queer populations elsewhere.[22]

The experiences of queer artists of colour often involve the conceptualisation of an alternative spatial reality, a sort of 'elsewhere.' In prevailing narratives, South Asian queer individuals and their experiences are often portrayed as difficult to reconcile with idealised queer notions of belonging. They are frequently situated within restrictive familial and communal frameworks, subject to social pressures and psychological conflicts that impede the realisation of fully articulated, contemporary, self-identified sexual subjectivities.[23] Such contested representations are part of a queer utopian vision including how queer racialised selves are created and contested.

Global labour and capital movements, nationalisms that uphold heteronormative norms, racism and colonialism, all influence queer diasporic subjectivity. The artists and their works described in this section offer a sophisticated viewpoint on the ways in which queer racialisation functions in the UK. Their work examines the various ways that art and visual culture create a sense of belonging and help to make sense of sexuality in relation to race, ethnicity and religion. It also dispels the myth that a person's sexual orientation is incompatible with their race, ethnicity or religion. It is critical to recognise how lived experiences and cultural variations force new kinds of queer diasporic belonging to be imagined and created. In the next section, the focus will shift towards contemporary artists, exploring how their creative work contributes to challenging norms, advocating for intersectional change, and critiquing the nation state.

5

CONTEMPORARY QUEER CULTURAL ACTIVISM

Queer South Asian diasporic art in Britain serves not only as a medium of expression but also as part of a wider discussion on issues of racialisation, class solidarity and critiquing the nation state. Drawing parallels with the cultural resistance of those artists that came before, as discussed in the previous section, we will now examine the work of four contemporary artists, which serves as an informative and critical set of tools to explore structural difficulties and inequalities in an exploitative racialised environment. The artists we discuss in this chapter—Raisa Kabir, Shiva Raichandani, Asifa Lahore and Charan Singh—have used their work to critique the idea of home whilst also pushing back against assimilationist politics and logics of respectability. Their works provide critical frameworks for understanding the value of cultural activism, particularly in their portrayal of resistance aesthetics and emphasis on documenting queerness. They advocate for a comprehensive understanding of political motivations and artistic engagements, while also exploring transnational resistance efforts in the face of ongoing racialised and transphobic culture wars.

The notion of culture as a plentiful and mobile resource gains particular significance within the context of cultural activism undertaken by South Asian queer artists. This is inherent in the aesthetics employed by the works and artists discussed here in terms of interpretation, circulation and reception. The artists undertake what is called 'critical making', which Matt Ratto argues is a mode of productive engagement, noting: 'Critical making emphasises the shared acts of making rather than the evocative object. The final prototypes are not intended to be displayed and to speak for themselves. Instead, they are considered a means to an end, and achieve value though the act of shared construction, joint conversation and reflection.'[1]

Malik et al offer the term 'creative interruptions' for diverse forms of creativity at the margins of society which have the potential to interrupt the status quo. The artists discussed in this chapter are unhesitant in using their creative work as a means of undertaking anti-racist activism and queer community building. Through shared video art, photography and performance they visualise a distinct aesthetic and vocabulary for queer South Asians in Britain. Further, Khubchandani notes that individuals in the diaspora find themselves caught in the cultural and social politics of multiple nations, which means these artists must navigate laws and norms—including racism, casteism, Islamophobia and homophobia, amongst others.[2]

In her discussion of the queer visual artist Chitra Ganesh, Gayatri Gopinath illuminates how Ganesh's work unveils the intricate layers of repression surrounding subaltern histories, memories, desires and subjectivities, which often form the foundation of diasporic nationalist ideologies. She introduces the concept of 'queer diasporic affect' as a distinct structure of feeling that serves to resurface obscured histories, genealogies and narratives from the past within the diasporic context. This framework highlights elements that challenge normative perspectives and foregrounds the perverse and antinormative aspects of these narratives.

Whilst all four artists described in this section work within a liminal space as queer and trans* brown people who reject homonormativity, they also foreground their work within an 'impossibility' of the British state which regulates queer and racialised people within a capitalist structure of extraction and exploitation. Nayan Shah has noted the deliberate deployment of South Asian historical narratives in defence of South Asian queerness, often contextualised within colonialist frameworks and migration logics. He further notes that 'queer relations cross boundaries of space, class, race and gender in ways that make the practice of democratic, egalitarian, and humane relationships both imaginable and viable'.[3]

The artists discussed in this chapter overtly characterise their creative endeavours as influenced by their anti-racist (Kabir, Lahore and Raichandani) and anti-caste (Singh) ideologies. While some of these artists incorporate elements of Bollywood into their visual expressions and performances, they employ this artistic platform to disrupt and contest the prevailing construction and representation paradigms within Bollywood. These interventions aim to confront and subvert the homophobic, racist and misogynistic narratives entrenched within Bollywood's cultural discourse. Performance offers a significant avenue for enacting South Asian queer diasporic politics, embodying aspects of intimacy, spectacle and South Asian identity. Through the deliberate placement of their South Asian queer bodies within familiar spaces and surroundings, performers such as Lahore and Kabir assert ownership and recognition of these spaces as sites of legitimacy and belonging.

Queer cultural activism serves as a response to what Caitlin Rimmer terms 'queer aphasia,' which she posits as the phenomenon wherein queer history is not only erased but also rendered invisible, even when it exists in plain sight, creating a disconnection between recognition and identification of queerness. Rimmer acknowledges aphasia as a multifaceted action across knowledge production, particularly emphasizing its impact on queer subjectivity.[4] Through staging queerness in visual and performance contexts, these artists embody queer resistance, employing a nuanced approach to the visibility of queer heritage and the integration of queerness into the South Asian historical narrative.

While Kabir and Lahore were born in Britain and have spent a significant portion of their lives there, Singh and Raichandani migrated to the UK within the last decade. All of these individuals produce and perform their work across Britain, North America and South Asia, aligning with our adoption of Gopinath and Desai's concept of the 'Brown Atlantic,' a region defined by the enduring influence of British colonialism. However, our utilisation of the framework of queer South Asian diaspora as a theoretical construct is not without its challenges. Jasbir Puar raises pertinent inquiries regarding how one might queer the diaspora or diasporicise queerness, as well as how processes of inclusion and exclusion operate within this context, and how diasporic subjects form queer identities through displacement.[5] While not all of these questions can be fully addressed within this chapter or the broader scope of the book, our discussion here strives to grapple with the complexities of cultural nationalism and avoid complicity in its perpetuation. The static portrayal of South Asia as the epicentre of a homogenised global South Asian queer identity is not without its drawbacks, as it excludes certain individuals who may feel marginalised due to factors such as religion, caste and class positioning in their countries of origin, thereby rendering them 'out of place'.

Weaving, performance and decolonial resistance

Raisa Kabir is an artist, writer and weaver based in London who self-identifies as a 'South Asian queer disabled femme'. Born to Bangladeshi parents in Britain, Kabir's art reflects her experiences navigating complex intersections of culture, sexuality and activism. Her experiences as a queer woman of colour navigating multiple intersecting identities deeply influence her work, driving her to explore themes of displacement, resilience and empowerment through art.

Her exhibition, *In/Visible Spaces: Reflections on the Realm of Dimensional Affect, Space and the Queer Racialised Self*, which debuted in 2014 at Rich Mix in Brick Lane, stands as a testament to her commitment to challenging prevailing narratives and offering a nuanced perspective on the experiences of queer individuals of South Asian descent in contemporary Britain. In Kabir's title, the slash serves both to delineate a paradigm and to highlight the oppositional nature of the two words—'visible' and 'invisible'—which hold significant associations within queer representation and queer communities of colour in the UK. The slash symbolises the potential for various interpretations of visible and invisible existence embodied by South Asian queers in the UK.

Kabir articulates her motivation for the exhibition as an exploration of the complex interplay between visibility and invisibility within the lived experiences of queer individuals of South Asian descent. By creating a space for dialogue and reflection, Kabir invites viewers to interrogate their own perceptions of queer identity and to recognise the multiplicity of experiences within South Asian queer communities. Through a combination of visual elements, textual narratives and immersive installations, Kabir offers a multifaceted exploration of the intersections between race, gender, sexuality and space, challenging viewers to confront their assumptions and preconceptions.

The exhibition showcased a series of visual essays that prompted self-identified queer and trans* individuals of South Asian descent to reflect on their perceptions of visibility and safety within the diverse urban spaces they inhabit across London. Rather than merely identifying such spaces, Kabir delves into the notion of whether these spaces are imagined constructs or tangible realities that can be actively created.

Kabir's work challenges the prevalent notion of 'brown' or 'ethnic' spaces as inherently homophobic or incompatible with diverse sexual orientations. Through her montages, Kabir actively confronts stereotypes that suggest an inherent conflict between religious affiliation and sexual identity. Her photographs portray the complex interplay between queer South Asian diasporic identities and the enduring legacies of colonialism, racialisation and Islamophobia in Britain. In the montage titled 'Sita' (see Figure 12), Kabir captures her subject in a local barber shop, a setting traditionally associated with masculinity and Pakistani cultural norms. For Sita, a masculine-presenting lesbian of South Asian descent, undergoing a buzzcut in this predominantly heterosexual and male-dominated environment evokes a sense of solidarity and belonging. Contrary to prevalent assumptions that such 'brown' spaces may harbour homophobic sentiments, Sita feels a palpable sense of safety and acceptance here, in contrast to the perceived alienation often experienced in predominantly white queer spaces.

Kabir's exploration challenges the misconception that visibly expressing queerness within a Muslim barbershop inevitably invites homophobic encounters and disrupts narratives surrounding queer experiences in culturally specific environments. Kabir's decision to situate Sita within the public space of a barbershop as a queer woman is significant. It serves not only as a form of resistance against gendered expectations but also as a means of navigating and negotiating her queer sexuality within the context of this male-dominated environment.

In the second montage, 'Girl in Hijab' (see Figure 13), Y is depicted in the predominantly Bangladeshi Brick Lane area of East London. Brick Lane holds a rich history as a haven for refugees and migrants, dating back to the arrival of French Huguenots, followed by the Jewish community and ultimately the Bangladeshi population. Brick Lane Mosque serves as a testament to the transformation of the area. Initially established in 1743 as a Protestant chapel, it later functioned as a synagogue in the nineteenth century, before being repurposed as a mosque in 1976.

Y grew up in the predominantly working-class Bangladeshi community in the lower south end of Brick Lane. Upon entering the upper north Shoreditch end of the street, which has undergone gentrification beyond the markers of its Bangladeshi migrant settlers from the 1950s and 1970s, Y describes feeling invisible or rendered invisible. This process of gentrification has displaced working-class and minority ethnic and religious communities, establishing a middle-class white cultural norm intertwined with an 'edgy' art/fashion scene and small business establishments. Despite experiencing invisibility, Y also finds a sense of freedom in this newfound invisibility, feeling less self-conscious of her Bangladeshi community. This sentiment is reflected in her dress, as she navigates the upper Shoreditch end of Brick Lane while wearing a hijab. However, she maintains markers of her hybrid visibility by donning a Ramones punk T-shirt, jeans and Converse sneakers, as she explores less gentrified and personalised corners of Brick Lane adorned with art and graffiti.

Kabir explains that in this montage we observe a strong inclination towards self-regulation of appearance. In her daily life, the hijab was not a fixed garment for Y; she would occasionally don and remove it. This behaviour reflects her endeavour to navigate the expectations of her deeply religious family while asserting her individual queerness. Her eclectic dress choices are influenced by a blend of factors, including her awareness of the community's norms regarding attire, her reluctance to openly express her queerness and her desire to reconcile cultural expectations with her own identity amid the prevailing white cultural dissonance. Y also shares her discomfort in mainstream queer spaces, where rampant racism and Islamophobia render her visible as a Muslim woman yet simultaneously render her invisible as a bisexual individual. The notion of finding refuge in the private space of a friend's car emerges as a poignant symbol of safety for Y and other queer South Asian women. Here, they can freely indulge in activities like smoking or having a drink without feeling scrutinised or judged for their Muslim and queer identities.

Gopinath's scholarship on South Asian queer diasporas is pertinent in this context. Gopinath suggests that the refusal of queer South Asian identities to conform neatly to predefined templates has enabled their survival within the 'cracks and fissures' of a broader pan-South Asian identity.[6] Kabir's montages serve as a lens through which we can examine how diasporic queer sexual identities are intertwined with ongoing legacies of colonialism, racialisation and the escalating Islamophobia in Europe following the events of 9/11 and the subsequent arrival of refugees from conflict-ridden regions in the Middle East and Western Asia. Describing her motivation for the exhibition, Kabir explains:

> It came out of my need for community and South Asian queerness. I was 22 and was experiencing isolation whilst finishing my BA in Textiles at Chelsea College of Art. I felt that specific kinds of queer South Asian identities at the time were really not very visible

> in contemporary art practice—I didn't see images of trans, queer, lesbian, bisexual transgender nonbinary people that didn't focus on gay men. Through my art practice I began to question what does a multidimensional queer South Asian identity mean. I felt the world that I was seeing and feeling at the time was not being reflected, and this project was a way for me to engage with my own trauma of being in a predominantly white art institution, being of Bangladeshi South Asian diaspora, with a disability, and identifying as a queer femme.[7]

Kabir's multidisciplinary approach to her artistic practice reflects a commitment to various forms of cultural resistance, deeply rooted in a queer politics of labour, intergenerational trauma and a disruptive stance towards the nation-state. Raised in Manchester, a city renowned for its textile and industrial legacy, Kabir's upbringing plays a significant role in her connection to her cultural heritage in Bangladesh and the ongoing negotiation of her identity within the framework of diaspora. Her piece নীল. *Nil. Nargis. Blue. Bring in the tide with your moon...* (see Figure 14) is a film installation created using footage from a performance on the Scottish coast, where British nuclear submarine warheads are stored underwater. In this performance, Kabir utilised natural Bengali indigo dye, along with items crafted from linen and jute, to weave on a backstrap loom within the sea. This act of weaving amidst the depths of the ocean symbolises a juxtaposition of the violent beauty of the sea with the militarised landscape and occupied indigenous territories. Kabir brings attention to the issue of occupation, one intimately tied to colonialism. The colonial project, as Priyamvada Gopal (2020) aptly puts it, was a process of 'making the globe and colonised people suitable for the spread of capitalist freedom'.[8] Artists such as Kabir challenge the notion of queer liberalism inculcated through colonialism and capitalism.

Through the incorporation of natural materials, the artwork unveils the historical and material connections between Scotland, Bengal and the Caribbean. The use of natural dye particularly evokes the legacy of forced labour in colonial Bengal's indigo production, which inflicted transgenerational trauma on the region. During the nineteenth century, indigo farmers in colonial Bengal were subjected to exploitation and perpetual debt under a harsh system established by colonial planters. The piece also delves into the history of the *Nil Bidroha* or Indigo Revolt in 1859, which emerged as a response to decades of oppression and violence perpetrated by colonial forces.

The genesis of the performance emerged from Kabir's discovery of the Indigo Revolt and subsequent conversations with her mother, who shared familial anecdotes about the significance of indigo in their lives. Kabir poignantly illustrates the interplay between personal grief and historical resistance, intertwining narratives of loss and resilience within the indigo-dyed fabric. Furthermore, Kabir traces indigo and jute production from Bengal to the Caribbean and Scotland, and illuminates the interconnectedness of global trade networks and the exploitation of Bengali labour. The performance serves as a poignant reminder of the enduring legacies of colonial exploitation and the resilience of marginalised communities in the face of adversity. Through her artistic intervention, Kabir invites viewers to reexamine the intertwined narratives of indigo production, transatlantic slavery and global trade, fostering a deeper understanding of the interconnectedness of human experience across time and space.

The performance, conducted on 14 August, coincided with the Independence of India and Pakistan, which also led to the trauma of Partition. The piece became more poignant still with the passing of Kabir's aunt, Nargis, who wore blue saris, which is how the piece got its name. By embodying the narratives of indigenous resistance and resilience, Kabir weaves a complex tapestry of material histories, drawing connections between disparate geographies and historical epochs.

The performance video titled *Gather your spools, let your hair down for me. Gently. Here. Undo* (see Figure 15) was showcased at an exhibition hosted by the Centre for Contemporary Art in Glasgow, *ambi*, in 2021. This title, derived from Punjabi, signifies the paisley pattern recognised in Scotland. Additionally, *ambi* conveys the notion of 'both,' thereby accommodating multiple narratives and recognizing the diverse origins and appropriations inherent within the archived works. The video shows Kabir wearing a sari in an empty field. Kabir has her back to the camera in a contemplative gesture looking ahead. The video cuts to shots of her sitting on the ground with her loom and various colourful fabric and threads scattered around her as she performs her craft. The video moves again a few times where we see her standing, her face away from the camera with threads. The final scene ends with her sitting, this time facing the camera as she works on her hand-held loom.

In this performance piece, Kabir responds to the textile geographies of labour between Britain and South Asia. She draws attention to colonial boundaries, created through trauma and capital in the name of nationhood. Textile techniques across Kashmir, Punjab, Sylhet, Lahore and Calcutta are shared across the borderlands. Much of the South Asian diaspora who ended up working in textile and garment mills in Britain came from this displaced diaspora affected by the trauma of colonialism and Partition.

> The Kashmiri textiles, which are shared between Pakistan and India, encompass techniques practiced on both sides of the border in Kashmir as well as in Punjab. Similarly, the jamdani weaving tradition is found on both sides of the border. Contrasting this with the northeastern border regions such as Assam and Rangamati, where the border cuts

> through indigenous lands, reveals a complex geopolitical landscape. In these border regions, indigenous peoples weave using backstrap looms, employing specific techniques unique to their cultural heritage. However, the colonisation and settlement by ethnically Bengali dominant groups have led to the appropriation of indigenous lands and the imposition of their own textile traditions, such as jamdani weaving, which is portrayed as superior to indigenous techniques. This phenomenon illustrates a form of textile cultural imperialism, perpetuated by the colonisers. Additionally, the partition of these regions and the violence associated with border-making further complicates the narrative, with nationalism often intertwined with these conflicts.[9]

These discussions highlight the multifaceted dynamics of cultural identity, land ownership and political boundaries in border regions affected by colonial legacies and nationalist ideologies. Kabir draws inspiration from her work in Rangamati, in the Chittagong Hill Tracts, which became part of East Pakistan post-Partition. This sudden shift in geopolitical boundaries caused major upheaval to the indigenous population, who were discriminated against for their non-Bengali language and religious practices and who faced immense challenges in obtaining citizenship.

In the video Kabir embodies, in her own words, a form of queer drag reinterpreting South Asian narratives through the lens of craft labour. Situated within a conceptualised natural setting, the portrayal detaches the labour of weaving from its geographical origins, particularly in relation to the production of paisley designs. Originating in Kashmir and prevalent across the northwestern region of South Asia extending into Afghanistan and Punjab, the motif holds cultural significance. The figure representing the craft labourer symbolises displacement, performing weaving actions amidst specific materials and surroundings to construct a narrative based on the mythos of the artisan. This portrayal does not seek to recreate reality but rather challenges viewers to reconsider the historical narratives imposed upon or erased from the origins of textiles and their patterns. It prompts reflection on the intimate connection between textile provenance and border violence, particularly in regions where traditional textile heritage has been diminished, and the continuation of hand weaving, such as brocade shawls, has declined. Additionally, it explores the relationship between Scottish and British engagement with these textiles, highlighting the consumption of paisley-patterned cloth divorced from its cultural context.

Kabir's reflections on cultural resistance echo the insights of Edward Said, particularly his analysis of cultural imperialism, drawing parallels between Said's reference to Palestine and the situation in Rangamati, where Adivasi textiles and weaving traditions are marginalised. Despite the denigration of their craft and knowledge, Adivasi communities in Rangamati engage in weaving as a form of cultural and archival preservation, resisting the loss of their lands and heritage. Through the act of weaving, these communities transmit their cultural legacy to younger generations, embodying a form of resistance that is deeply rooted in their matrilineal traditions. This mode of resistance, characterised by queer making and weaving, underscores a unique knowledge system that diverges from patriarchal frameworks, emphasizing the embodied nature of craft and archival practices within these communities.

South Asian trans and nonbinary narratives*

Shiva Raichandani, a BAFTA-nominated nonbinary filmmaker of South Asian origin, won the Iris Prize for their film *Queer Parivaar* in 2022. Born in Hong Kong, Raichandani's grandparents migrated from Pakistan during the Partition, travelling across India before settling in Indonesia while seeking work. They grew up in Hong Kong, Dubai and Indonesia before finally moving to Leeds in 2016.

The historical and political cartography of the region constructs South Asian transnational migration as part of the wider colonial project. Raichandani's migration history can be seen within this wider complex lens of oppression, conflict and global capitalism. Their own experience also provides an opportunity to critique the Western imaginary, which often consolidates South Asian diasporic subjectivity as homogenous and singular. Desai notes that strategically identifying oneself as South Asian/Asian can create (or not) meaningful alliances within certain contexts.[10] This is certainly the case with Raichandani. They tell us how living across these different places had an impact on them as an artist:

> I believe that all those experiences have truly granted me a sensitivity to various cultures, identities and people from diverse backgrounds. They have given me a bit of an international worldview perspective on things. Indeed, all of these experiences have shaped who I am. I consider myself fortunate and privileged to have learned from such a range of diverse experiences.

Raichandani's documentary film, *Peach Paradise*, funded by a Netflix Talent Fund, documents the experience of The Bitten Peach, a pan-Asian queer collective founded in 2019 with the aim to 'empower the queer Asian community by providing safe spaces, diversifying Asian representation and educating non-Asians on racial issues.'[11]

The film begins with ShayShay, one of the founders of Bitten Peach, as they prepare for 'their biggest show ever.' ShayShay narrates their experience of growing up as an effeminate young kid who was called 'girly' and laughed at by other kids at school. However, it was only when ShayShay moved to London, framed as a place with queer utopian possibilities, that they discovered drag could be a medium for not just political possibilities but also a lifesaver. In one scene, ShayShay says: 'Life for a femme, Asian nonbinary trans person is risky from the moment I walk out my front door. And to be on stage and be visible, that's even riskier. I'm willing to take that risk because I don't want to hide trying to exist in the shadows.'

Here, they are not just describing an individual experience but rather one faced by many queer performers of Asian descent. Through a diversity of stories and voices, the film critiques the racial nature of the drag and cabaret scene, where diversity can be tokenistic. The film also emphasises the importance of spaces for queer Asians, as often many of them 'cannot be their authentic selves outside of these spaces'. Raichandani tells us about the everyday impact of transphobia in contemporary Britain:

> We live in a time where there is rampant transphobia, even in our British context. Identifying in a way that people are accustomed to, or even fearful of, is not an excuse. It's a reflection of those who aren't open to understanding experiences different from their own. This vulnerability can lead to various forms of violence—emotional, mental and physical—due to the negative thoughts and beliefs projected onto individuals. Even today, walking down the streets of London as I do and expressing myself can be daunting. I am hyper-aware and hyper-vigilant of myself and the way I present myself, constantly prioritizing my safety.

Raichandani's sensitive film provides an alternative to the white-dominated queer entertainment spaces in the city. Through celebrating pan-Asian queerness, the filmmakers extend the concept of the Brown Atlantic by prioritizing the role of queer kinship and collective community-making. In fact in an interview with *Attitude* magazine, ShayShay notes that the film is stronger because it was 'made by someone who is actually a part of the collective, and not an outsider coming in to try and capture a world that they're not actually a part of. It was very much a family effort.'[12]

It would be worthwhile to note communications scholar Shinsuke Eguchi's critique of 'queer Asia' which could obfuscate and contradict the complexities of the region, noting that intra-Asian cultural influences like racialisation, empire and capitalism change and strengthen political rivalries, economic competition and historical conflicts. These forces make the timing and nature of interactions within the region more complex.[13] Indeed, it may be more beneficial to consider Asia not merely as a geographical location, but rather through a social and cultural lens, as ShayShay and Raichandani suggest. Raichandani further emphasises the importance of immersing oneself in this broader Asian culture. They also highlight how dominant media often simplifies the complexity of the 'Asian' identity category by failing to feature Asian characters in a nuanced manner that celebrates the layers and intersectionality inherent in these identities. They say:

> It was important for us to show that not in the sense of it being complex, because I think the mainstream non-Asian, white-dominant media tend to perceive our identities as complex and therefore use that as an excuse to not feature us. Whereas, we believe that we have all of these layers. Yes, we have all of these multiple intersectional identities, but they all coexist.

Another documentary that Raichandani is very proud of is *Always, Asifa*, a BAFTA nominee. It follows trans* drag artist and activist Asifa Lahore's journey towards gender affirmation surgery, reflecting on her life as a Muslim, South Asian disabled artist navigating life in Britain.[14] The film begins with an emotional clip from 2017 when Asifa first went public that she had been questioning her gender identity and now identifies as a trans* woman who was beginning the process of transitioning. Similar to *Peach Paradise*, Raichandani's focus is on empowering the voice of their interlocutor, and through that process, provides a powerful platform to showcase the power of trans* Asian lives in Britain. Asifa declares at the very outset of the documentary that her identity as South Asian and Muslim has played a massive role in her drag identity. Discussing the film, Raichandani says:

> In many ways the film is a love letter to South Asian, trans nonbinary, gender nonconforming people out there because we don't really get to see ourselves in this light. A lot of the stories around queerness are through white narratives but the ways in which we experience transition is so different. To see someone like Asifa visibly documenting her journey is so empowering because it's such a great educational point to humanise the experience. If anything, there's so much fun and joy to be found through it because she's a performer and not every story around transitioning needs to be sad and dramatic.[15]

In a poignant scene from the film, Asifa stands proudly on stage during Pride in London, her voice ringing out as she declares her multitude of intersectional identities. The audience responds with thunderous applause, acknowledging and celebrating the complexity and richness of her identity.

> I am British!
> I am South Asian!
> I am Pakistani!
> I am queer!
> I am a transgender!
> I am Muslim!
> I am disabled!

Raichandani's short feature film *Queer Parivaar* delves into the intricacies of multiple identities with depth and nuance. This lively and dramatic short musical portrays the romance between Sufi, a British gay man of Pakistani origin portrayed by Raimu Iftam, and

Madhav, a Hindu nonbinary individual played by Raichandani. Set amidst wedding preparations for the couple, the narrative takes an unexpected turn when Madhav's grandmother, Dadi, portrayed by Taru Devani, unexpectedly appears at the festivities. Madhav, previously under the impression that their grandparents were deceased, learns that they were in fact disowned due to their queerness. Further revelations unfold as it is disclosed that Dadi is in a relationship with a woman, while Madhav's late grandfather had undergone a gender transition, living as Saraswati, portrayed by Asifa Lahore, and finding happiness with a man named Janak. Unable to reconcile with having two queer parents, Madhav's father declared them both deceased. The ensuing dialogue between Madhav and their grandmother serves as a poignant exploration of family dynamics, religious identity and personal narratives. The film notably celebrates diversity across various dimensions, including religion, generation, gender and sexuality, albeit at times in a manner that may appear contrived. Raichandani tells us:

> It was a deliberate choice for us to approach this project with a default lens of inclusivity, creating a space where all genders, identities and expressions of gender could be represented. Personally, as a nonbinary individual, it was important for me to write a character that reflected this identity, as such representations are rare to find. There are many layers to consider in this approach—it's inherently intersectional. In the film, I portray a nonbinary Indian person, while Shamir portrays a Pakistani gay man. Moreover, within our wider team, we have individuals who identify as intersex, transgender, bisexual and lesbian, spanning different age groups.
>
> This diversity was crucial for us to showcase, from teenagers who are transgender to elder women who are lesbian. This dynamic reflects the essence of the film's title, *Queer Parivaar*, which underscores the notion of family beyond biological ties. It challenges and expands our understanding of what constitutes a family, encompassing chosen

> families, friends and those whom we consider family, recognizing that family structures are not always heteronormative or nuclear.

While the film hints at queer trauma and familial violence, there was a deliberate decision not to focus extensively on those aspects. Instead, the emphasis was placed on celebrating queer joy. This choice is particularly poignant considering the current climate in Britain, where there have been numerous attacks on the lives of queer and trans* individuals, alongside the rise of anti-trans legislation. Described as reminiscent of the era of Section 28 and resulting in stigmatisation within political and educational settings, this legislation has created a challenging environment for queer and trans* communities. In response, *Queer Parivaar* seeks to prioritise celebration over oppression, offering a narrative that uplifts and empowers queer identities.

> I feel like we have a very huge lack of positive imageries of queerness out there in mainstream media, especially within the South Asian context. A lot of our narratives, while not obviously discounting the trauma and struggles that we have as queer Asians, but they tend to centre a lot on the negative sides of being queer and Asian. And we tend to be sort of stereotyped as caricatures and reduced to just, yeah, just whatever is palatable, I guess, to a straight audience, and there aren't many queer films created by queer people, for queer people, and that are centred around our joy. So I think that was the driving force for this to sort of create space for ourselves, create an opportunity for ourselves to see ourselves on the big screen.

Sara Ahmed argues that the potentiality of 'not following' some traditional scripts of family, inheritance and childrearing is central to queer existence.[16] For Raichandani, the film shows that queer South Asians can thrive and that their narratives do not only revolve around trauma, with its focus being on love and kinship. While celebrating marriage, it diverges from the heteronormative ideals of respectability and normativity. Instead, it emphasises the creation of families of choice, highlighting the thriving nature of queer South Asian lives in Britain.

> MADHAV: What holds a family together,
> If not love?
> The kind of love that honours you,
> that nourishes you,
> that celebrates you for all that you are
> and all that you will be.
> SUFI: Whatever that family may look like,
> their love sets you free.
> Just like a marriage should.
> Marriage doesn't mean anything besides what we make of it.

A poignant flashback scene in which Dadi sings 'Aftaab' (Sun) shows tender moments from Saraswati's life with Janak, featuring them holding hands, sharing laughter and enjoying tea, all set against the backdrop of an uplifting song.

> Come make peace with your tears
> Wipe out the crumples on your pillow
> You are the embodiment of love and the medium of love

The film ends with an interreligious marriage ceremony where prayers are read from the Holy Quran, followed by an exchange of garlands.

Raichandani's films present a range of diverse South Asian queer and trans* narratives. While elevating the visibility of queer Asians has been a central aspect of their work, Raichandani also recognises visibility as a two-sided coin. They caution that creating visible platforms without considering the safety and protection of Asian queer and trans* individuals is futile. Furthermore, they emphasise that these films portray specific characters and their unique experiences rather than serving as comprehensive representations of the entire community. Raichandani underscores the importance of films as a means of preserving the lives of queer Asians:

> It's exhilarating to immortalise our experiences on celluloid because I believe our stories deserve to be preserved in some form. Capturing them through film and fiction is particularly beautiful because it ensures they endure over time. It becomes something that people can revisit and engage with, allowing our narratives to persist and resonate.

This observation aligns with the perspective of Syrus Marcus Ware, who highlights the ongoing erasure of racialised and indigenous histories from white queer and trans* archives. Ware emphasises how power and privilege shape which stories are deemed worthy of preservation and dissemination. Furthermore, they critique how narratives of queer struggle and resistance frequently centre on whiteness, serving what Ware terms 'gay imperialism.'[17] Artists like Shiva Raichandani contribute to the effort of reinstating Asian trans* and nonbinary histories and stories. Through their art, they aim to preserve and transmit intergenerational memory, ensuring that the contributions of Asian individuals to British queer organising and activism are not overlooked or forgotten.

Drag as politics

In the previous section we discussed Shiva Raichandani's film *Always Asifa* which featured Asifa Lahore, Britain's first Muslim drag queen. Prior to this, Asifa worked as a South Asian sexual health worker for Naz Project London, an organisation focused on HIV and sexual health within minority communities. She later transitioned into hosting queer parties for Urban Desi, Club Kali and other events. Asifa's journey into drag began when she first appeared as Asifa at London Pride. Following this debut, she began performing regularly and released several music videos on various social media platforms, further solidifying her presence in the South Asian LGBTQ+ community and the drag scene.

Asifa's family's migration to the United Kingdom during the 1970s and 1980s was initially intended as a temporary arrangement, with eventual plans to return to Pakistan. However, the family's dynamic shifted significantly when Asifa's older brother was diagnosed with autism shortly after her birth, presenting considerable challenges compounded by the limited understanding of autism within the South Asian community.

Confronted with these difficulties, Asifa was sent to Pakistan as a young child, where she remained until approximately the age of two before returning to the UK. The family had relocated from Southall to Tooting and subsequently to Brixton in South London during her absence. Asifa reflects on the significance of this transition, noting both the sense of security found within immigrant communities and the inherent tensions arising from cultural diversity.

The move to Brixton immersed Asifa in Black culture, which she describes as feeling 'familiar' and providing a space where aspects of her own culture, such as foreign food markets, spices and halal butchers, could be encountered. Despite this, her parents ultimately made the decision to return to Pakistan when Asifa was around eleven years old, leading to a period of living between Karachi and Lahore. This period proved pivotal for Asifa's development, as she became increasingly acquainted with South Asian music and culture, experiences that would profoundly influence her creative trajectory in subsequent years.

> Those years from eleven to fourteen were incredibly formative for me and played a huge role in shaping who I am today. My love for Bollywood and Bhangra really blossomed during that time. Before my time in Pakistan, I had been exposed to bits and pieces of South Asian

> culture through sources like Sunrise Radio and occasional cultural events, but I hadn't been particularly interested. However, when I went to Pakistan, everything changed. I had access to international cable channels, including American and UK channels, but it was Bollywood that captured my heart.
>
> I found myself immersed in Bollywood culture, dancing at weddings, and just enjoying the vibrant expressions of it all. Karachi was an eye-opening experience for me. While Lahore, where my dad's family is from, was a more polished and affluent area, my mom's side of the family hailed from the slums of Karachi. When I visited Karachi or spent holidays there, I was left to explore the bustling streets, public transport, and the raw essence of the city on my own. In Lahore, on the other hand, I was always accompanied and chaperoned everywhere. This exposure to different parts of Asian culture, from the opulence of Lahore to the grittiness of Karachi's slums, gave me a deep appreciation for the diversity within my own heritage.

Asifa's family, like many others, bore the scars of Partition, which deeply impacted their lives. Her maternal family originated from Aligarh in Uttar Pradesh and experienced the upheaval of migration during that turbulent period. Asifa fondly recalls her childhood visits to India with her grandfather, where she had the opportunity to immerse herself in the rich tapestry of Indian culture. She emphasises that these journeys held particular significance for her, especially in terms of gaining a deeper understanding of her own sexuality.

> I deeply cherish that period because it was not only instrumental in shaping my understanding of my sexuality, but also marked a significant phase of personal growth. It was during this time that I became acutely aware of my attraction to men. Additionally, I found myself captivated by the Khwaja Sira or Hijra community, as I encountered them during my travels. Despite feeling a sense of identification with them, I was hesitant to explore my own sexuality further due to my youth and the potential consequences I anticipated. Deep down, I sensed that

> engaging in sexual experiences at that time could lead to complications and challenges that I wasn't prepared to confront.

During her formative years, Asifa experienced a heightened awareness of her own attractiveness, attributed to a blend of Punjabi and northern Indian features. This awareness, coupled with attention from men, prompted reflection on the power of her appearance. Returning to the UK for her GCSEs, she encountered severe bullying, which introduced her to the term 'gay' for the first time. This marked a departure from her prior experiences in Pakistan, where terms like *Khwaja Sira* and *Hijra*, for transgender, nonbinary and gender non-conforming people, were more prevalent, reflecting a different cultural understanding of gender identity. The bullying she endured was exacerbated by institutional apathy and homophobia, leaving her isolated and vulnerable.

The adoption of Western patriarchal norms, influenced by legal and religious frameworks, contributed to the emergence of homophobia in South Asia. Colonial encounters introduced sodomy laws and religious doctrines that fuelled animosity towards sexual minorities. Drawing on Mary Louise Pratt's concept of a 'contact zone,' where colonisers and colonised interact under conditions of coercion and inequality, we can directly surmise that this interaction, marked by colonialism, played a pivotal role in shaping South Asian attitudes towards homosexuality.[18] The homophobic sentiments witnessed in South Asia can be traced back to the imposition of British penal laws and the introduction of Western religions, notably Christianity, during the colonial period. At the same time Asifa's experience pushes back on the narrative of brown Asian/Muslim spaces being inherently homophobic.[19] Asifa reflects on how the expressive and flamboyant nature acquired during her time in Pakistan clashed with the expectations of British culture upon her return. She recalls instances where expressing admiration for someone of the same gender led to derogatory remarks from peers, highlighting the cultural disparity between the two environments. Overall, Asifa suggests that her experience in Pakistan and exposure to desi culture allowed her to embrace her expressive tendencies more freely during her teenage years. However, this newfound expressiveness also subjected her to bullying and negative reactions from peers upon returning to the UK.

Discovering the term 'gay' represented a pivotal moment of self-recognition and acceptance. It enabled Asifa to contextualise her experiences and find solidarity within the queer community. Despite the trauma endured during those years, she found solace and refuge in creative pursuits such as drama and music, which ultimately facilitated her enrolment in the Brit School for her A-Levels.

Asifa sees her creative process being directly influenced by her own identity and experience so whilst some of her songs are celebratory and powerful, she also sings about loneliness and failure, all of which are part of the South Asian queer experience. She says:

> Certainly, many of the lyrics I've penned stem from personal experiences, whether it's about heartache, love or empowerment. Being part of minority communities, and navigating issues of sexuality and gender on top of that, has heightened my desire for self-empowerment and inspiration. I aim to inspire not only myself but also others through my music and performances. When I reflect on the roughly twenty songs I've composed in the last fifteen months, many of them are upbeat anthems about empowerment, euphoria and embracing pride. Conversely, there are also heartfelt ballads exploring themes of loneliness, yearning for love and the pain of heartbreak. Experiencing the contrast between being alone and feeling lonely, or the aftermath of a failed relationship, has taught me valuable lessons about self-

> discovery. Additionally, drawing from my past experiences, particularly when I lived a compartmentalised life before coming out, has influenced much of my lyrical content. It delves into the struggle of not being able to fully express oneself, adding depth and authenticity to my music.

In an editorial Asifa claimed that she was censored on BBC Free Speech when she spoke about being Muslim, gay and a drag queen. The controversy pushed her to national fame, giving her a platform to discuss issues such as sexuality and religion, which alongside making her a key figure of the South Asian queer scene in London also led to threats of violence. Gosett et al argue that trans* visibility can often be a trap accompanied by violence on trans* bodies of colour. They use the trap and the door as metaphors to illustrate the dual nature of trans* representation, highlighting both its threat and promise. By examining the ambivalent space where trans* identity intersects with visual representation, they suggest the existence of an alternative and clandestine modality—the trapdoor. This metaphor suggests the possibility of trans* bodies finding an unexpected means of escape from the complexities and challenges inherent in their representation.[20]

Asifa reminisces about a happier time in her life, particularly during her university years around 2006 to 2007. This period coincided with her involvement with the Naz Project, where she not only came out but also engaged in counselling and volunteering. It was during this time that she ventured into the London club scene, notably at venues like Club Kali. These experiences were transformative for Asifa, as they allowed her to discover a sense of belonging within the LGBTQ+ South Asian community. Prior to her involvement with Club Kali, Asifa recalls feeling like an outsider within both the LGBTQ+ and South Asian communities. She struggled to find peers who shared her cultural background and interests, often feeling alienated in predominantly white or Westernised spaces. However, her time at Queen Mary University of London, located in a vibrant Bengali community, provided her with a sense of connection to her Asian heritage.

Club Kali, with its unique blend of South Asian music and queer expression, became a sanctuary for Asifa too. Here, she could freely embrace her identity as a queer South Asian and express herself through dance and music. The club's inclusive atmosphere empowered Asifa to explore her sexuality and feel comfortable in her own skin. One memorable moment stands out in Asifa's memory: witnessing a group of attractive British South Asian boys dancing to a remix of the song 'Dus Bahane' from the film 'Dus', seamlessly mixed with 'Don't Cha' by The Pussycat Dolls. This experience sparked a newfound sense of confidence and pride in her sexuality, as she revelled in the realisation that she, too, could be desirable. She highlights the importance of inclusive spaces like Club Kali in fostering self-acceptance and empowerment within marginalised communities.

The drag figure of Asifa is a hyphenated in-between within the global diaspora where South Asian-ness is celebratory as well as contradictory. Asifa's chosen surname Lahore also situates her geographically as she celebrates her place within a global South Asian queer space. Asifa's drag performance in videos such as 'Punjabi Girl' and 'You and I' offer visibility to a kind of queer femininity that has often been sidelined on queer social media spaces. At the same time, the popularity of these videos are testament to how digital media offers a space for South Asian queer drag performance. Asifa's performance displays a kind of femininity and queerness that resists South Asian gender expectations. Queer drag performance can be a transformative experience, as scholars such as Khubchandani have noted. Asifa tells us:

> You know I am in a career that I am really happy in. I have a good relationship with my family but the thing is whether I like it or not my career itself is political and to become a successful drag artist from a South Asian and Muslim background in the UK is activism in itself and that is what I have come to realise. We have a lot to deal with—fight barriers of language and explaining ourselves to our older generation through their language.

Despite her popularity as a drag artist, Asifa initially hesitated to explore her trans* identity. During this period, Asifa observed several fellow Club Kali performers transitioning, including Anjali, whose visibility in the community sparked conversations about gender identity. Asifa felt apprehensive about the potential challenges of transitioning publicly. Her traumatic experience coming out as a gay man and the fear of jeopardizing her burgeoning drag career were significant factors influencing her decision.

Furthermore, Asifa's long-term relationship and subsequent marriage added another layer of complexity to her journey. The prospect of transitioning while married raised numerous questions and uncertainties for Asifa, further delaying her decision. However, a transformative experience at an LGBT Muslim activist conference in South Africa in November 2016 marked a turning point for Asifa. Hearing the stories of Hijras and Khwaja Siras from around the world inspired her to embrace her transgender identity fully. Upon returning to London, Asifa made the decision to come out as a trans* woman to her family and friends, ultimately leading to the end of her marriage. Asifa acknowledges the progress made in South Asia regarding transgender rights and visibility, citing Pakistan's enactment of employment laws for trans* individuals in 2018 as a significant milestone which might have impacted how she was accepted by some members of her family.

Asifa's work pushes against the boundaries of respectability politics within the South Asian community. At the same time she uses her heritage to point towards the hypocritical nature of liberal politics itself, which has seen increased Islamophobia and racism within the mainstream gay community that continues to invisibilise South Asian queer performers. Asifa's use of drag and media activism is part of her personal and political resilience to the hostility that South Asian queers face within an increasingly xenophobic Britain exacerbated through government policies and homophobia. Performers such as Asifa perform a distinctly hybrid form of drag, which infuses Bollywood and Punjabi music with disco and RnB. Whilst her name Asifa Lahore inscribes her within a distinct South Asian/Pakistani heritage, she pushes against her identity of being within a nation-state. As she herself mentions in her interview, her work is not just about performing and bringing representation for South Asian queers but also creating spaces of solidarity and community-making through her cultural activism.

> Certainly, I understand that societal issues such as racism and white privilege are currently in the spotlight. Yet, it's worth noting that I've been advocating for these causes for years, even incorporating them into my artistic expression, such as my rendition of Jimmy's 'Disco Dancer' song. This longstanding commitment to raising awareness about social issues remains unchanged. Moving forward, I intend to continue speaking out about important issues, albeit perhaps in a more artistic manner. Additionally, I recognise a significant gap in the empowerment of South Asian queer movements and communities as a whole. In the coming years, I believe it's essential to address the specific challenges and nuances faced by individuals within these communities, including language barriers and the need to educate older generations.

Asifa's artistic expression serves as a critical examination of oppressive patriarchal constructs prevalent within South Asian communities, while also shedding light on the underlying racism present within mainstream LGBT circles. By directing her focus inward, she utilises certain stereotypes as a means to convey broader societal commentary regarding the limitations of liberal queer culture. Her involvement in Shiva Raichandani's film *Queer Parivaar* and the documentary *Always Asifa* underscores her commitment to assuming a cultural activist role, and positions her as a potential icon for South Asian queer individuals to identify with. Notably, her participation in the BBC's 'Free Speech' programme, where she candidly discussed her identity as a Muslim, gay and British individual, garnering significant backlash, highlighted the challenges she faces in navigating intersecting identities.

Asifa's approach to creative activism is characterised by inclusivity rather than self-exceptionalism. This is exemplified in her facilitation of collaborative efforts and provision of platforms for others, as evidenced in Channel 4's *Muslim Drag Queens*, where numerous performers were featured, working with Asifa as their mentor.

'Your India is very different from my India'

The final artist we will discuss is Charan Singh, who hails from Delhi, where he spent his formative years. He initially worked for a charity organisation there before transitioning to community consultation roles with various international organisations, including the UN. His work primarily focused on addressing issues related to sexual health and poverty alleviation. Despite his extensive experience, Singh felt there was a gap in knowledge at the grassroots level. It was during this time, while attending an HIV conference, that he crossed paths with Sunil Gupta, leading to a personal and professional relationship.[21] Eventually, Singh and Gupta entered into a civil partnership and relocated to Britain. The decision to move happened very suddenly for Singh. A significant turning point came with Sunil's exhibition at Alliance Française which was shut down by the police following an anonymous complaint about its content being 'obscene', as discussed earlier. Singh and Gupta had envisioned Delhi as their primary home, but the exhibition closure and the couple becoming vulnerable to the changing political situation prompted them to reconsider their situation abruptly.[22]

Singh decided to give the UK a try, moving there in 2012. While initially considering the move a temporary one, enrolling in a photography course that same year was a turning point. He was also reflecting on the changes in laws back in India and the uncertainties surrounding their future plans. The repeal of Section 377 in India by the Delhi High Court in 2009 which was reversed following intense opposition by the Supreme Court in December 2013 was a further factor affecting Singh's decision to remain in the UK.[23] Activists planned a Global Day of Rage in eighteen cities across the world. A protest was held in London outside the High Commission, which Singh attended.[24] At this point, Singh and Gupta began to consider the UK their primary base while maintaining visits to India to visit family.

As an artist Singh is well aware of the limits of safety when it comes to creating art, especially with greater surveillance on dissent and cultural productions in the diaspora by an increasingly authoritarian government:

> Even now, I cannot emphasise enough the importance of safety, particularly in the context of my work. When operating within public spheres, such as the one I inhabit as an artist, one becomes more vulnerable. Unlike academia, where my activities are more contained, the nature of artistic expression exposes me to greater risks, especially considering the ease with which content can be shared across various platforms like Instagram. Consequently, I exercise caution in determining what I create and choose to showcase.

Singh doesn't view art and activism as diametrically opposed or disruptive forces; rather, he sees them as complementary mediums through which he can narrate stories about the communities he engages with. A central theme in Singh's work, as well as his political stance, is class consciousness. While discussions on contemporary South Asian migration often overlook class dynamics, Singh deliberately places class experiences at the forefront of his work.

> Leaving India as an adult, having lived a significant portion of my life there, I still grapple with uncertainty regarding where home truly lies. There's a strong connection to my roots there, both culturally and politically. My understanding of the world, my political awareness, it's all framed by my experiences in India. Even while residing here, I view India as my foundational framework for engaging with the world. The stark socio-economic disparities I witness here often draw parallels to those back home, reinforcing my ties to India.

Singh's most recent work, a video project 'They Called it Love, But Was it Love?' was commissioned by Visual AIDS for Day With(out) Art 2020: TRANSMISSIONS. It sets out to explore issues of economic and sexual precarity faced by *kothis* in India.[25] According to Singh, this community described as a 'risk group' by public health campaigns is often misinterpreted; their authentic selves and ability to pursue happiness and fulfilment disregarded. Singh argues that categories such as MSM (men who have sex with men) and *kothis*, which arrived with discourse about HIV/AIDS funding and public health, refer implicitly to 'underclass' queer and trans* men. For Singh they were not seen as objects of desire, always being pushed to the periphery.

The film opens with an accented voiceover from 'Mohini,' who reads aloud: 'Acquired Immuno Deficiency Syndrome.' This is followed by our introduction to the first of three characters, who sings 'Ye pyar hai ya kuch aur tha' from Raj Kapoor's renowned film 'Prem Rog' (Sickness of Love, 1982). The English translation of the song serves as the title of this artwork. Singh rejects the often-limited portrayal of *kothis* found in media and literature. Instead, leveraging artistic freedom, he crafts a fresh narrative, fashioning a new story for them. In one scene of the film we read, 'Love is a place where we find ourselves, through language and intimacies.'

The three characters' accented pronunciation of AIDS is also part of Singh's own interest in language and how the hegemony of English, especially through public health discourse, has impacted the lives of subaltern queer people in India. HIV education programmes often relied on English-language materials, which presented a challenge for those who were not literate or had limited education, particularly among marginalised groups like the *hijras*.[26] Singh recalls a moment during which he endeavoured to teach individuals how to pronounce 'immunodeficiency syndrome' by breaking down the words into manageable segments. This exercise, aimed at individuals with little to no formal education, served as a poignant reminder of the intersection between language, knowledge production and power dynamics.

From outdoor prayer spaces for Muslim men to benches used for cruising, bustling streets, vibrant market vendors and intimate bedroom scenes, each locale in the film serves as a canvas for queer encounters and identity expression. These spaces not only facilitate interactions but also provide avenues for the characters to authentically perform their identities, process grief and embrace moments of joy and happiness.

Singh's *Kothis, Hijras, Giriyas and Others* constitutes another intervention in queer subaltern storytelling, simultaneously challenging the class-based origins of Indian photography. This series of carefully posed photographs, often in portrait format, showcases a diverse array of queer individuals adopting postures inspired by popular Indian films and television culture. Given the widespread accessibility of popular Indian cinema in the country, many of the subjects found it natural to use it as a means of defining their subjectivity and style.[27] Rachel Dwyer famously argues that Bollywood cinema offers the best insight into the realities of modern India, reflecting the thoughts, aspirations and attitudes of its people.[28] These portraits can be viewed as imaginative representations, depicting how individuals can inhabit, conceive and sustain societies, while also exploring shared expectations and norms. In many ways these portraits can also be seen as a unique repository of queer subaltern imaginings, shaped by caste, class and sexuality.

The figures also challenge the supremacist nature of the history of Indian photography where studio portraiture was the domain of the dominant caste and class. Singh is quick to point out that his work is not 'representative' of all queer subaltern experience. In fact he is quite critical of the art scene in Britain where South Asian artists are expected to be repositories of their culture. When discussing his work in the diasporic setting, Singh has often challenged the notion that there is only one migrant or queer narrative in India. His work is a reminder that India encompasses a multitude of experiences and realities, far beyond the idyllic perceptions held by some: 'When discussing my work in academic settings, I often find myself starting from the very basics, needing to elucidate fundamental concepts about India before delving into more nuanced discussions.'

Despite being based in Britain for more than a decade now, Singh has however chosen not to do work on the diaspora yet, noting it is not an experience he shares with second or third generation South Asian migrants:

> The Indian diaspora is diverse, encompassing individuals from various backgrounds, including those from the Caribbean and Africa, whose

> ancestors left India generations ago. Their experiences differ vastly from mine, and I'm mindful not to conflate them with my own. While I'm often urged to explore themes related to my current environment in my work, I hesitate to do so, feeling it's not my place to appropriate their struggles.

He feels his work can continue to challenge the misrepresentations of subaltern queer Indian communities in Britain. Even within South Asian communities he encounters challenges related to the perception and representation of various identities and cultures. He describes an incident when he was invited to participate in a panel discussion about a film from India that portrayed transgender individuals. However, the introductory material accompanying the film contained inaccurate and sensationalised descriptions of the *hijra* community, which he felt compelled to address:

> When I suggested contextualizing the film within the diversity of Indian cultures and communities, the response was dismissive, with the organiser insisting that the portrayed individuals were 'real people.' While acknowledging the authenticity of the individuals depicted, I emphasised the need to recognise the cultural nuances and regional variations within India, especially given the diverse experiences of transgender individuals across different cities and states. Furthermore, I proposed discussing contemporary issues affecting the transgender community in India, such as the proposed trans bill, which was met with resistance. It became evident that there was a reluctance to engage with perspectives that challenged existing notions about India and its queer communities.

This experience highlighted for Singh the tendency for individuals to uphold oversimplified or sensationalised portrayals of India and its diverse cultures, often influenced by Western perspectives. There seemed to be a resistance to acknowledging the complexity of Indian society, as well as a reluctance to engage in nuanced discussions about contemporary issues affecting marginalised queer communities within India. Singh reflects on how people in the diaspora attempt to place one within certain hierarchies and structures based on their name and background, shedding light on the complexities of identity politics and the ways in which individuals negotiate their identities within social contexts especially within the diaspora. Singh argues that focusing more on these intersections can provide valuable insights into the multifaceted nature of queer South Asian identities and the challenges individuals face in navigating complex social landscapes. This is the reason why Singh continues to make important work on issues related to marginalised queer people in India.

This chapter has explored the work of four contemporary South Asian artists in Britain who make a significant intervention in redefining the South Asian queer diasporic imagination, distinct from the artists discussed in the previous chapter. Their work highlights the transformative power of performance and visual art in challenging Britain's imperial and racialised history, as well as in fostering queer collectives and communities within a frequently hostile environment. In an era where queer identities often lean towards homonormativity, respectability and neoliberal politics, these artists offer a powerful critique of such trends. Rejecting nationalist politics, they instead pursue a politics of intra-Asian solidarity, though not without its complexities.

This work seems quite urgent given the right-wing backlash against trans* liberation politics. The long history of South Asian internationalism in terms of political struggle is crucially important in relation to the works discussed here, whilst situating them within sexual liberation politics also evokes the complexity of South Asian diasporic identities in Britain with respect to class, caste, faith and in/visibility. Gayatri Gopinath, writing about Parminder Sekhon's work, describes it as 'unimaginable' within diasporic and dominant nationalist frameworks; Kabir, Singh, Raichandani and Lahore take up this mantle of decentring their work from the logics of colonial modernity and liberal visibility politics.

CONCLUSION

When we received the British Academy Grant for our project, 'Cross Border Queers: The Story of South Asian Migrants in the UK', we had a slightly different book in mind. We were keen to look at the realities of queer migration, in particular queer people from South Asia migrating to Britain, who have been made invisible in stories in mainstream media. Whilst in Britain we have seen tremendous changes in terms of legislation around sexuality, we are also aware this has had little effect when it comes to the experiences of South Asian queer people and those concerns that were raised decades ago remain. The purpose of that project was to document these histories towards potential advocacy and social change.

Before lockdown, we were fortunate to hold one workshop in Kolkata in 2019 with the support of Varta Trust, community organiser Pawan Dhall, and the British High Commission, where several micro-histories of migration and archival material were shared with us. Significantly, Pawan made the archives of Counsel Club, an erstwhile queer support forum that existed between 1993 and 2002, available to us. This archive included letters written to Counsel Club by visitors and South Asian migrants who were living in Britain requesting a copy of their magazine, *Naya Pravartak*.[1] These letters were meticulously archived with the dates they were received and replied to.

We had hoped to take this form of collaborative and action-based research through workshops and archival study to other South Asian countries but as we started to plan those journeys the Covid-19 pandemic began and travel became impossible. Given the precarious financial and social future many respondents in India and other sites were facing, we decided to shift the focus of our research and instead make some of the issues raised at the Kolkata workshop, around cultural activism, belonging and community amongst the British South Asian diaspora our focus.

Participants at that workshop discussed the difficulties of receiving visas and the surveillance they were subject to when they attended visa interviews. With the uncertainties around the discriminatory Citizenship Amendment Act many participants were also worried about how that would add further exclusionary barriers—having to prove their gender and 'domicile' when for many queer people without access to 'property' and 'home', there was no way to prove there is no 'fixed home'. The very idea of home is complicated when there exists no social acknowledgement of their relationship with same sex partners and 'proof of cohabitation'. Many participants discussed the need for trans-affirmative care as a major reason for migrating, especially with the passage of the regressive and controversial Transgender Persons (Protection of Rights) Act in 2019 which would act as a further barrier for trans* people not just wanting to migrate to a different country but also relocate within India to different cities.

Puar, Rushbrook and Schein have rightly argued that non-normative sexuality often leads to, or is equated with, spatial displacement. By this they mean that queer people experience both physical and social displacement due to trauma, violence and marginalisation.[2] This sense of non-belonging, as Debanuj Dasgupta and Rohit K. Dasgupta rightly note, is racialised where queer people of colour represent a limit to the West's liberal modernity in which religious and raced bodies are made to reside on the very margins as migrants navigate structural racism and heteronormativity.[3] Another participant at the workshop pushed back on the narrative of the West being a more accommodating place for queers, recalling their experience of visiting the United States on a cultural exchange to discover how policed his brown body was from the moment he entered the country.

The stories we have shared in this book are not new; they've just been pushed to the margins. These narratives reveal uncomfortable truths that challenge the gatekeepers who have long crafted more homogenous and mainstream depictions of 'their' communities. But for us, these stories are a vibrant and essential unearthing of lives that deserve to be seen and celebrated. As South Asian diasporic Britons, who have had to challenge racism in mainstream queer spaces and homophobia in many brown spaces, these stories remind us of the importance of amplifying voices that are silenced and reclaiming histories and experiences that have been conveniently neglected. In this book we challenge both the whitewashing of British queer history and the heterowashing of migrant history.

One of the key insights throughout the work has been the importance of collectivisation when it came to organising. Through grassroots activism, cultural production and the creation of spaces for communities to unite, a new vocabulary has emerged. In this book, we have intentionally adopted a transnational perspective. The politics of where knowledge is produced and how it circulates is crucial, but what truly matters is who generates this knowledge, why it is created, and where it originates. Transnational feminist queer methodologies creating knowledge through collaboration and embracing networks and flows of information in creative ways can contest the power relations that exist between the researcher and object and the hierarchy of the Global North/South.[4]

This is not to suggest that collaborative research is without challenges, but it does allow us to acknowledge both the joy and frustration inherent in our critical engagement with this work. The period discussed in the book represents a significant moment of transnational organising, where South Asian queer diasporic communities across North America, Europe and South Asia came together in solidarity. Friendship is an important aspect of social justice activism. It is a mode of activism in our quotidian lives and a disruption of the heteronormative ordering of life. As the various narratives of organising and cultural production in this book attest, friendship and love played a crucial role in sustaining and enriching queer diasporic organising and cultural production. For those involved in activism, these bonds provide not only emotional support but also a foundation for ethical engagement, mutual accountability and resilience. Friendship and love helped navigate the challenges of activist struggles, organisational conflicts, heartbreaks and moments of burnout. They created life-worlds where kinship and care were central, allowing activists to build trust and solidarity across local and transnational spaces. Within these relationships, desires were lived, shared and mapped, fostering a deeper commitment to collective goals.

We go back to signpost the queer 'Brown Atlantic'. Loosely referred to as the geographical area bound by British colonialism, the Brown Atlantic as Alpesh Kantilal Patel notes can refer to a much more diverse group of South Asian populations who live outside of, but trace their ancestry to, the South Asian subcontinent.[5] South Asian diasporic queer organising during this period (and to some extent even today) was happening across the Brown Atlantic. *Trikone*, founded in 1986, was an organisation for queer desis that spanned North America, Europe and India.

Similarly, festivals such as Desh Pardesh were bringing together queer artists and organisers from across the diaspora.

Throughout this book, we've collected snapshots of queer South Asian life in Britain spanning five decades. We've traced the threads that connect these diverse voices across time and continents, exploring who Britain's desi queers are and why their history might be unsettling for communities today that seek to imagine different pasts. Much of South Asian migrant history and heritage in Britain has focused on a class-based narrative, often depicting working-class migrants bringing their 'traditional' food and 'culture' to British shores. But there is more to it; as Banerjea et al remind us, 'life after all is an unruly vector, always escaping empires, biopolitical attempts to discipline and regulate our bodies and pleasure'.[6]

There is a historical context within which these narratives have emerged, which is the colonial encounter. This is important not just to locate this work geographically but also subjectively. Rahul Rao notes that one of the most significant impacts of colonial governmentality was the inclination of native elites to perceive their identity, their bodies, through the same lens as their colonisers.[7] This is significant given queer subjectivity has been so deeply informed by rigid imperial heteronormative structures which privileged certain forms of identity and belonging.

The story of queer liberation takes on a new dimension in this book where we centre the experiences of South Asian queers who fought against both racism and homophobia on the streets of Britain. Instead of focusing solely on pivotal moments like Stonewall in the US or the miners' strikes in the 1980s, these narratives highlight the struggles and resilience of those who navigated the intersection of race and sexuality in a hostile environment. They come from cultures with rich histories of sexual diversity, yet they were often labelled as homophobic and made to feel like they were the problem. By incorporating their stories, we gain a fuller, more nuanced understanding of queer liberation—one that acknowledges the unique challenges and contributions of those who have been marginalised not only for their sexuality but also for their race and cultural background. As Churnjeet Mahn in her exploration of queer postcolonial travel writing notes, gay rights have often been seen as belonging to the Global North, with everywhere else being incredibly homophobic; she rightly questions this idea, given the central importance of homoeroticism in Orientalism and the Empire.[8]

The narratives in our book are a testament to how South Asian queer migrants through collaboration, activism and art countered the heteronormative and racist discourse of Britishness and belonging. The chapters interrogate critical activist collectives and the postcolonial structures that reify differences in contemporary Britain. The scholarly trajectory for this book begins in the 1980s through the turbulent Thatcherite era up until contemporary austerity Britain. The stories we tell are messy—they interrogate power structures; community fractures; funding regimes and social structures, but through it all, hold space for queer care and kinship. As we mention in our introduction and reiterate again now, these are stories pushed to the periphery of the history of queer organising; we question why the structures of power pushed away such figures. As Syrus Marcus Ware powerfully points out: 'we need to consider what we want to remember and how we want to remember it, building an archive of our movements going forward to ensure that intergenerational memory can inform our activism, community building and organising.'[9]

This is our small contribution to that endeavour. We hope that this book and the larger project it is part of will serve as an evolving body of knowledge which will centre the important role queer South Asians have played in organising and building solidarity and resistance movements to combat racism and homophobia in Britain.

POSTSCRIPT

RESEARCHING DESI QUEER LIVES

As we discussed in the conclusion to the previous chapter, our original project focusing on desi queer solidarity and collectives in the context of different types of hostile environment was abruptly cut short by Covid-19 lockdowns. As we began talking about how we might shift the focus of our work to the UK, we were met with a steady flow of people volunteering their experience of being queer and South Asian, alongside younger generations and queer migrants curious about the queer elders, the auntie jis and uncle jis, and big sisters and brothers, who had come before them. We hope that this book gives them the tools to imagine the desi queer genealogies they want or need to thrive. This postscript addresses the larger research framework behind why British queer history has been so whitewashed, and why the history of British South Asians has been so straight. This postscript is primarily intended for students and scholars, particularly of gender, queer and diaspora studies, to outline the scholarly contexts undergirding *Desi Queers*.

The economic migrants of the 1960s, many of them born as subjects of the British Empire, have become the template for historicising the first-generation South Asian experience in the UK, despite earlier waves of migration. The story of their resilience in the face of racism, their commitment to 'getting on' and not just 'getting by', has become a powerful mythology still deployed by politicians to vaunt the success of supposedly entrepreneurial-minded South Asian migrants. If you work hard enough, you too can be a success. Needless to say, this story rarely touches on the majority for whom precarity and discrimination is a multi-generational inheritance. We are interested in configuring first-generation queer South Asians as a distinct group whose shared consciousness and social concerns framed a distinct experience. Our use of this term stems from the Gay Black Group/Gay Men's Press Book Project in 1981 which called for the collection of 'Conversations: with first generation black gays, accounts of experiences of being gay in a colonial situation and the differences/similarities in being gay in Britain.'[1]

This book is part of the ongoing response to this call but extended across generations of racialised South Asian queers from migrant backgrounds. These first-gen desi queers tell a different story, one of anti-racist activism, working-class solidarity and the everyday labour to imagine and live in more hopeful worlds. We approach this book as more than a static output; rather, we hope it will offer community activists, scholars and queer South Asians some new tools and resources to hack dominant narratives that have cast queer South Asians as 'minor' or 'invisible' figures in South Asian and queer life in Britain. As part of our commitment to providing new routes into this work for others, we are in the process of depositing many of our interviews with the Bishopsgate Institute in London as we write. We hope this will help to turn the cache of material that often underpins books into resources that others can use to create new ways of seeing and understanding queer South Asian life in the diaspora.

We use 'story' throughout the book to extend the frame beyond conventional methodological approaches to the humanities and social sciences that use different orders of (social or narrative) form and (social or aesthetic) value to categorise social movements which through their work create and imagine different orders of social life and possibility. Drawing on the work of Ramzi Fawaz, we consider the work of desi queers as socially minded left-aligned aesthetic and cultural experiments orientated towards horizons of survival and possibility, while being concretely located in the specificities of time and place.[2]

Departures

We do not read queer as a point of departure from accounts of South Asian life in Britain, as a threshold to be crossed; we read queer as a part of the story of South Asian life in Britain. By framing this story in a broader analysis of the queer South Asian diaspora in the UK, we ask, who are Britain's desi queers? How have they navigated the lines between racism and homophobia in UK life? The 1960s mark the beginning of an organised LGBTQ civil rights movement in the UK, as well as larger waves of migration to the UK, with those of South Asian descent arriving from India, Pakistan, Kenya and Uganda. However, there is little research on queer South Asians who arrived in the UK and how their experiences of racism, homophobia and their transnational connections in South Asia shaped their (inter)national experience of being queer. In this book we show how histories and accounts of South Asian life in the UK have assumed heteronormativity while accounts of queer life in the UK have only recently become attuned to its whiteness. Our book argues that an account of queer lives of colour beyond the past ten years is vital for understanding histories of racism and homophobia in the UK.

In the wake of Brexit and a resurgence of the alt right movement in the UK, there has been much subsequent backlash against migrants and a resurgence of homophobia. This has also led to renewed attention towards precarious queer migrants of colour, who are framed as a threat to conservative nationalist projects.[3] This characterisation has come to perform a powerful truth claim as queer migrants from South Asia are framed as a specific kind of problem, seen as 'out of place' both within queer and South Asian communities. Social anxieties stemming from the 'problem' of South Asian migrants inform structural racism within present day UK.[4] However, the imagining of South Asian migrants and refugees as heteronormative figures also erases the racialised narratives of queer migrant subjects. In these circumstances issues of racialised queer migration require urgent attention.

The movement of people is also historically constructed through colonialism and imperialism, with South Asians over the years migrating in waves, forming ethnic neighbourhoods and communities and taking part in the process of shaping Britain.[5] Whilst there are a number of books on South Asian history and culture in the United Kingdom exploring it from historical,[6] cultural[7] and literary perspectives,[8] no book-length work exists so far which tells the story of South Asian queer migration and diasporic life in Britain. Major studies of South Asian migration such as Rozina Visram's important volume *Asians in Britain* (2002) gloss over issues of queer belonging and identity. While there are a number of studies addressing queer migration and issues of detention and deportation in the context of the United States,[9] there are no major studies which analyse the experience of queer sexualities within South Asian migrant communities in the UK, with a notable exception being Avtar Brah's recent work on intersectional and decolonial approaches to theorisations of mobility.[10]

While there are recent volumes which have explored the experience and cultural production of some queer South Asian communities, they have had a focus on faith communities rather than taking an expansive approach to South Asia (Carbajal 2017, Peumans 2017).[11] Our study works across faith and ethnic communities and imagines South Asia expansively to think about the difference between historical accounts of movement (in the wake of decolonisation) and more recent formations of nation and identity which have reworked ideas of 'British Asians' to foreground other aspects of identity (British Muslim, Scottish Asian, etc).

Desi Queers does not follow the confines of so-called LGBTQ+ 'liberatory' narratives that invariably cast communities of colour as problematic 'others'. Instead, our orientation is towards South Asian projects in Britain that critique racist and imperialist structures and the use of gender and sexuality as modalities of oppression.[12] The material we draw on counters the non-value of queer South Asians in liberal projects of LGBTQ+ recognition and inclusion in the state. Such knowledge regimes, invested in underwriting the value of their liberal democracies, cast less-desirable bodies as problems to be solved in societies where 'non-Western practices are marginalised and cast as "premodern" or unliberated. Practices that do not conform with Western narratives of development of individual political subjects are dismissed as unliberated or coded as "homophobic."'[13]

Queer South Asians are perennially on the wrong side of civilising missions. Under colonial rule, the historically diverse practices of gendered and sexual life in South Asia were characterised as aberrations to modernity, with visible communities such as *hijras* (a historical third gender community) proscribed through new legislation, and practices of queer intimacies policed through the exportation of British anti-sodomy law (incarnated as the infamous Section 377).[14] But as the LGBTQ+ civil rights movement gained traction, cultures that had been 'too queer' were now incubators for virulent homophobias that threatened liberal politics of inclusion.

While our research is based in the UK, it links to other studies of South Asian queer diasporas, especially in the US. Gayatri Gopinath's work on South Asian queer diasporas is of particular importance here. Gopinath for instance writes that it is the queer South Asian figure's stubborn failure to cohere and neatly fit an identity template that has helped it survive within what Gopinath calls the 'cracks and fissures' of a pan-South Asian identity.[15] A prevailing narrative of queer migration from South Asia is about escaping oppressive social conditions. Ruth Vanita calls this the homoerotics of travel. She argues that queer people move from the rural to the urban and to other countries 'in search of more congenial climes and of the hidden self'.[16] Our research suggests that 'escape' and 'migration' are important concerns and a prevailing part of queer life narratives, but that the recent work of scholars such as Kareem Khubchandani on queer performance,[17] Omar Kasmani on queer intimacy and affect in syncretic practice,[18] and Maya Bhardwaj's work on queer solidarities,[19] have helped to produce ever more intricate tapestries of diasporic queer South Asian life.

Arrivals

While the book is structured around specific periods and case studies, they coalesce in the three inter-connected arguments of the book: (1) The emergence of a visible queer South Asian identity in 1980s Britain was a unique formation in the broader South Asian diaspora and based in the specificities of working-class anti-racist second-generation migrant politics. The enabling factors for its emergence were tied to UK-specific contexts, for example increased local authority funding for racially and sexually minoritised groups, the Black Women's Movement in the UK, and the space for creative counter-cultural scenes supported by low/no rents and grants. (2) The specificity of racial politics in the UK, combined with the legacy of Empire, produced a distinct political, cultural and aesthetic lexicon for organising emerging from political blackness that was reflected in art and community organising. (3) South Asian queer and feminist women shared unexpected terrains and solidarities through their shared work to challenge patriarchal violence in the diaspora. This history is 'unexpected' because of enduring narratives that segregate the supposedly 'straight' politics of South Asian feminism from the broader politics of queer-feminist liberation in the UK.

Desi Queers builds on the queer scholarship of Roderick A. Ferguson who has demonstrated the ways in which 'multidimensional and intersectional interests were overtaken by single-issue formulations of queer politics'.[20] We do not trace the emergence of queer South Asian life, community making, politics or culture as a distinct thread within historical projects of (primarily) gay and lesbian liberation in the UK since the 1960s. Instead, from the early 1980s, we look to the interstices of social movements which used anti-imperialism, anti-racism and black feminism as the language that critically unpicked the specific seams of oppressive realities playing out in the heart of the British Empire, but which also drew on philosophy and practice from class-conscious international movements reaching beyond British colonies, including black and brown diasporas. From the late 1980s, we follow the turn to global queer South Asian diasporas that attempted to queer relationships within a South Asian imaginary overdetermined by differences of class, ethnicity, cultural belonging and politics.

We also draw on the work of queer of colour scholars such as José Esteban Muñoz and Gayatri Gopinath who analyse creativity and performance to illuminate the ways in which artistic experiments can queer dominant forms by revealing structures of violence and power. In his seminal work on the topic, Muñoz describes this as an aesthetic practice which engenders 'disidentification': 'decoding mass, high, or any other cultural field from the perspective of a minority subject who is disempowered in such a representational hierarchy.'[21] If creative material and performances can begin to decode fields of power, the affective power of interpretation can be felt by individuals who catch glimpses of recognition. Queer formations emerge through racialised, gendered, sexed and classed realities.

Desi Queers brings together a series of experiments in community, politics and aesthetics which drew on class-conscious anti-imperial international movements, including across black and brown diasporas. We use 'British' loosely to concurrently sequence the layered temporalities of the British Empire and the United Kingdom (from 1922, after the Partition of Ireland).[22] We do not propose or celebrate a distinct British history of queer South Asian life. We argue that its lives, parameters and times always extend beyond narrow conceptualisations of the nation state. We do, however, cleave to the specificity of a desi queer experience in Britain that is grounded in its role in Empire, its migration histories, and the lived experience of racialised minorities. As the writer Nadya Ali has pointed out, 'The idea that "Britishness" is synonymous with whiteness is rooted in the way we selectively remember and forget histories of British colonialism.'[23] Part of the impetus behind our work is to de-centre whiteness from the history of queer life, especially when understood through experiments in social and cultural ordering, and the parsing of queer possibility and hope for other futures.

Another way of conceptualising the location of this work is through thinking about 'home,' which carries the dual connotations of intimate home life, and where home really is ('but where are you from?'). Gayatri Gopinath touches on the popularity of 'leaving home' as the first step in coming out in Western art. For Gopinath, 'home' for the queer South Asian diaspora is always and already a site of contested belonging: 'For queer racialised migrant subjects, "staying put" becomes a way of remaining within the oppressive structures of the home—as domestic space, racialised community space and national space—while imaginatively working to dislodge its heteronormative logic.'[24] While we do not underestimate the real threats of violence and family exclusion, *Desi Queers* does not advocate for queer South Asians to exit brown closets and join rainbow dancefloors and communities that occlude the work of whiteness.

The coining and expanded uses of 'homonationalism' have opened a highly productive field centred on how the politics and practices of LGBTQ+ inclusion have been used to bolster national projects embedded in imperialism.[25] We are indebted to the body of scholarship that has been at the forefront of articulating how and why the allegiance to LGBTQ+ inclusion is instrumentalised to mask the operations of renewed iterations of state racism, namely Islamophobia.[26] Part of the work of *Desi Queers* is to identify how the national work of LGBTQ+ inclusion has codified good sexual citizenship, and how this values system has, in turn, created a hierarchy of national desirability, dividing desi queers along ethno-religious lines.

Throughout the book, we use desi as a conceptual framework that speaks to a specific experimentation in aesthetic or cultural formations tied to diasporic life, while keeping South Asia as geographical marker. This conceptual framing is tied to the earlier work of Gayatri Gopinath, who identified the potential for the 'Brown Atlantic' to illuminate the similarities and differences between the British and North American queer South Asian diasporas.[27] Adapting Paul Gilroy's formulation, the Brown Atlantic encapsulates South–South relations through longer histories of the South Asian diaspora, starting with the movement of indentured labour in the nineteenth century across the Indian Ocean, Africa and the Caribbean.[28] In her study of the Brown Atlantic, especially in the context of Martinique, Devi Hardeen reflects on the difficulty of holding memory in the Brown Atlantic:

> the inter-ethnic tensions between the actors of the Black and Brown Atlantic remained like an open scar until the 1970s. With the passing of time, and the ignorance of youth, younger generations in Martinique have become 'colour-blind' and unburdened by history. [...] History repeats itself. Inhumanity and injustice continue. The Past is Present.[29]

The flows of the Black and Brown Atlantic place bodies in relation to one another through racialised histories measured against their proximity to whiteness. In Hardeen's pessimistic take on the Brown Atlantic, these relations became unmoored from history, and in that unmooring, invite new and invasive forms of injustice predicated on hoarding resources along community lines divided by forces that are harder to name, and so become harder to undo.

We foreground desi queer formations which have found plenitude in queer economies outside mainstream regimes of recognition. We deliberately use 'story' rather than another term like 'history'. A 'story' is an account which often holds second-order legitimacy. Stories are resistant towards the desires of empirical methods to provide veracity. But they are also the vehicles to pass on knowledge, especially from one generation to the next, about a set of experiences that offer moral or philosophical instruction through care-laden narrative efforts.

Queer approaches

Three types of research informed this monograph: interviews, archival research and literary and media critical analysis informed by postcolonial queer theory. Interviews with South Asian-origin queer people in the UK formed one of the most original contributions of this book. We were given unique access to private archives detailing decades of queer connections between South Asia and the UK which contributed to writing this 'missing' story of transnational connection, love, activism and cultural belonging across the borders of nation and sexuality.

Methodologically speaking, this book attends to the interdisciplinary and critical nature of doing queer research, which does not lend itself to neat methodological specificities of knowledge production. Given the anti-disciplinary features of queer theory, we hold multiple and opposed ideas together in how we frame this work. In this we are guided by scholars such as Kath Browne and Catherine J. Nash who argue that research methods can only partially capture the messiness of queer social worlds. They ask a provocative set of questions around linking epistemology and ontological positions in our choice of methods and queer conceptualisations.[30] Ghaziani and Brim note that 'methods are queered when we use the tenets of queer theory to tweak or explode what is possible with our existing procedures. The most common pursuits include making strange the otherwise commonplace or familiar; interrogating alternate possibilities for worldmaking and liveability.'[31]

Spending a long time in the 'field' has become nearly impossible due to the pandemic, neoliberal labour conditions, expectations of work-life balance, family and professional obligations, and on the academic side, the important intervention made by Gunel et al. about the changing nature of fieldwork. In response to these obstacles in fieldwork, they propose patchwork ethnography which is creative and unconstrained by the rigid requirements of traditional ethnography.[32] They further argue that whilst ethnographers have been adapting to various fieldwork challenges there has been very little attention paid to how these practices are being reshaped by our own lives and personal concerns.

Taking this further, we argue for queer patchworks—a way of not just attending to the new demands of fieldwork realities but also the very act of ethnographic writing given multiple disruptions and the need for creative interpretation of the data collected. We use assemblage and patchwork ethnography as a critical lens to observe how connections and relations are forged, interrupted and modified within the new realities of the present. In alignment with assemblage thinking and modes of inquiry, the stories we present centralise the lived experience of the participants as non-uniform and contested.[33]

We have attempted to foreground the work of queer, feminist and racialised community members, workers, activists and scholars. Our approach to queer patchwork aims to bring minoritised positions that are often pitted against one another into dialogue through the cultural, political and aesthetic experiments of the past and present. Some readers will identify this queer patchwork in the structure of our chapters which work across the different real and imagined scales of queer South Asian life. At some points, we offer overviews of movements, and at others we focus on single lives. While scholarly training emphasises the importance of robust arguments always braced against inevitable criticism, we hope our readers find space in the arguments and material of the book to elaborate our patchwork. Following in the steps of queer and feminist activists calling for more public forms of thinking, our queer patchwork is designed to leave some hanging threads for readers to pull or pick up.

We have been inspired by broader work theorising queer approaches to archives, including Muñoz's work on queer ephemera,[34] Sedgewick's work on the queer structure of open secrets,[35] and the very different approaches from Anjali Arondekar and Laurie Marhoefer to archives of minoritised life in/of decay.[36] During the larger project that preceded this book, we had begun to consider the challenge of apprehending different forms of queer migrant and refugee archives in the South Asian context. One of our collaborators, the artist Shashank Peshawaria, began with the very literal approach of asking major archives and projects of Partition whether they had any evidence of queer life. In Peshawaria's words:

> The project explores the absence and invisibility of queer voices in the narratives surrounding the Partition of India. When the borders between India and Pakistan were drawn in 1947, they wrecked people's lives and cleaved families and friendships across a communal axis. But the history of friendships and of the people who were separated from each other due to the upheaval has not considered gay and lesbian lives and their bonds of friendship and perhaps intimacy that may have been torn asunder. Their identities and the unspeakability of their desires, then, add to the silences surrounding Partition testimonies.[37]

Peshawaria was met with a series of non-replies, refusals (there could not be any such material), and questions about the appropriateness of his line of enquiry. He had used India's Right to Information Act (similar to the UK's Freedom of Information Act) to frame some of his enquiries to larger organisations. But in the end, evolving queer networks brought him to a story of queer migration and Partition through a conversation with the late historian and activist Saleem Kidwai a few days before he passed away. As we elaborate in Chapter 1, scavenging for primary material in itself reflects the methodological difficulty of apprehending lives that have been marginalised or missed out in existing research or frameworks for making bodies of knowledge legible.

Our methodological approach is informed by the queer right to access the resources, materials and stories that have contributed to queer worldmaking and resistance. This partly involves identifying the conceptual frameworks for identifying this material, which we do in the book through queer black-brown coalitions; queer nightlife; and political and cultural projects informed by queer and decolonial aesthetics. But as we continued our work, we became acutely aware of the difficulty of easily accessing some of the real archival material available in universities, museums and libraries. Haringey Vanguard (a BME LGBTQ+ archive housed at the Bruce Castle Museum, London); the Lesbian Archive (with significant black lesbian collections from the 1980s at Glasgow Women's Library); the rukus! archive (a Black LGBT archive at London Metropolitan Archive); and significant collections of photographs and print material from 1980s queer South Asian organising (at the Bishopsgate Institute, London) are just a few of the places which have material relevant to queer South Asian lives, often included as part of larger black queer collections. Part of our approach was to identify a through line to these significant collections, to assemble a composite story of queer South Asian life that avoided essentialising what being queer or South Asian means in the diaspora. We view configurations of queer South Asians as contextually contingent and often fraught formations which emerge in response to distinct community-focused and societal shifts. We hope this approach will help others to build their own accounts of queer South Asian life in the diaspora.

ACKNOWLEDGEMENTS

It took a village to make this book happen. Thank you to everyone who supported us or believed in the project along the way.

Before the book, the three of us were working on a British Academy-funded project called 'Cross Border Queers: The Story of South Asian Migrants to the UK'. We are incredibly grateful to the BA for their support, especially as we had to re-conceptualise the work after the first UK lockdown. Thanks to Rukhsar Hussain who supported part of that work.

We were lucky to have the assistance of some incredible museums and archives. These are archives held by and for the communities they serve. We want to extend a heartfelt thanks to Nicola Maksymuik, Mae Moss and Adele Patrick at the Glasgow Women's Library (GWL); Stef Dickers and all the team at the Bishopsgate Institute; and Julie Melrose and Valerie Crosby at the Haringey Archive and Museum Service. In every single case, the extra time, care and generosity of individuals helped us to make breakthroughs in the project. Thanks to Nicola who pulled down a slim and uncatalogued file that contained a long run of *Shakti Khabar* (which forms much of the work behind Chapters 2 and 3). Thanks to Stef, who took us to incredibly rare pictures of Shakti and ASIA (a club night) from the 1980s. Thanks to

Julie, who knew exactly where to point us to in the material intersecting the Haringey Lesbian and Gay Unit and Haringey Black Action. Thanks to GWL for making the Camden Lesbian Centre and Black Lesbian Group Archive more accessible; much of our research for Chapter 1 came from this archive.

We also thank Kris Black, Pawan Dhall, Sunil Gupta, Raisa Kabir, Gordon Rainsford, Parminder Sekhon and Charan Singh for the permission to reproduce images of their work/material from personal collections. We tried, several times, to find the person who took the cover image of this book (Shakti marching at Pride in 1989 with a banner, we think, partly designed by the artist Zahid Dar) by asking around our networks and appealing on social media. We were unable to find the person who took the picture but if they recognise it as theirs, we would ask them to get in touch with the publisher of this book so they can be credited.

We were also very fortunate to have countless conversations with and feedback from many individuals. There are too many to name here, but we would like to single out a few. Savi Hensman, who was one of our interviewees, kindly read an early version of Chapter 1 and offered feedback, and helped us secure permissions for some of the work featured in this book. After spending hours reading about her time at the Black Lesbian and Gay Centre from 1985, being part of the UK's first black queer national demonstration in 1987, and being part of the black feminist takeover of the Lesbian Archive and Information Centre in 1988, it was a privilege to have her insight and thoughtful engagement. Gilli Salvat, who supported the Young Lesbian Group in 1979, and worked at the Haringey Lesbian and Gay Unit in 1986, took the time to sit down for two long interviews, and worked with us on the section of the book about her (generously accompanied by a delicious lunch). Many of the people we name as interviewees did more than just agree to be interviewed. They pointed us towards other material, helped source material, but most importantly opened up the incredible world of desi queer life in Britain. Thank you for your time and generosity.

For Pawan Dhall and Shashank Peshawaria, we have many thanks. Pawan led the work to organise our first in-person event for the BA project in Kolkata in collaboration with the Deputy High Commission (UK). This was during a period of protests in reaction to the Citizenship Amendment Act (CAA) which had a direct impact on many of the trans* and queer folk attending the workshop. We return to the project we were not able to pursue in the Conclusion. Here, we would like to thank the presenters in the workshop, Kaustav Bakshi, Anil Pradhan, Andronicus Aden, and the many contributors including representatives from SAATHII and the Amitie Trust. Pawan was a central part of the BA project and a constant source of knowledge, support and inspiration. His stewardship of the Counsel Club Archive in Kolkata, which includes countless letters from queer people across India, is a carefully attended and invaluable resource of queer life. Shashank was also part of the BA project and had begun work to source accounts of queer displacement during Partition. Shashank, thank you for your critical and creative insight, intuition and artistic eye.

A huge thanks to Moya Lothian-McLean who commissioned us to write a short piece about the heterowashing of South Asian migrant history for gal-dem. Without that nudge, and the interest the article generated, we may never have started this book project. Thank you to Aswin Punathambekar for hosting Rohit at CARGC, University of Pennsylvania. This gave Rohit the time and space to work on parts of this book.

We presented earlier snippets of work in this book in different forums. Sincere thanks to fellow speakers and audiences for consistently generous and thought-provoking questions. Thanks include: South Asian Heritage Month (UK) who hosted our panel 'Desi Diasporas and LGBTQ+ Activism' in 2021 which featured Pawan Dhall, Jasbir Puar, Ian Iqbal Rashid and Sandip Roy; South Asian Sisters Speak for their invitation to speak on the 'Lost Histories: Queer Asia' panel in 2021 alongside Anjali Arondekar and Alia Romagnoli; Amal Malik and Chandan Mahal for the invitation to contribute to the 'Finding Queer South Asian Voices in the Archives' event at the British Library in 2022 alongside Kuljit Singh and Hafsa Qureshi; The World That Belongs to Us exhibition at the New Gallery Walsall curated by Aziz Sohail; Debanuj Dasgupta and Jigna Desai and the Center for Feminist Futures at UCSB; Somak Biswas, Shashank Peshawaria, Pawan Dhall and the Bishopsgate Institute for a panel event in 2022; and Radha Kapuria and Shamira Meghani for their invitation to speak at the University of Durham in 2024. A special note about the British Library event: thanks for the incredible opportunity to listen to rare archival sound recordings of queer South Asians talking about their lives in the 1980s. We were unable to revisit this material for the book as the sound archive was part of the cyberattack that brought the British Library's information systems to a halt in 2023.

To Michael Dwyer, thank you for believing in this book and taking it on. To our editor, Mei Jayne Yew, thank you for your keen eye and insightful comments. Your feedback and editorial direction made this a better work. We apologise for every time we were annoying and difficult; you were a patient pro throughout! Sincere thanks to the team at Hurst who were instrumental in its production including Tom Feltham, Becca Hirst, and Daisy Leitch.

Inevitably, there are a lot of people missing from the thanks here, and we hope you will let us thank you in person and in other forums. Writing collectively requires a very different kind of labour than writing on your own. In some ways it's easier, in other ways it's harder. The three of us come from very different backgrounds and with very different kinds of experience. This book has been the process of finding the common ground that speaks to a queer diasporic experience of being South Asian. Just like us, that is not singular. It's filled with difference and diversity. We hope the book offers a range of entry points for different readers.

We were determined not to write a book structured by painful exile from families and communities, stories which have for too long stood as dominant narratives of queer South Asian life in Britain. Part of our intention in the book is to show the plenitude of queer South Asian life, in forms, desires, loves and orientations. But we are mindful of all the queer South Asians, including many people in our own lives, who didn't make it. Who disappeared after coming once to a club or meet-up. Who disappeared from their families and communities. Or who couldn't bear to be here. We dedicate this book to them.

NOTES

INTRODUCTION

1. For a brief summary and digital reproduction of selected items that includes this leaflet see 'Smash the Backlash: LGBT+ Rights Campaigning in Haringey', *LSE History*, 2024 <https://blogs.lse.ac.uk/lsehistory/2024/05/01/smash-the-backlash-lgbt-rights-campaigning-in-haringey/> [accessed 7 September 2024].
2. Ibid.
3. Ibid.
4. Anjali R. Arondekar, *Abundance: Sexuality's History* (Duke University Press, 2023).
5. Sara Ahmed, *Living a Feminist Life* (Duke University Press, 2017), 'Part II. Diversity Work', p. 93.
6. 'Trouble and Strife' was the name of a radical feminist magazine published 1982–2002. See 'T&S Journal Archive—Trouble and Strife' <https://www.troubleandstrife.org/articles/> [accessed 21 April 2024].
7. Anandi Ramamurthy, *Black Star: Britain's Asian Youth Movements* (Pluto Press, 2013).
8. Amrit Wilson, *Finding a Voice: Asian Women in Britain*, New and expanded edition, 2nd edition (Daraja Press, 2018).
9. Rima Saini, *Politics, Identity and Belonging across the British South Asian Middle Classes: Between Privilege and Prejudice* (Palgrave Macmillan, 2024).

10. Vazira Zamindar, *The Long Partition and the Making of Modern South Asia: Refugees, Boundaries, Histories*, Cultures of History (Columbia University Press, 2010).
11. Wilson, pp. 12–13. Pratibha Parmar was critical of the original publication for precisely this point, that the characterisation of South Asian women through poverty impoverished the complexity of South Asian women's experience. See Natalie Thomlinson, *Race, Ethnicity and the Women's Movement in England, 1968–1993*, Palgrave Studies in the History of Social Movements (Palgrave Macmillan, 2016), pp. 81–82.
12. Wilson, p. 216.
13. The *kala pani* is a taboo rooted in Hindu mythology, but passing into broader South Asian vernacular folklore, where the crossing of the black water is a threshold event from which there is no return. It can be a literal or figural social death. Crossing the threshold threatens to upend inscribed social orders of caste and social order that render the travellers who undertake these transgressive journeys, ultimately, unrecognisable. The figurative threat of crossing the *kala pani* was made literal for nineteenth-century indentured labourers who faced the real prospect of what crossing the *kala pani* to unimaginably distant places might mean for them. See Vijay Mishra, 'Theorising the Troubled Black Waters', in *Kala Pani Crossings*, ed. by Ashutosh Bhardwaj and Judith Misrahi-Barak, 1st edn (Routledge India, 2021), pp. 19–30, doi:10.4324/9781003247463-3.
14. *Vilayat* is a version of the nickname Blighty (Britain) and was used in the early twentieth century.
15. Anisha Sircar, 'Is the Term "Desi" Offensive? Some South Asian Americans Think So', *Scroll.In* (https://scroll.in, 2020) <https://scroll.in/global/975071/is-the-term-desi-offensive-some-south-asian-americans-think-so> [accessed 20 April 2024]. There are several reddit threads with strong opinions about the geographical, ethnic and cultural coordinates of *desi*, for which there is no consensus.
16. Gayatri Reddy, 'Queer Desi Formations: Making the Boundaries of Cultural Belonging in Chicago', in *Pakistan Desires: Queer Futures Elsewhere*, ed. by Omar Kasmani (Duke University Press, 2023).
17. Maya Bhardwaj, '"That's What We Think of as Activism": Solidarity

through Care in Queer Desi Diaspora', *Journal of Lesbian Studies*, 28.1 (2024), pp. 100–124, doi:10.1080/10894160.2023.2228652.

18. Naveen Minai, 'Desi Butch (Where the 'Twain Shall Meet)', *Journal of Autoethnography*, 3.2 (2022), pp. 160–68, doi:10.1525/joae.2022.3.2.160.
19. Kareem Khubchandani, *Ishtyle: Accenting Gay Indian Nightlife* (University of Michigan Press, 2020), doi:10.3998/mpub.9958984.
20. Shivananda Khan, *Khush: A Shakti Report*, 1991.
21. *'Queer' Asia: Decolonising and Reimagining Sexuality and Gender*, ed. by Jennifer Ung Loh and J. Daniel Luther (Zed Books Ltd, 2019).
22. 'How the Creative Punjabi Diaspora Turned out in Support of the Indian Farmers' Protest' <https://www.itsnicethat.com/features/punjabi-disapora-sikh-farmers-protests-illustration-photography-070521> [accessed 11 August 2024].
23. Selina Chen, Middle East Eye, 'LGBTQ+ groups "opt out" of Pride in London over partners' links to Israel's occupation', 28 June 2024: https://www.middleeasteye.net/news/lgbtq-groups-pride-london-pride-partners-israel-occupation
24. 'Many Voices, One Chant: Black Feminist Perspectives', ed. by Valerie Amos and others, *Feminist Review*, 17 (1984). Throughout the book we use 'black' to refer to political blackness and 'Black' to refer to Afro-Caribbean heritage communities. We have not changed capitalisation within direct quotations. The people and sources we quote take different approaches to capitalisation.
25. Valerie Amos and others, 'Editorial', *Feminist Review*, 17(1984), pp. 1–2 (p. 1).
26. Carmen and others, 'Becoming Visible: Black Lesbian Discussions', *Feminist Review*, 17(1984), pp. 53–72 (p. 72), doi:10.2307/1395010.
27. Carmen and others, p. 54.
28. Ibid.
29. Ibid.
30. Ibid.
31. For an example of how 'triple jeopardy' has been explored in terms of lesbian identity, see Beverly Greene, 'Lesbian Women of Color: Triple Jeopardy', *Journal of Lesbian Studies*, 1.1 (1996), pp. 109–47, doi:10.1300/J155v01n01_09.

32. See *Feminist Review*'s thirty year anniversary edition which revisited the state of Black British feminism: Jay Bernard, Sita Balani, and Camel Gupta, 'Many Voices, One Chant: 30th Anniversary Roundtable', *Feminist Review*, 108(2014), pp. 26–43.
33. Jasbir K. Puar, *Terrorist Assemblages: Homonationalism in Queer Times* (Duke University Press, 2007), doi:10.1215/9780822390442.
34. Ahmed, *Living a Feminist Life*, pp. 15–16.
35. Stuart Hall, *Selected Writings on Race and Difference* (Duke University Press, 2021), p. 247.
36. Ibid., p. 248.
37. Tariq Modood, 'Political Blackness and British Asians', *Sociology*, 28.4 (1994), pp. 859–76 (p. 869).
38. For an overview of the changing use of political blackness in Britain, see Claire Alexander, 'Breaking Black: The Death of Ethnic and Racial Studies in Britain', *Ethnic and Racial Studies*, 41.6 (2018), pp. 1034–54, doi:10.1080/01419870.2018.1409902.
39. Ibid., p. 1037.
40. Heidi Safia Mirza and Yasmin Gunaratnam, '"The Branch on Which I Sit": Reflections on Black British Feminism', *Feminist Review*, 108(2014), pp. 125–33 (p. 126).
41. See Sara Ahmed, *On Being Included: Racism and Diversity in Institutional Life* (Duke University Press, 2012).
42. Mirza and Gunaratnam, p. 131.
43. feministkilljoys, 'Black Feminism as Life-Line', *Feministkilljoys*, 2013 <https://feministkilljoys.com/2013/08/27/black-feminism-as-life-line/> [accessed 29 April 2024]. For another envisioning of lines/threads that can bind, see Poulomi Desai and Parminder Sekhon, *Red Threads: The South Asian Queer Connection in Photographs* (Millivres-Prowler, 2003).
44. bell hooks, 'Choosing the Margin as a Space of Radical Openness', *Framework: The Journal of Cinema and Media*, 36(1989), pp. 15–23. This is expanded in our discussion of 'creative interruptions' in Chapters 4–5.
45. Gloria Anzalduá, *Borderlands: The New Mestiza = La Frontera*, 1st edn (Aunt Lute Books, 1991).
46. Rozina Visram, *Asians in Britain: 400 Years of History* (Pluto Press,

2002); *A Postcolonial People: South Asians in Britain*, ed. by N. Ali, Virinder S. Kalra, and S. Sayyid (Hurst & Co, 2006); Dan Glass, *United Queerdom From the Legends of the Gay Liberation Front to the Queers of Tomorrow* (Bloomsbury Publishing, 2022); Dan Glass, *Queer Footprints: A Guide to Uncovering London's Fierce History* (Pluto Press, 2023).

47. Amin Ghaziani, *Long Live Queer Nightlife: How the Closing of Gay Bars Sparked a Revolution* (Princeton University Press, 2024).
48. Sita Balani, *Deadly and Slick: Sexual Modernity and the Making of Race* (Verso, 2023).
49. For an excellent consideration of this issue in a transnational setting see Kareem Khubchandani, 'Caste, Queerness, Migration and the Erotics of Activism', *South Asia Multidisciplinary Academic Journal*, 20 (2019), doi:10.4000/samaj.7173.
50. Sandeep Bakshi, 'A Comparative Analysis of Hijras and Drag Queens', *Journal of Homosexuality*, 46.3–4 (2004), pp. 211–23 (p. 214), doi:10.1300/J082v46n03_13.
51. Nat Raha, 'Transfeminine Brokenness, Radical Transfeminism', *South Atlantic Quarterly*, 116.3 (2017), pp. 632–46, doi:10.1215/00382876-3961754.
52. Matt Brim, *Poor Queer Studies: Confronting Elitism in the University* (Duke University Press, 2020), doi:10.1215/9781478009146.
53. *Queer Sharing in the Marketized University*, ed. by Churnjeet Mahn, Matt Brim, and Yvette Taylor (Routledge, 2023)."
54. Niharika Banerjea, Debanuj Dasgupta, Rohit K. Dasgupta and Jaime Grant, *Friendship as Social Justice Activism* (Kolkata: Seagull, 2018).

1. BLACK, SOUTH ASIAN AND QUEER IN 1980S BRITAIN

1. For an excellent discussion of the potential and conflict in framings of black feminism, especially in OWAAD, see Nydia A. Swaby, '"Disparate in Voice, Sympathetic in Direction": Gendered Political Blackness and the Politics of Solidarity', *Feminist Review*, 108.1 (2014), pp. 11–25, doi:10.1057/fr.2014.30.
2. For an overview of the GLC and its initiatives for progressive social change see Stephen Brooke, *London, 1984: Conflict and Change in the Radical City* (Oxford University Press, 2024).

3. Ruth Wilson Gilmore, *Golden Gulag: Prisons, Surplus, Crisis, and Opposition in Globalizing California* (University of California Press, 2007), p. 28.
4. Anandi Ramamurthy, *Black Star: Britain's Asian Youth Movements* (Pluto Press, 2013).
5. The racist murder of Altab Ali in 1978 provoked a series of protests from a community that had faced an onslaught of organised racist violence emboldened by the small but significant electoral traction of fascist groups like the National Front. Between 1979 and 1981, there were anti-racist protests across major UK cities including Bristol, London, and Birmingham. When the National Front came to Southall for a public meeting ahead of the 1979 general election, they were met with protests which quickly escalated into violence after the death of one of the protesters, Blair Peach, at the hands of the police.
6. The seminal text on South Asian youth movements of the period is Anandi Ramamurthy, *Black Star: Britain's Asian Youth Movements* (London: Pluto Press, 2013). For a more recent overview of Black and South Asian anti-racist solidarity in the period, see Preeti Dhillon, *The Shoulders We Stand on: How Black and Brown People Fought for Change in the United Kingdom* (Dialogue Books, 2023).
7. Paul Gilroy, *After Empire: Melancholia or Convivial Culture?*, Repr. (Routledge, 2009), p. xi.
8. Yvette Taylor, *Working-Class Queers: Time, Place and Politics* (Pluto Press, 2023).
9. For a recent account of the history of black queer organising in the UK see Stephanie Davis, *Queer and Trans People of Colour in the UK: Possibilities for Intersectional Richness*, Transforming LGBTQ Lives (Routledge, 2023).
10. For an account of the group's formation see the interview with Zahid Dar in the LSE Hall-Carpenter Oral History Archive, C456/19/01.
11. Ahmed Farooqui, Black Gay Group [1981–1983]. Haringey Vanguard Archive, Bruce Castle Museum, VAN/10/001.
12. Ibid.
13. Ibid.
14. 'Watch Gay Black Group Online – BFI Player' <https://player.bfi.

org.uk/free/film/watch-gay-black-group-1983-online> [accessed 27 April 2024].

15. Haringey Vanguard Archive, Bruce Castle Museum. Box 1, File ii.
16. The seminal text in this field remains Gayatri Gopinath, *Impossible Desires: Queer Diasporas and South Asian Public Cultures*, Perverse Modernities, 2nd edn (Duke Univ. Press, 2006). For more recent studies of the queer South Asian life at 'home' and in the diaspora, see Kareem Khubchandani, *Ishtyle: Accenting Gay Indian Nightlife* (University of Michigan Press, 2020).
17. Haringey Vanguard, Bruce Castle Museum, Van/03/17/01/001.
18. For an account of how LAIC found itself at the centre of the 1980s 'sex wars' and legal battles to control the archive, see Sarah Green, 'Urban Amazons', *Trouble & Strife*, 35(1997) <https://www.troubleandstrife.org/articles/issue-35/urban-amazons/>; Sarah F. Green, *Urban Amazons: Lesbian Feminism and beyond in the Gender, Sexuality, and Identity Battles of London* (Macmillan [u.a.], 1997).
19. For a brief account of the acquisition see Glasgow Women's Library, 'Papers of the Camden Lesbian Centre and Black Lesbian Group' <https://archive.womenslibrary.org.uk/papers-of-camden-lesbian-centre-and-black-lesbian-group>.
20. For an analysis of local authority funding and queer grassroots activism in the 1980s see Davina Cooper, *Sexing the City: Lesbian and Gay Politics and the Activist State* (River Orams Press, 1994).
21. Glasgow Women's Library, GB 1534 CLCBLG/6/1.
22. Ibid.
23. Ibid.
24. For a digital example of the code, see Glasgow Women's Library, *SAD Access Code* <https://womenslibrary.org.uk/collection-item/sad-access-code/> [accessed 4 April 2024].
25. 'Black and Asian Diaspora Feminism and Black Lesbian Feminism', Glasgow Women's Library, CLCBLG/18, Black lesbian anti-racist campaigns. See Natalie Thomlinson, '"Second-Wave" Black Feminist Periodicals in Britain', *Women: A Cultural Review*, 27.4 (2016), pp. 432–45, doi:10.1080/09574042.2017.1301129.
26. Clare Hemmings, *Why Stories Matter: The Political Grammar of Feminist Theory* (Duke University Press, 2011), p. 2.

27. Jack Halberstam, *In a Queer Time and Place: Transgender Bodies, Subcultural Lives*, Sexual Cultures (New York University Press, 2005), pp. 169–70.
28. Joan Nestle, 'Coda: Who Were We to Do Such a Thing? Grassroots Necessities, Grassroots Dreaming: The LHA in Its Early Years', in *Turning Archival: The Life of the Historical in Queer Studies*, ed. by Daniel Marshall and Zeb Tortorici, Radical Perspectives (Duke University Press, 2022), pp. 347–56 (p. 355).
29. Sophie Marie Niang, 'In Defence of What's There: Notes on Scavenging as Methodology', *Feminist Review*, 136.1 (2024), pp. 52–66 (p. 54), doi:10.1177/01417789231222606.
30. Femi Otitoju, 'The Should We, Shouldn't We? Debate', in *Radical Records: Thirty Years of Lesbian and Gay History, 1957–1987*, ed. by Bob Cant and Susan Hemmings (Routledge, 1988), pp. 222–31 (p. 222).
31. Otitoju, p. 226.
32. Hostile environment is also the name of a 2012 Conservative Party policy designed to target illegal immigration but which was criticised for triggering broader racism and xenophobia.
33. 'Historic Moments', in *Talking Black: Lesbians of African and Asian Descent Speak Out*, ed. by Valerie Mason-John (Cassell, 1995), pp. 4–22 (p. 4).
34. Valerie Mason-John and Ann Khambetta, *Making Black Waves* (Scarlet Press, 1993), p. 47.
35. Mason-John and Khambetta, p. 25.
36. For a discussion of the significance of OWAAD in the black women's movement, see Davis.
37. Mason-John, p. 7.
38. Ibid., p. 18.
39. Ibid., p. 12.
40. South Asian women were involved in running key groups, for example see Rani Kaur's work at Peckham Women's Centre: Metro, *Pride Firsts* <https://metrocharity.org.uk/news/2022/jun/01/pride-firsts> [accessed 4 April 2024].
41. The Black Lesbian Support Network emerged from the conference but had to close in 1986, giving its material to the Lesbian Archive.

42. Mason-John, p. 14.
43. Valerie Amos and Pratibha Parmar, 'Challenging Imperial Feminism', *Feminist Review*, 17(1984), pp. 3–19 (p. 4), doi:10.2307/1395006.
44. Savitri Hensman, 'A Retrospective: Black Together under One Banner', in *Talking Black: Lesbians of African and Asian Descent Speak Out*, ed. by Valerie Mason-John (Cassell, 1995), pp. 23–51 (p. 29).
45. Hensman, p. 24.
46. See Ramamurthy.
47. Pratibha Parmar, 'Hateful Contraries: Media Images of Asian Women', *Ten. 8*, 116 (1984), pp. 71–78 (p. 75).
48. We discuss Keith Khan in more detail in Chapter 4. For an interview with Poulomi Desai who founded the Hounslow Arts Co-Operative, see 'Poulomi Desai—Unfinished Histories' <https://www.unfinishedhistories.com/interviews/interviewees-a-e/poulomi-desai/> [accessed 5 April 2024].
49. Where the funeral for Blair Peach, a protestor killed during an anti-racist demonstration, was held a few years earlier
50. See Shaheen Haq, Pratibha Parmar, and Ingrid Pollard, 'Images of Black Women Organizing', *Feminist Review*, 17(1984), pp. 90–95, doi:10.2307/1395019. The Sari Squad were a group of South Asian women living in the East End of London who took direct action against anti-immigration threats and intimidation. When Afia Begum, a young widow, was threatened with deportation to Bangladesh in 1984, they took her case to the European Commission of Human Rights (she was deported before a ruling was made).
51. Mandana Hendessi, 'In Conversation', in *Against the Grain: A Celebration of Survival and Struggle, 1979–1989*, ed. by Southall Black Sisters (Glasgow Women's Library, CLCBLG312), pp. 10–12 (p. 10).
52. See Gita Sahgal, 'Fundamentalism and the Multi-Cultural Fallacy', in *Against the Grain: A Celebration of Survival and Struggle, 1979–1989*, ed. by Southall Black Sisters (Glasgow Women's Library, CLCBLG312), pp. 16–24.
53. See 'Introduction', in *Against the Grain: A Celebration of Survival and Struggle, 1979–1989*, ed. by Southall Black Sisters (Glasgow Women's Library, CLCBLG312), pp. 3–6.
54. Sahgal, p. 16.

55. Southall Black Sisters, p. 3.
56. For Southall Black Sisters' involvement in the 1984 Miners' Strike see Diarmaid Kelliher, *Making Cultures of Solidarity: London and the 1984–5 Miners' Strike*, Routledge Studies in Radical History and Politics (Routledge, 2021).
57. See Sahgal.
58. Sahgal, p. 20.
59. Pratibha Parmar, 'Fighting Back: An Interview with Pratibha Parmar', in *A Lotus of Another Color: An Unfolding of the South Asian Gay and Lesbian Experience*, ed. by Rakesh Ratti (Alyson Publications, 1993), pp. 34–40 (p. 36).
60. Hannana Siddiqui, 'BMWs & Samosas at the Seaside', in *Against the Grain: A Celebration of Survival and Struggle, 1979–1989*, ed. by Southall Black Sisters (Glasgow Women's Library, CLCBLG312), pp. 37–42 (p. 38).
61. Sahgal, p. 17.
62. Rahila Gupta, 'Automony and Alliances', in *Against the Grain: A Celebration of Survival and Struggle, 1979–1989*, ed. by Southall Black Sisters (Glasgow Women's Library, CLCBLG312), pp. 55–61 (p. 61).
63. Hensman, p. 42.
64. Mason-John, p. 6.
65. A. Sivanandan, *Communities of Resistance: Writings on Black Struggles for Socialism*, [New edition] (Verso, 2019), p. 77.
66. Sivanandan, p. 84.
67. Julia Sudbury, *'Other Kinds of Dreams': Black Womens's Organisations and the Politics of Transformation* (Routledge, 1998), pp. 154–56.
68. Haringey Black Action, 'Haringey Black Action Ephemera' (Glasgow Women's Library, CLCBLG 3/14, Back Lesbian and Gay Activism).
69. Glasgow Women's Library, CLCBLG 3/14.
70. See Stephen Brooke, 'A Thirty Years War?: Gay Rights and the Labour Party, 1967–97', in *Sexual Politics: Sexuality, Family Planning, and the British Left from the 1880s to the Present Day*, ed. by Stephen Brooke (Oxford University Press, 2011), <https://doi.org/10.1093/acprof:oso/9780199562541.003.0009>.
71. In the wake of the Brixton Riots in 1985, prompted by the killing of Cherry Groce by the police, the Broadwater Farm Estate Riot in

1985 was another response to dispensability of black lives in policing 'problem' communities.

72. Sivanandan, p. 51.
73. For a lecture covering Haringey Black Action and Section 28 through connected social justice issues (tax, racial capitalism, apartheid), see *Wolfson's 2023 Berlin Lecture – Dr Nathaniel Adam Tobias Coleman*, dir. by Wolfson College, Oxford, 2023 <https://www.youtube.com/watch?v=1wN98xUffjs> [accessed 5 April 2024].
74. For a discussion of Sunil Gupta's work responding to Section 28, see Chapter 5.
75. The original poster is reproduced in Susan Reinhold, 'Through the Parliamentary Looking Glass: "Real" and "Pretend" Families in Contemporary British Politics', *Feminist Review*, 48.1 (1994), pp. 61–79, doi:10.1057/fr.1994.42.
76. Haringey Black Action Ephemera in 'Black Lesbian and Gay Activism', Glasgow Women's Library, CLCBLG 3/14.
77. Davina Cooper, 'Positive Images in Haringey: A Struggle for Identity', in *Learning Our Lines: Sexuality and Social Control in Education*, ed. by Carol Jones and Pat Mahony (Women's Press, 1989), pp. 46–78 (p. 55).
78. Haringey Black Action Ephemera in 'Black Lesbian and Gay Activism', Glasgow Women's Library, CLCBLG 3/14.
79. For more information and resources on Haringey Black Action see the Haringey Vanguard history project: 'BME LGBTQ+ History Project', *Haringey Vanguard* <https://www.hqbh.co.uk/> [accessed 5 April 2024].
80. Haringey Black Action Ephemera in 'Black Lesbian and Gay Activism', Glasgow Women's Library, CLCBLG 3/14.
81. Ibid.
82. Ibid.
83. Ibid.
84. Black Lesbian and Gay Centre Annual Reports, Bruce Castle Museum, Van/01/02/03/001.
85. Ibid.
86. Paul Baker, *Outrageous!: The Story of Section 28 and Britain's Battle for LGBT Education* (Reaktion Books, 2022).

87. Mason-John and Khambetta, p. 17.
88. For a longer analysis of the incident see Sita Balani, *Deadly and Slick: Sexual Modernity and the Making of Race* (Verso, 2023).
89. Hemmings, p. 42.
90. Cooper, *Power in Struggle*; Beverley Bryan and others, *The Heart of the Race: Black Women's Lives in Britain* (Verso, 2018).
91. Anamik Saha, 'Return to Innocence? Diaspora Screen Media and "New Ethnicities" in the Moment of Diversity', *Journal of Postcolonial Writing* (2024), pp. 1–15, doi:10.1080/17449855.2024.2312360.
92. Claire Alexander, 'Breaking Black: The Death of Ethnic and Racial Studies in Britain', *Ethnic and Racial Studies*, 41.6 (2018), pp. 1034–54 (p. 1048), doi:10.1080/01419870.2018.1409902.
93. Glasgow Women's Library, CLCBLG/17.
94. 'Black and Asian Diaspora Feminism and Black Lesbian Feminism'.
95. Ibid.

2. SHAKTI DISCO TO CLUB KALI

1. Shivananda Khan, *Khush: A Shakti Report*, 1991, p. 35.
2. There were other Shakti Discos, for example Leicester ran a Shakti Disco in 1989.
3. Amin Ghaziani, *Long Live Queer Nightlife: How the Closing of Gay Bars Sparked a Revolution* (Princeton University Press, 2024), p. 7.
4. 'Introduction', in *Queer Nightlife*, ed. by Kemi Adeyemi, Kareem Khubchandani and Ramón H. Rivera-Servera (University of Michigan Press, 2021), p. 2.
5. Nirmal Puwar, *Space Invaders: Race, Gender and Bodies out of Place* (Berg, 2004).
6. Tara Joshi, 'By the Light of Day: How "daytimers" Created a South Asian Club Scene', *Rolling Stone UK*, 2022 <https://www.rollingstone.co.uk/music/by-the-light-of-day-how-daytimers-created-a-south-asian-club-scene-10416/> [accessed 3 August 2024].
7. 'Remembering Daytimers – the Secret South Asian Day Raves of the '80s and '90s', *AZEEMA*, 2021 <https://www.azeemamag.com/stories/daytimers> [accessed 3 August 2024].
8. While Shakti was up and running in 1988, discussions to set up

a gay and lesbian South Asian network were taking place in 1987. The Fallen Angel was a gay pub in Islington that had a long history of community organising, including being one of the homes for Lesbians and Gays Support the Miners in 1984.

9. The Asian Lesbian Group (mid 1980s) and the Gay Asian Group (which lasted only a few weeks before becoming the Gay Black Group) are two examples.
10. Sunil Gupta, 'Correct Singularities', *Gay Times*, 131 (1989), pp. 40–41 (p. 41).
11. See Chapter 1.
12. 'South Asian Queer Pride', *Inspirate – Inspiring Creativity* <https://www.inspirate.org/south-asian-queer-pride> [accessed 28 April 2024].
13. Arun Kundnani, 'The Death of Multiculturalism', *Race & Class*, 43.4 (2002), pp. 67–72, doi:10.1177/030639680204300406.
14. 'An Unholy Alliance? Racism, Religion and Communalism', *Institute of Race Relations*, 2005 <https://irr.org.uk/article/an-unholy-alliance-racism-religion-and-communalism/> [accessed 25 April 2024].
15. Jennifer V. Evans, *The Queer Art of History: Queer Kinship after Fascism* (Duke University Press, 2023), p. 182.
16. Evans, p. 4.
17. This critique of feminism, gender and drag was playing out around the same time as Judith Butler's 1990 critique of the imagined relationship between sex and gender that extensively drew on the figure of drag and would become so foundational for queer theory, see Judith Butler, *Gender Trouble: Feminism and the Subversion of Identity*, Routledge Classics (Routledge, Taylor & Francis Group, 2015).
18. Avtar Brah, *Cartographies of Diaspora: Contesting Identities*, Reprinted (Routledge, 2010).
19. Ibid.
20. Paul Gilroy, *The Black Atlantic: Modernity and Double Consciousness* (Verso, 1993), p. 16.
21. Stuart Hall, *Selected Writings on Race and Difference* (Duke University Press, 2021), p. 261.
22. Gayatri Gopinath, *Impossible Desires: Queer Diasporas and South Asian*

Public Cultures, Perverse Modernities, 2nd edn (Duke Univ. Press, 2006), p. 11.

23. Gayatri Gopinath, *Impossible Desires: Queer Diasporas and South Asian Public Cultures* (Duke University Press, 2006), p. 31.
24. Kareem Khubchandani, '"People Bring Their Histories to the Club": An Interview with DJ Rekha', in *Queer Nightlife*, ed. by Kemi Adeyemi, Kareem Khubchandani and Ramón H. Rivera-Servera (University of Michigan Press, 2021), p. 85.
25. Maya Bhardwaj, 'Embodying transnational queer Black and Brown utopia in alternative QTPOC nightlife spaces', *Agenda: Empowering Women for Gender Equity*, 36 (4), 2022, 122–137 (p. 122).
26. Kareem Khubchandani, *Ishtyle: Accenting Gay Indian Nightlife* (Ann Arbor: University of Michigan Press, 2020), p. 4
27. Ibid., p. xiv.
28. Gayatri Reddy, 'Queer Desi Formations: Making the Boundaries of Cultural Belonging in Chicago', in *Pakistan Desires: Queer Futures Elsewhere*, ed. by Omar Kasmani (Duke University Press, 2023).
29. Khubchandani, *Ishtyle*, pp. xx–xi.
30. *Shakti Khabar* (Glasgow Women's Library South Asian Lesbian and Gay Network Shakti Khabar Box 1, 1990), 10: Oct/Nov, p. 10.
31. *Shakti Khabar* (Glasgow Women's Library CLCBLG 3/4 Asian Women's Groups, 1991), 15: August/September, p. 2; *Shakti Khabar*, 15: August/September, p. 13.
32. *Shakti Khabar*, 15: August/September, p. 8.
33. 'Nasreen Memon', *Speak Out London*, 2021 <https://www.speakoutlondon.org.uk/oral-histories/nasreen-memon> [accessed 4 April 2024].
34. *Shakti Khabar*, 15: August/September, p. 8.
35. 'Khush' was also a report on gay and lesbian South Asians in Britain commissioned by Camden Council and written by Shiv Khan in consultation with Parmar, see *Shakti Khabar* (Glasgow Women's Library South Asian Lesbian and Gay Network Shakti Khabar Box 1), xvii, p. 1.
36. Pratibha Parmar, 'That Moment of Emergence', in *Queer Looks*, ed. by Martha Gever, Pratibha Parmar, and John Greyson, 1st edn (Routledge, 2013), pp. 3–11 (p. 10).

37. *Shakti Khabar*, 15: AUGUST/SEPTEMBER, p. 8.
38. *Shakti Khabar*, XVII, p. 8.
39. Ibid.
40. *Shakti Khabar* (Glasgow Women's Library South Asian Lesbian and Gay Network Shakti Khabar Box 1), XIX, p. 2.
41. *Shakti Khabar*, XIX, p. 9.
42. Ibid., p. 2.
43. For example, see Ryan Persadie, 'Queering "Queer" Toronto Space: Transgressive QTBIPoC Drag Artists and Disrupting homonormativity' *Canadian Theatre Review*, 185 (2020), 22–28.
44. Shaka McGlotten, *Dragging Or, In the Drag of a Queer Life*, (Routledge, 2019), xiv.
45. See Chapter 4, for example.

3. *SHAKTI KHABAR*

1. Shivananda Khan, *Khush: A Shakti Report*, 1991, p. ii.
2. For an excellent recent overview of queer print culture in Europe see *Queer Print in Europe*, ed. by Glyn Davis and Laura Guy, presented at the Between the Sheets: Radical Print Cultures (Symposium), Bloomsbury Visual Arts, 2022.
3 See Francesca Sobande, 'By Us, for Us? Past and Present Black Feminist Publishing Narratives and Routes', *Women: A Cultural Review*, 32.3–4 (2021), pp. 395–409, doi:10.1080/09574042.2021.1973763. Beverley Bryan and others, *The Heart of the Race: Black Women's Lives in Britain* (Verso, 2018); Brixton Black Women's Group, *Speak Out!: The Brixton Black Women's Group* (Verso, 2023).
4. 'I got the impression that many such parents were relatively uneducated. Their values were 30–50 years behind the times.' *Shakti Khabar* (Glasgow Women's Library South Asian Lesbian and Gay Network Shakti Khabar Box 1, 1990), 9: AUG/SEP, p. 9.
5. *Shakti Khabar* (Glasgow Women's Library South Asian Lesbian and Gay Network Shakti Khabar Box 1, 1990), 7: APR/MAY, pp. 7–8.
6. For more detailed work on HIV/AIDS activism in the UK during this period see George Severs, *Radical Acts: HIV/AIDS Activism in Late Twentieth-Century England* (Bloomsbury Academic, 2024).

For an interview with Shivananda Khan that covers his activism, see 'Project Bolo – Shivananda Khan – YouTube' <https://www.youtube.com/watch?v=cE8o7oHNWMU> [accessed 7 September 2024].

7. *Shakti Khabar*, 7: Apr/May, p. 3.
8. Ibid.
9. Pratibha Parmar, 'Fighting Back: An Interview with Pratibha Parmar', in *A Lotus of Another Color : An Unfolding of the South Asian Gay and Lesbian Experience*, ed. by Rakesh Ratti (Alyson Publications, 1993), pp. 34–40 (p. 39).
10. A short-lived publication called *Gay Scene: An Indian Newsletter on Gay Communication* was produced in India in 1978.
11. Khan estimated that copies, especially in India, were being passed between different people and he estimated a regular readership of a thousand as more realistic.
12. 'Houston LGBT History' <https://www.houstonlgbthistory.org/> [accessed 11 April 2024].
13. For example, although there were several appeals to readers to produce 'gay guides' to major South Asian cities (the published guides focused on India), there were no attempts to develop a regional approach to South Asian queer life and identity in Britain.
14. An example of this is the Red Rose Group in Delhi which used *Trikone* and *Shakti Khabar* to document their experiences and recruit new members.
15. Gayatri Gopinath, *Impossible Desires: Queer Diasporas and South Asian Public Cultures*, Perverse Modernities, 2nd edn (Duke Univ. Press, 2006).
16. Sunil Gupta, 'Conversations with Gay Men in India', *Shakti Khabar*, April/May 1, 1989. p.1.
17. For an example of a full list see 'Aims and Objectives of Shakti', *Shakti Khabar*, Feb/March (1990).
18. *Shakti Khabar* (Glasgow Women's Library South Asian Lesbian and Gay Network Shakti Khabar Box 1, 1990), 6: Feb/Mar, p. 3.
19. *Shakti Khabar* (Glasgow Women's Library South Asian Lesbian and Gay Network Shakti Khabar Box 1, 1990), 8: June/July, p. 7.
20. 'Can you come up with positive terms for being lesbian or gay in any of our languages? Send us your terms in Hindi, Urdu, Punjabi,

Gujarati, Bengali, Tamil or Sinhalese, with their English equivalents.' *Shakti Khabar*, 9: AUG/SEP, p. 7. Words like Shamakami (Bengali), Sam Laingik, Sam Bandhan (Hindi), Samjincee (Urdu), Sam Premi/ Sam Kami (Gujarati) were suggested.

21. *Shakti Khabar*, 9: AUG/SEP, p. 5.
22. See *Shakti Khabar*, 7: APR/MAY; *Shakti Khabar* (Glasgow Women's Library South Asian Lesbian and Gay Network Shakti Khabar Box 1, 1990), 10: OCT/NOV; *Shakti Khabar* (Glasgow Women's Library South Asian Lesbian and Gay Network Shakti Khabar Box 1, 1990), 11: DEC–JAN.
23. Sue O'Sullivan and Pratibha Parmar, *Lesbians Talk (Safer) Sex* (Scarlet Press, 1992), pp. 48–49.
24. *Shakti Khabar* (Glasgow Women's Library South Asian Lesbian and Gay Network Shakti Khabar Box 1, 1991), 12: FEB–MAR, p. 13.
25. Chaitanya Lakkimsetti, *Legalizing Sex: Sexual Minorities, AIDS, and Citizenship in India* (New York University Press, 2020).
26. *Shakti Khabar* (Glasgow Women's Library South Asian Lesbian and Gay Network Shakti Khabar Box 1), XVIII.
27. The Naz Project (India) would become instrumental in challenging Section 377 of the Indian Penal Code.
28. *Shakti Khabar*, 11: DEC–JAN, p. 13.
29. See Chapter 4 for our discussion of Pratibha Parmar's film on the same topic.
30. Khan, *Khush: A Shakti Report*, p. 11.
31. Ibid., p. 19.
32. Ibid., p. 37.
33. Ibid., p. 38.
34. Ibid., p. 36.
35. 'Some of Us Are Younger', in *Talking Black: Lesbians of African and Asian Descent Speak Out*, ed. by Valerie Mason-John (Cassell, 1995), pp. 94–107.
36. K.A.H. Charsley and M.C. Benson, 'Marriages of Convenience or Inconvenient Marriages: Regulating Spousal Migration to Britain', *Journal of Immigration, Asylum and Nationality Law*, 26.1 (2012), pp. 10–26. Also, Katharine Charsley and others, *Marriage Migration and*

Integration, Palgrave Macmillan Studies in Family and Intimate Life (Palgrave Macmillan, 2020).

37. Perveez Mody, 'Marriages of Convenience and Capitulation', in *Routledge Handbook of the South Asian Diaspora*, ed. by Joya Chatterji and David Washbrook (Routledge, 2014), pp. 374–87, doi:10.4324/9780203796528-31.
38. *Trikone*, 1995, p. 5.
39. *Shakti Khabar*, 10: Oct/Nov, p. 3. Through his work on HIV/AIDS, Khan spent a significant amount of time advocating for men who had sex with men: 'The fluidity of South Asian males' sexual experience, the framework of sexual invisibility, gender segregation, South Asian homosocialability, male ownership of public space, South Asian shame cultures, sexual invisibility, community 'izzat', compulsory marriage and procreation, the current lack of personal identity-based sexual behaviours, South Asian gender constructions, male and female roles as frameworks of adulthood, and so on have a central impact on sexual behaviours'. Shivananda Khan, *Making Visible the Invisible: Sexuality and Sexual Health in South Asia* (Naz Foundation).
40. *Shakti Khabar*, 6: Feb/Mar, p. 7.
41. While marriages of convenience were generally used to define marriages where the 'convenience' was known from the outset, the discussion in *Shakti Khabar* stretched this definition to include a broader range of marriages which became marriages of convenience.
42. *Shakti Khabar*, 8: June/July, p. 2.
43. Ibid.
44. Ibid., p. 3.
45. Ibid., p. 3.
46. *Shakti Khabar*, Glasgow Women's Library, South Asian Lesbian and Gay Network, Shakti Khabar, Box 1, 1991, 14: June/July, p. 6.
47. *Shakti Khabar*, 11: Dec–Jan, p. 7.
48. See Ruth Vanita, 'Same-Sex Weddings, Hindu Traditions and Modern India', *Feminist Review*, 91(2009), pp. 47–60. Also see Paola Bacchetta, 'Rescaling Transnational "Queerdom": Lesbian and "Lesbian" Identitary–Positionalities in Delhi in the 1980s', *Antipode*, 34.5 (2002), pp. 947–73, doi:10.1111/1467-8330.00284.
49. *Shakti Khabar*, 14: June/July, p. 3.

50. *Shakti Khabar*, 11: Dec/Jan, p. 7.
51. *Shakti Khabar*, 8: June/July, p. 5.
52. *Shakti Khabar*, Glasgow Women's Library, CLCBLG 3/4, Asian Women's Groups, 1991, 15: August/September, p. 12.
53. Mumtaz Karimjee and Amina Patel's *Aurat Shakti* was a community-based photographic exhibition in 1987.
54. Sara Ahmed, *Living a Feminist Life* (Duke University Press, 2017).
55. Ibid., p. 222.
56. Ibid., p. 224.
57. This includes Gilli Salvat (see Chapter 1) and Poulomi Desai, see 'Poulomi Desai—Unfinished Histories' <https://www.unfinishedhistories.com/interviews/interviewees-a-e/poulomi-desai/> [accessed 5 April 2024].
58. *Shakti Khabar*, 6: Feb/Mar, p. 1.
59. Ibid.
60. Ibid., p. 9.
61. See Armrget in, *Shakti Khabar*, 9: Aug/Sep, p. 2.
62. *Shakti Khabar*, 11: Dec–Jan, p. 3.
63. See *Shakti Khabar*, Glasgow Women's Library, South Asian Lesbian and Gay Network Shakti Khabar, Box 1, 1991, 13: Apr–May, p. 9.
64. *Trikone*, p. 5.
65. Xine Yao, *Disaffected: The Cultural Politics of Unfeeling in Nineteenth-Century America*, Perverse Modernities (Duke University Press, 2021), p. 16.
66. Rahul Gairola, 'Capitalise houses, queer homes: National belonging and transgressive erotics in My Beautiful Laundrette', *South Asian Popular Culture*, 7.1 (2009), pp. 37–54.
67. *Shakti Khabar*, 12: Feb–Mar, p. 12.

4. QUEER ART AND VISUAL CULTURE IN THE DESI DIASPORA

1. Sarita Malik et al, *Creativity and resistance in a hostile world* (Manchester University Press, 2020).
2. Gayatri Gopinath, *Unruly Visions: The Aesthetic Practices of the Queer Diaspora* (Duke University Press, 2018), 6.

3. Ranajit Guha, 'The Migrant's Time', *Postcolonial Studies*, 1.2 (1998), pp. 155–160, 155.
4. Sunil Gupta, 'Culture Wars: Race and Queer Art' in P. Horne and R. Lewis (eds.), *Outlooks: Lesbian and Gay Sexualities and Visual Cultures* (Routledge, 1996), pp. 170–177.
5. Mumtaz Karimjee, 'In Search of an Image', *Trouble & Strife*, 20 (1991), 22–27.
6. E. Ann Kaplan, 'An interview with Pratibha Parmar', *Quarterly Review of Film & Video*, 17.2 (2000), pp. 85-105, (101).
7. Gayatri Gopinath, *Impossible Desires* (Durham: Duke University Press, 2005).
8. Kaplan, p. 89.
9. Maggie Warwick interviewing Pratibha Parmar. Available at: https://sites.dundee.ac.uk/rewind/wp-content/uploads/sites/146/2021/03/PP510.pdf
10. David Bailey, Ian Baucom and Sonia Boyce, *Shades of Black: Assembling Black Arts in 1980s Britain* (Duke University Press, 2005).
11. Natasha Bissonauth, 'A Camping of Orientalism in Sunil Gupta's Sun City', *Art Journal*, 78.4 (2019), pp. 98–117.
12. Glyn Davis, 'The Queer Archive in Fragments: Sunil Gupta's London Gay Switchboard', *GLQ: A Journal of Lesbian and Gay Studies*, 27.1 (2021), pp. 121–140, 131.
13. Sunil Gupta, *India Postcard: or Why I Make Work in a Racist, Homophobic Society*.
14. Gopinath (2005), p. 192.
15. Jin Haritaworn, Adi Kuntsman, and Silvia Posocco (eds), *Queer Necropolitics* (Routledge, 2014).
16. Lauren Berlant, 'Slow Death (Sovereignty, Obesity, Lateral Agency)', *Critical Enquiry*, 33.4 (2007), pp. 754–780.
17. Jigna Desai, *Beyond Bollywood: The Cultural Politics of South Asian Diasporic Film* (Routledge, 2003), p. 5.
18. Sharon Fernandez, 'More than Just an Arts Festival: Communities, Resistance, and the Story of Desh Pardesh', *Canadian Journal of Communication*, 31:1 (2006), pp. 17–34.
19. Debanuj Dasgupta and Rohit K. Dasgupta, 'Being Out of Place:

Non Belonging and Queer Racialization in U.K', *Emotion, Space and Society*, 27 (2018), pp. 31–38.

20. Ian Iqbal Rashid, 'Three Poems', *Wasafiri*, 10.20 (1994), pp. 14–15.
21. Sara Ahmed, *The Promise of Happiness* (Duke University Press, 2010), p. 121.
22. Sara Ahmed, *The Promise of Happiness* (Duke University Press, 2010), p. 121.
23. Paul Boyce and Rohit K. Dasgupta, 'Alternating Sexualities: Sociology and Queer Critiques in India', in S. Srivastava, Y. Arif and J. Nair (eds.), *Critical Themes in Indian Sociology* (Sage, 2019), pp. 330–345.

5. CONTEMPORARY QUEER CULTURAL ACTIVISM

1. Matt Ratto, 'Critical Making: Conceptual and Material Studies in Technology and Social Life', *The Information Society*, 27.4 (2011), pp. 252–260
2. K. Khubchandani, 'Queer South Asian Diasporas', Oxford Research Encyclopaedia of Literature (Oxford University Press, 2019). Available at: https://oxfordre.com/literature/view/10.1093/acrefore/9780190201098.001.0001/acrefore-9780190201098-e-807.
3. Nayan Shah, *Stranger Intimacy: Contesting Race, Sexuality, and the Law In the North American West* (University of California Press, 2011).
4. Caitlin Rimmer, 'On Queer Remembering and Misremembering: Exploring Queer Aphasia', *Journal of Folklore Research*, pp. 37–66.
5. Jasbir Puar, 'Transnational Sexualities: South Asian (Trans) nation(alism)s and Queer Diasporas', in David Eng and Alice Y. Hom (eds), *Q &A: Queer in Asian*), pp. 405– 422.
6. Gopinath (2005), p. 153.
7. Raisa Kabir, Lipi Begum, and Rohit K. Dasgupta, 'In/visible space: reflections on the realm of dimensional affect, space and the queer racialised self', in L. Begum, R.K. Dasgupta and R. Lewis (eds.), *Styling South Asian Youth Cultures: Fashion, Media & Society* (Bloomsbury, 2018), pp. 86–95.
8. Priyamvada Gopal, *Insurgent Empire: Anticolonial Resistance and British Dissent* (Verso, 2019), p.1.

9. https://cca-annex.net/entry/gather-your-spools-let-your-hair-down-for-me-gently-here-undo/
10. Desai (2003), p. 5.
11. https://www.shayshay.show/bitten-peach
12. Will Stroude, 'Peach Paradise: There are so many ways of being queer and Asian', *Attitude Magazine*, 2002.
13. S. Eguchi, 'What is "Queer Asia?": A struggling pathway to globalizing queer Studies in communication', *Communication and Critical/Cultural Studies*, 18.2 (2021), pp. 196–203, 197.
14. We interviewed Asifa for this book and discuss her work in more detail in the next section.
15. 'Destigmatising Transitioning with Shiva Raichandani', *TogetherTV*. Available here: https://www.togethertv.com/blog/destigmatising-transitioning-shiva-raichandani.
16. Sara Ahmed, 'Orientations: Toward a Queer Phenomenology,' *GLQ: A Journal of Lesbian and Gay Studies*, 12.4 (2006), pp. 543–574.
17. Marcus Syrus Ware, 'All Power to All People? Black LGBTTI2QQ Activism, Remembrance, and Archiving in Toronto', *TSQ: Transgender Studies Quarterly*, 4.2 (2017), pp. 170–80.
18. Mary Louise Pratt, *Imperial Eyes: Travel Writing and Transculturation* (Routledge, 1992).
19. Also see Debanuj Dasgupta and Rohit K. Dasgupta, 'Being Out of Place: Non Belonging and Queer Racialisation in the UK', *Emotion, Space and Society*, 27 (2018), pp. 31–38.
20. Reina Gossett, Eric Stanley and Johanna Burton (eds.), *Trap Door: Trans Cultural Production and the Politics of Visibility* (MIT Press, 2017).
21. Singh and Gupta have collaborated many times including, for example, their groundbreaking exhibition 'Delhi: Communities of Belonging' which chronicles LGBTQ life in Delhi and the publications: Sunil Gupta and Charan Singh, *Dissent and Desire*, Houston: Contemporary Arts Museum (2018); and Sunil Gupta and Charan Singh, *Delhi: Communities of Belonging* (The New Press, 2016).
22. Neha Alawadhi, 'Police force closure of photo exhibition on Paris gay life', *Hindu* (2012). Available at: https://www.thehindu.com/news/

cities/Delhi/police-force-closure-of-photo-exhibition-on-paris-gay-life/article3257108.ece

23. Section 377 of the Indian Penal Code was a colonial-era law that criminalised sexual acts deemed 'against the order of nature.' Although the law did not explicitly mention homosexuality, it was often used to prosecute LGBT individuals. The punishment for violating this law ranged from a minimum of ten years to life imprisonment.
24. More details about this protest can be found in Rohit K. Dasgupta, Sunil Gupta and Rahul Rao 'Global Day of Rage in London: Reflecting on Queer Activisms, New Media and Friendship', in N. Banerjea, D. Dasgupta, R.K. Dasgupta and J.M. Grant (eds.), *Friendship as Social Justice Activism: Critical Solidarities in a Global Perspective* (Seagull Books, 2018).
25. The origins of this term are unclear. Aniruddha Dutta notes that it is a category for socioeconomically marginalised gender variant or 'feminine' same sex desiring males that gained visibility within the emerging institutional movement for LGBT rights in the late 1990s. See, Aniruddha Dutta, 'An Epistemology of Collusion: Hijras, Kothis and the Historical (Dis)continuity of Gender/Sexual Identities in Eastern India', *Gender & History*, 24.3 (November 2012), pp. 825–849.
26. Also see, Charan Singh: https://www.charansingh.net/they-called-it-love-but-was-it-love.html
27. Ibid.
28. Rachel Dwyer, *Bollywood's India: Hindi cinema as a guide to contemporary India* (Reaktion Books, 2014).

CONCLUSION

1. This was a bilingual queer magazine published between 1991 and 2000 by Counsel Club which circulated privately and mostly by word of mouth. Pravartak and the latter Naya Pravartak has been described by a journalist as 'In the pre-Internet era... aa connecting link for queer people spread across India and abroad' (https://www.telegraphindia.com/opinion/no-more-silence/cid/1462210).

2. J. Puar, D. Rushbrook and L. Schein, 'Guest editorial', *Environment and Planning D: Society and Space* 21 (2003), pp. 383–387, 386.
3. Debanuj Dasgupta and Rohit K. Dasgupta, 'Being out of place: Non-belonging and queer racialisation in the UK', *Emotion, Space and Society*, 27 (2018), pp. 31–38.
4. K. Browne, N. Banerjea, N. McGlynn et al, 'Towards transnational feminist queer methodologies', *Gender, Place and Culture*, 24.10 (2017), pp. 1376–1397.
5 A.K. Patel, *Productive failure: Writing queer transnational South Asian art histories*, (Manchester University Press, 2017).
6. N. Banerjea, D. Dasgupta, R.K. Dasgupta and J. Grant, *Friendship as Social Justice Activism: Critical Solidarities in a Global Perspective* (Seagull, 2018), p. 7.
7. R. Rao, *Out of Time: The Queer Politics of Postcoloniality*, (Oxford University Press, 2020).
8. C. Mahn, 'Queering postcolonial travel writing', *Studies in Travel Writing*, 24.2 (2020), pp. 170–182.
9. Syrus Marcus Ware, 'All Power to All People?: Black LGBTTI2QQ Activism, Remembrance, and Archiving in Toronto', TSQ, 4.2 (2017), pp. 170–180, 171.

POSTSCRIPT

1. Ahmed Farooqui, Black Gay Group [1981–1983]. Haringey Vanguard Archive, Bruce Castle Museum, VAN/10/001.
2. Ramzi Fawaz, *Queer Forms* (New York University Press, 2022).
3. Jasbir K. Puar, *Terrorist Assemblages: Homonationalism in Queer Times* (Duke University Press, 2007), doi:10.1215/9780822390442; Gayatri Gopinath, *Impossible Desires: Queer Diasporas and South Asian Public Cultures*, Perverse Modernities, 2nd edn (Duke Univ. Press, 2006).
4. For an account of racialised queer feelings 'out of place', see *Out of Place: Interrogating Silences in Queerness/Raciality*, ed. by Adi Kuntsman and Esperanza Miyake (Raw Nerve Books, 2008).
5. See Rozina Visram, *Asians in Britain: 400 Years of History* (Pluto Press, 2002); Susheila Nasta, *Home Truths: Fictions of the South Asian Diaspora in Britain*, first publ. (Palgrave, 2002).

6. See Visram; *A Postcolonial People: South Asians in Britain*, ed. by N. Ali, Virinder S. Kalra, and S. Sayyid (Hurst & Co, 2006); *South Asian Resistances in Britain 1858–1947*, ed. by Rehana Ahmed and Sumita Mukherjee, first publ. (Continuum, 2012).
7. Examples of performance culture include Jerri Daboo, *Staging British South Asian Culture: Bollywood and Bhangra in British Theatre* (Routledge, 2018); *Critical Essays on British South Asian Theatre*, ed. by Graham Ley and Sarah Dadswell (University of Exeter Press, 2015).
8. See Sara Upstone, *British Asian Fiction: Twenty-First-Century Voices*, first publ. (Manchester Univ. Press, 2010); *Writing the City in British-Asian Diasporas*, ed. by Sean McLoughlin and others (Routledge, 2017).
9. *Queer Migrations: Sexuality, U.S. Citizenship, and Border Crossings*, ed. by Eithne Luibhéid (Univ. of Minnesota Press, 2005); *Queer and Trans Migrations: Dynamics of Illegalization, Detention, and Deportation*, ed. by Eithne Luibhéid and Karma R. Chávez, Dissident Feminisms (University of Illinois Press, 2020).
10. Avtar Brah, *Decolonial Imaginings: Intersectional Conversations and Contestations* (Goldsmith Press, 2022).
11. Alberto Fernández Carbajal, *Queer Muslim Diasporas in Contemporary Literature and Film* (Manchester University Press, 2019); Wim Peumans, *Queer Muslims in Europe: Sexuality, Religion and Migration in Belgium* (I. B. Tauris, 2018).
12. 'Race is the modality in which class is lived. It is also the medium in which class relations are experienced.' See Stuart Hall and others, *Policing the Crisis: Mugging, the State, and Law and Order* (Macmillan, 1978), p. 394.
13. Martin F. Manalansan, 'In the Shadows of Stonewall: Examining Gay Transnational Politics and the Diasporic Dilemma', *GLQ: A Journal of Lesbian and Gay Studies*, 2.4 (1995), pp. 425–38 (p. 486), doi:10.1215/10642684-2-4-425.hy.
14. Jessica Hinchy, *Governing Gender and Sexuality in Colonial India: The Hijra, c.1850–1900* (Cambridge University Press, 2019).
15. Gopinath, p. 153.
16. Ruth Vanita, 'The Homoerotics of Travel: People, Ideas, Genres', in

The Cambridge Companion to Gay and Lesbian Writing, ed. by Hugh Stevens, Cambridge Companions to Literature (Cambridge University Press, 2010), pp. 99–115, doi:10.1017/CCOL9780521888448.007.

17. Kareem Khubchandani, *Ishtyle: Accenting Gay Indian Nightlife* (University of Michigan Press, 2020).
18. Omar Kasmani, *Queer Companions: Religion, Public Intimacy, and Saintly Affects in Pakistan* (Duke University Press, 2022).
19. Maya Bhardwaj, '"That's What We Think of as Activism": Solidarity through Care in Queer Desi Diaspora', *Journal of Lesbian Studies*, 28.1 (2024), pp. 100–124.
20. Roderick A. Ferguson, *One-Dimensional Queer* (Polity, 2019), p. 3.
21. José Esteban Muñoz, *Disidentifications: Queer of Color and the Performance of Politics* (University of Minnesota Press, 1999), p.25..
22. As one of our interviewees points out in Chapter 1, affiliating with anti-colonial politics in Ireland and Palestine was a vital part of anti-racist and queer organising in the 1980s.
23. Nadya Ali, *The Violence of Britishness: Racism, Borders and the Conditions of Citizenship* (Pluto Press, 2023), p. 3.
24. Gopinath, pp. 14–15.
25. For the original work on homonationalism, see Puar.
26. See Puar; Fatima El-Tayeb, *European Others: Queering Ethnicity in Postnational Europe*, Difference Incorporated (University of Minnesota Press, 2011); Jin Haritaworn, *Queer Lovers and Hateful Others: Regenerating Violent Times and Places*, Decolonial Studies, Postcolonial Horizons (Pluto Press, 2015).
27. Gopinath, p. 70.
28. For a recent discussion of the intersection between queer and the Brown Atlantic, see Amar Wahab, 'Introduction', *Journal of Indentureship and Its Legacies*, 2.1 (2022), pp. 1–14.
29. 'Black Atlantic Resource Debate', *Black Atlantic Resource Debate* <https://blackatlanticresource.wordpress.com/> [accessed 20 April 2024].
30. Kath Browne and Catherine J. Nash, 'Queer Methods and Methodologies: an introduction' in *Queer Methods and Methodologies: Intersecting Queer Theories and Social Sciences Research*, ed. by Kath Browne and Catherine J. Nash (Ashgate, 2010), pp. 1–24.

31. Amin Ghaziani and Matt Brim, 'Queer Methods: Four provocations for an Emerging Field' in *Imagining Queer Methods*, ed. by Amin Ghaziani and Matt Brim (New York University Press, 2019), pp. 3–27, 15.
32. G. Günel. S. Varma and C. Watanabe, 'A Manifesto for Patchwork Ethnography', Member Voices, *Fieldsights*, 9 June. Available from: https://culanth.org/fieldsights/a-manifesto-for-patchwork-ethnography. [Accessed on 25 April, 2024].
33. See Rohit K. Dasgupta, 'Viral Assemblages and Witnessing Extraordinary Times: Queer Patchworks of Intimacy, Precarity and Affect in an Indian City', *Journal of Intercultural Studies*, 43.6 (2022), pp. 880–96 and G. Deleuze and C. Parnet, *Dialogues* (Columbia University Press, 1987).
34. José Esteban Muñoz, 'Ephemera as Evidence: Introductory Notes to Queer Acts', *Women & Performance: A Journal of Feminist Theory*, 8.2 (1996), pp. 5–16, doi:10.1080/07407709608571228.
35. Eve Kosofsky Sedgwick, *Epistemology of the Closet*, A Centennial Book, Updated with a new Preface (University of California Press, 2008).
36. Anjali R. Arondekar, *Abundance: Sexuality's History* (Duke University Press, 2023); Laurie Marhoefer, *Racism and the Making of Gay Rights: A Sexologist, His Student, and the Empire of Queer Love* (University of Toronto Press, 2022).
37. Email correspondence between Shashank Peshawaria and Churnjeet Mahn, 11 June 2022.

INDEX

INDEX

INDEX